M

WINTER

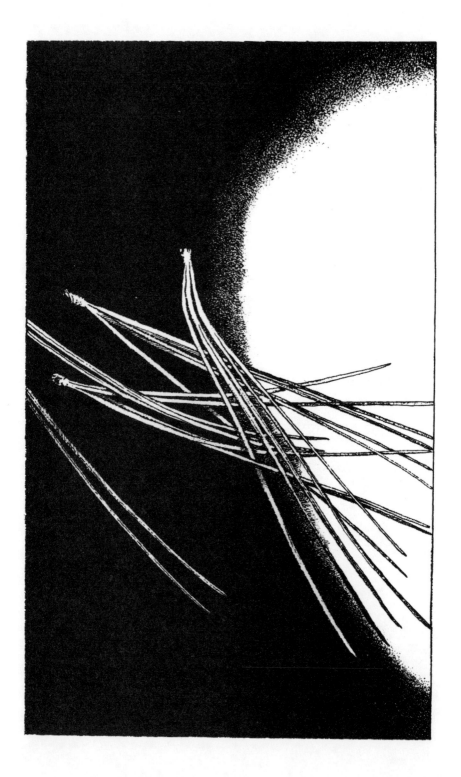

$\mathcal{W}$INTER

A SPIRITUAL BIOGRAPHY
OF THE SEASON

EDITED BY GARY SCHMIDT
AND SUSAN M. FELCH

ILLUSTRATIONS BY BARRY MOSER

Walking Together, Finding the Way
SKYLIGHT PATHS Publishing
Woodstock, Vermont

Winter:
A Spiritual Biography of the Season

© 2003 by Gary Schmidt and Susan M. Felch

Grateful acknowledgment is given for permission by Barry Moser for the reproduction of his drawings. These were first drawn for and published in Robert D. Richardson, Jr.'s *Henry Thoreau: A Life of the Mind,* published by the University of California Press in 1986.

Library of Congress Cataloging-in-Publication Data
Winter : a spiritual biography of the season / edited by Gary Schmidt and Susan M. Felch.
p. cm.
Includes bibliographical references.
ISBN 1-893361-53-5 (hardcover)
1. Winter—Literary collections. I. Schmidt, Gary, 1957– II. Felch, Susan M., 1951–
PN6071.W6 W53 2002
808.8'033—dc21
2002012993

10   9   8   7   6   5   4   3   2   1
Manufactured in the United States of America

SkyLight Paths Publishing is creating a place where people of different spiritual traditions come together for challenge and inspiration, a place where we can help each other understand the mystery that lies at the heart of our existence.

SkyLight Paths sees both believers and seekers as a community that increasingly transcends traditional boundaries of religion and denomination—people wanting to learn from each other, *walking together, finding the way.*

SkyLight Paths, "Walking Together, Finding the Way" and colophon are trademarks of LongHill Partners, Inc., registered in the U.S. Patent and Trademark Office.

Walking Together, Finding the Way
Published by SkyLight Paths Publishing
A Division of LongHill Partners, Inc.
Sunset Farm Offices, Route 4, P.O. Box 237
Woodstock, VT 05091
Tel: (802) 457-4000   Fax: (802) 457-4004
www.skylightpaths.com

For Peter and Betsy Stine,
who know that winter can never come
without Christmas.
—G. S.

In memory of my grandmother Lydia Foos,
who, for 101 years, graced our
winters with her presence.
—S. M. F.

CONTENTS

Contents

Contents

PREFACE

For many years, the most famous fireplace in North America was probably that in John Greenleaf Whittier's boyhood home in northern Massachusetts. It was the site of his first successful poem, "Snow-Bound," and the images from that poem—all drawn from the homestead—became part of American lore and myth. There is the family gathered around the hearth, sipping cider, telling stories, staying warm with the fire's "tropic heat," the red logs beating back the north winds that spilled snow all about the beset but not defeated farmhouse. "What matter how the night behaved? / What matter how the north-wind raved? / Blow high, blow low, not all its snow / Could quench our hearth-fire's ruddy glow." The poem is, though, in some ways a eulogy, since every single soul but John and his brother had died by the time he wrote it, and the call to defeat the winter storm is set against the inability of anyone to defeat time and change.

But some things do resist time and change. Whittier soon after concludes that despite death and the cold snow that emblems it, "Life is ever lord of Death, / And Love can never lose its own!"

If you were to go to the house now, you would find it much the same as it was when Whittier was a boy, chafing at the duties of the farm. If you were to make your pilgrimage there most any

January, it would always be snowing—or at least seem to be snowing. You might bring wood with you from Michigan—maple grown on your own land that you yourself had cut and split the winter before. And so the energy and light of Michigan's short summer sun might glow at the hearth of the Haverhill homestead in winter, and you would sit in the rocker there and stretch out your feet, and winter would be a fine thing—though it is easy to imagine how Whittier and his family had a less romantic vision of it, and how eager they were that the "chill embargo of the snow" be "melted in the genial glow," hoping that soon the ice-locked door would open again and they could call, "All the world was ours once more!"

For Whittier, winter was a low, dormant time in the life of the farm. As a metaphor for our spiritual lives, it often strikes the same note. It is that time of a frozen spirit, or even a desolate spirit, a time when activity and life and love slow and then still; it is the winter of our discontent, and its temperature is invoked in ways generally unpleasant: "cold shoulder," "cold-blooded," "cold steel," "cold comfort." Winter summons up images of barrenness, of frigidity, of discomfort, of flights to Florida and the Carolinas, and, on a more internal plane, of spiritual dryness and depression, of a cold and unmoving spirit and a hardened heart.

But if winter is frigidity, it is also sliding down the hill by Whittier's house, laughing with the snow in your face, and running in to the fireplace, where the cider is heating well and the maple logs are sending their sweet smoke up a chimney they have warmed for three and a half centuries. It is the quiet time in the rhythm of life, a time of thoughtfulness and looking forward, a time of hope and even celebration, a time when we gather together (the old word was "croodle"), and stamp the ice off our boots and dash into the kitchen—or perhaps by the wood stove—to be warm together and to remark on how cold this winter has been and how much colder it is than last year but not nearly as cold as it used to be in winters past. It is never as cold as it used to be in winters past.

Winter is the seat of what will come, the freeze that reminds us of the thaw, the hope pensively waiting, the moment pausing, the rhythm at its nadir but poised to begin its upward swing. "We felt the stir of hall and street, / The pulse of life that round us beat," writes Whittier. This is winter too: the pulse of life halting at its proper point, but still a pulse, and still a life.

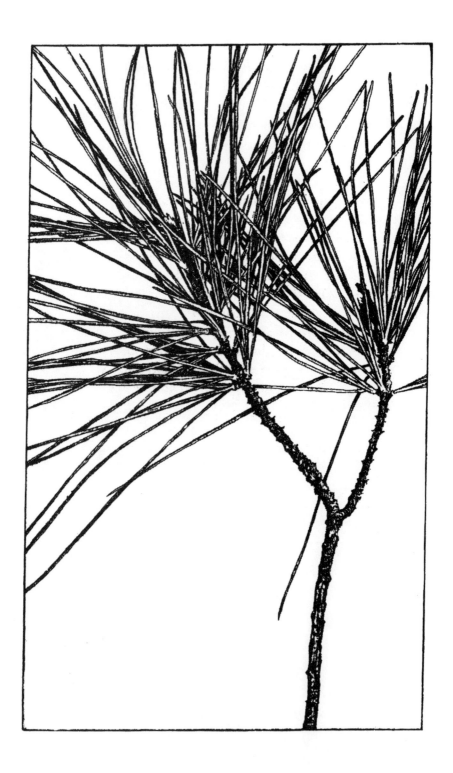

PART ONE

Winter As a Time of Sorrow and Barrenness

INTRODUCTION

Spiritual reflection upon the cycle of seasons has a long history, from Roman and Sufi philosophic poems and medieval meditations on the brevity of life to our contemporary picture postcard calendars. Though the year begins and ends with winter, moving from January's icy landscape to December's white mountain peaks, we often regard winter only negatively—as the antithesis to spring—or, at best, as the season we hurry past in order to reach April's blooms. It is the great "no" that cancels travel plans, forces us to rely on underdeveloped internal resources, and mutes the busy noise of social commerce. Folk rhymes have captured our impatience with winter, our longing for signs that it will soon be over:

> *If New Year's Eve night wind blow south,*
> *It betokeneth warmth and growth;*
> *If west, much milk, and fish in the sea;*
> *If north, much cold and storms there'll be;*
> *If east, the trees will bear much fruit;*
> *If north-east, flee it, man and brute.*

We face winter only to flee it. The winter wind, says an ancient Sanskrit poem, is "as cruel / as a hypocrite's embrace."

The beginning of winter has a long tradition of representing the advent of a fearsome time. In ancient Egypt, the winter solstice was the time when the god-man Osiris was entombed. In ancient Greece, it was the time when the god Dionysos was torn in pieces so that he could later be reborn as an infant. Our medieval forebears, less insulated against the ravages of winter than we, are unrelenting in their depictions of the season's brutality. Winter is the time that "maketh old" as it draws its "sword of cold": "The soil in summer with flowers glad, winter's razor doth all away erase." It is a "crabbed season" whose poverty can be forgotten only when spring once again rejuvenates the earth. And Shakespeare opens his claustrophobic tragedy of decay and deceit with the bone-chilling cold of Danish winds and kingly ghosts. "'Tis bitter cold," says Francisco, a sentinel who guards old Hamlet's castle, "And I am sick at heart."

The spiritual biography of winter might be said to begin here, with the soul pitted against its harsh surroundings. When the *Pearl* Poet, a fourteenth-century religious writer, wants to examine the transformation of a sincere but callow youth into a wise man, he thrusts his hero, Gawain, into the fierce English winter. The bleak landscape dramatically accentuates Gawain's frailty and God's hidden though attentive care:

> *Had Gawain not been stouthearted and brave and*
> *trusted in God,*
> *Doubtless he would have died, slain full often.*
> *For if war afflicted him, winter was much worse,*
> *When the cold clear water from the clouds wept*
> *And froze before it fell to the frosted earth;*
> *Near slain with sleet he slept in his iron armor*
> *More than enough nights, among the naked rocks,*
> *Where the cold stream clattered from the hillcrest,*

And froze, hanging high over his head in hard icicles. . . .
The hazel and the hawthorn tangled together,
With rough, ragged moss arrayed about,
And many birds, mournful upon bare branches,
Piping piteously in pain from the cold.

This image of winter as a bleak white season, scouring the landscape with bitter winds and lowering clouds, is sharply etched on our minds. Winter is a time of stillness, darkness, and death, and while we know intellectually that this season will pass into the birth of a new year and then into spring, instinctively we hunker down, peering fearfully into the twilight toward a shadow whose shape we cannot discern. We stand like William Bradford at the prow of the *Mayflower*, staring for the first time at the cold tip of Cape Cod: "And for ye season it was winter, and they that know ye winters of y^t cuntrie know them to be sharp & violent & subjecte to cruell & feirce stormes, deangerous to travill to known places, much more to serch an unknown coast. Besids, what could they see but a hidious & desolate wildernes?"

For what do we watch? Perhaps it is not the start of a transformation as it was for Gawain, or the beginning of a new world as it was for Bradford, but an ending—an ending that must be both anticipated and endured. This, at least, is how Madeleine L'Englc thinks of it:

A new year can begin only because the old year ends. In Northern climates this is especially apparent. As rain turns to snow, puddles to ice, the sun rises later and sets earlier; and each day it climbs less high in the sky. One time when I went with my children to the Planetarium I was fascinated to hear the lecturer say that the primitive people used to watch the sun drop lower on the horizon in great terror, because they were afraid that one day it was going to go so low that it would never rise again; they would be left in unremitting night. There would be weeping and wailing and gnashing of teeth, and a terror of great darkness would fall upon them. And then, just as it seemed that there would never be another dawn, the sun would start to come back; each day it would rise higher, set later.

Somewhere in the depths of our unconsciousness we share that primordial fear, and when there is the first indication that the days are going to lengthen, our hearts, too, lift with relief. The end has not come: joy! and so a new year makes its birth known.

The eschaton conjures up images of primordial fear, but winter also provides the context in which we think of more personal sorrows, of the deaths of loved ones, and of our own impending mortality. The metaphors that we often use for winter—the ground is as hard as iron, snow blankets the landscape, the cold numbs, the frost whitens the locks—can be applied to the spiritual life as well: the winter of our discontent. We often see the season as a time when life retreats, as the time of old age, loss, sorrow, endings. It is not only our personal experience of death that chills us in the long nights, but the shock of cruelty that is exacerbated by winter's unrelenting, impersonal cold. Frozen fingers grasp the caged enclosures of death camps; blood stains the impeccable whiteness of fresh-fallen snow. Death in winter, as the Confucian poet Du Fu knows, carries with it an exquisite, almost unnamable sorrow:

> *Battles, sobbing, many new ghosts.*
> *An old man, I sadly chant poems.*
> *Wild clouds lower and touch the thin evening.*
> *Fast snow dances in swirling wind.*
> *A ladle abandoned, no green wine in the cask.*
> *Fire still seems to redden the empty stove.*
> *No news, the provinces are cut off.*
> *With one finger I write my sorrows in the air.*

In hunkering down to ride out the season, as we write our sorrows in the air, we feel the metaphor of the season speaking to our own lives. But in hunkering down, we recognize that the existence of such a season—in both an external and an internal sense—is inevitable in this world. In accepting the inevitability—even necessity—of winter, we find a way to live in its cold blows.

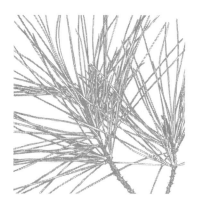

Jamaica Kincaid

"A Fire by Ice"

Jamaica Kincaid was born on the island of St. Johns in Antigua and, in moving to northern New England, experienced about the most dramatic climatic change that one might ever hope to undergo. Thus, for her, the cold of winter becomes an almost personal assault and a vigorous aggressor—particularly as she considers the havoc that the cold wreaks upon her garden.

> *Thus, for her, the cold of winter becomes an almost personal assault and a vigorous aggressor—particularly as she considers the havoc that the cold wreaks upon her garden.*

The images that she uses are telling: the snow is mounded like a grave; the season is dark and frosted, a season of death, a cold that is unnatural and unreal on some level. But she also asserts, from her life in Antigua, that the winter and the summer are not irreconcilable, that they form two very different times for the world, for the gardener, for the soul.

A Fire by Ice

It is winter in Vermont, and so my garden does not exist. In its place are mounds of white, the raised beds covered with snow, as in a graveyard—not a graveyard in New England, with its orderliness and neatness and sense of that's that, but a graveyard in the place I am from, a warm place. There, a grave is topped off with a huge mound of loose earth—carelessly, as if piled up in child's play, not serious at all—because death is just another way of being, and the dead will not stay put, and sometimes the actions of the dead are more significant, more profound, than their actions in life, and no structure of concrete or stone can contain them.

The whiteness of the snow is an eraser, so that I am in a state of near-disbelief. A clump of lovage, with its tall, thick stalks of cel-erylike leaves (with celerylike taste), did really stand next to the hedge of rhubarb; the potatoes were near the rhubarb, the broccoli was near the potatoes, the carrots and beets were together and near the potatoes, the basil and cilantro were together and near the peas; the tomatoes were in a bed by themselves (a long, narrow strip that I made all by myself this summer with a new little tiller I bought from Gardener's Supply Company), separating my garden from my daughter Annie's; the strawberries were in a bed by themselves, and so were all the salad greens; the sunflowers, tall and short, in various hues of yellow and brown, were clustered in groups over here, over there, and over here again. The scarecrow that scared nothing was here; the gun to shoot the things the scarecrow didn't scare was right here (unloaded, lying between the bundles of hay for mulching the potatoes). The line of silver (aluminum pie plates) was strung between the two tepees covered with lima-bean vines (whose pods remained empty of beans).

The colors (the green of leaf, the redpink stem of rhubarb, the red veins of beet leaves, the yellows and browns of sunflowers) start out tentatively, in a maybe-or-maybe-not way, and then one day, perhaps after a heavy rain, everything is strong and itself, twinkling, jewel-like. At that moment, I think life will never change: it will always be summer. The families of rabbits or woodchucks will eat the salad greens just before they are ready to be picked; I plot ways to kill these animals but can never bring myself to do it; I decide to build a fence around the garden and then decide not to. There are more or fewer Japanese beetles than last year—who can really care? There are too many zucchini—who can really care? And then, as if it had never happened before, I hear that the temperature will drop to such a low degree that it will cause a frost.

I always take this personally; I think a frost is something someone is doing to me—only to me. And this is how winter in the garden begins—with another tentativeness, a curtsy to the actual cold to come, a gentle form of it. The effect of the cold air on things growing in the garden is something I cannot get used to, cannot understand, even after so many years. How can it be that after a frost the entire garden looks as if it had been to a party in Hell? As if it had been picked up and set down just outside the furnace of a baker's oven, with the fire constantly fed and the oven door never shut?

I must have been about ten years old when I first came in contact with cold air. Where I lived (Antigua), the air was hot and then hotter, and if sometimes—usually in December—the temperature at night got down to seventy-five degrees you wore a sweater, and a flannel blanket was put on the bed. Once, the parents of a girl I knew got a refrigerator, and when they were not at home she asked me to come and put my hand in the freezer part. I was convinced then (and remain so now) that cold air is unnatural, man-made, associated with prosperity (refrigerators being common in the prosperous North), and more real (as the artificial always seems) and special than the warm air that was so ordinary to me. And then (when I moved to the prosperous North) I became suspicious of cold air, because it seemed also associated with the dark. With the cold comes the dark. In the dark, things grow pale and die, and no explanation, from science or nature, of how the sun can shine brightly in the deep of winter has ever been satisfactory to me. In my heart I know that the cold and the light, the winter and the summer, cannot be at the same time.

Summer: One afternoon, before I arrived for dinner at my friend Albert's, he and his mother were walking in his garden. Albert's garden is an enormous circle, subdivided into rectangular beds, half-circle-shaped beds, square beds; it is separated from his house by a wide sheet of obsessively well-cut grass and a deep border of iris, foxglove, and other June-and-July flower-bearing perennials. Albert was in a fretful mood (his mother's presence had made him that way); he was looking forward to feeding me (he later told me so), because I like the food he cooks (almost always something he has grown), and also, perhaps, because my presence would come as a relief (he did not tell me this). As Albert and his mother walked, they removed faded flowers and ripe vegetables (he plants flowers and vegetables freely together), and they exchanged the silences and sentences typical of people bound together in a way they did not choose and cannot help (and so do not like). When his mother came to a bed where Asiatic lilies were in bloom, she broke one of the exchanges of silence by saying, "Just look at these nigger colors." Albert was shocked but not surprised; after all, this was his mother, whom he had always known.

When I arrived, Albert made cocktails, and snacks of vegetables with a dip while his mother and I walked in the garden. We exchanged monuments of praise to Albert's gardening ability, and when we came to the bed of Asiatic lilies I wondered (since I did not know her very well) if I should be my natural and true self or unnatural and untrue. Without deciding, I blurted out something true. I said, pointing to the Asiatic lilies, "I hate these colors." Then I went back to being unnatural and untrue (polite, that is), and would have forgotten Albert's mother entirely, except that later, while Albert and I did the dishes alone, he was venting his irritation with the people in his life whom he loved but did not like, and he told me of what had happened before I arrived—of his mother's casual but hateful remark. Had I sensed the true character of the person with whom I was taking a walk in the garden, I would have embraced the Asiatic lilies and their repulsive, psychedelic hues.

Autumn: Visible from the back door of my house is a stone wall, sensibly separating a terrace and flower bed from a sudden downward slope (which my children like for sledding). The stone wall was dilapidated, and two men—one fat, the other thin (this Jack Sprat style in couples is not an unusual sight in Vermont)—came to rebuild it. One day, as they worked, I sat on a stone step (also in need of repair), revelling in my delicious position of living comfortably in a place that I am not from, my position of visitor, of not the native, of seeing my orders carried out by the two men who were stooped over before me. I had to tell one of the men to save Mrs. Woodworth's roses, which he had dug up in the process of dismantling the wall. Mrs. Woodworth was the previous owner of my house (she is now dead), and her roses had been in that spot for forty years and had come from her mother's house, in Maine, so I had a sentimental feeling about them, a false feeling that no native can afford to have.

After the man agreed to save the roses, he told me that he had been to New York City only once in his life and didn't wish to go there again. He said that when he was a boy he had been to New York City on a day trip with his class, and their bus had been pelted with stones by some people; not all the people who threw the stones were colored, he said; he liked colored people, but his father did not; his father had been in the Army with some colored men, and they had all got along very well until they were ordered into battle and all the colored men in unison turned and ran away. I said it was so sensible of the soldiers to run away; I would certainly have done the same; and it was just as well that the soldiers were colored, because if they had been white, his father would have come to dislike white people, and then certainly his mother would have looked like me. He stared at me and said he saw what I meant—but that couldn't have been true, because I couldn't see right away what I meant.

The next day, he brought me a small paper bag full of bulbs, each the size of three thimbles. He did not know the name of the flower the bulbs would bear, but he described it (small, white, star-shaped) and said it would bloom earlier than anything else in spring. I wanted to plant the bulbs quite near the stone wall, so I waited until the wall was finished, and left the paper bag of bulbs unprotected on the ground. The paper fell apart; the bulbs spilled out and scattered. Each morning, as I went to work in the garden, I planned to plant them, and at the end of each day I would resolve to do it the next day. And finally one day, with gestures completely free of anger, I put them not in the compost heap but in the rubbish bin.

Between the end of summer and the shortest day of the year, I battle a constant feeling of disbelief. All things come to a halt rapidly; they die, die, die; the garden is all brown stalks and the ground is tightening. What continues to grow and bloom does so in isolation. All the different species of chrysanthemums in the world grouped together (and I have seen more than a hundred and fifty strains of them on display at once in greenhouses at Smith College), all the sedum, all the rest of it—it's beautiful, but it takes place against a background of dead or almost so.

People will go on and on about the beauty of the garden in winter. They will point out scarlet berries in clusters hanging on stark brown brittle branches; they will maintain that this beauty is deep and unique, and that it will be even more so when brought inside. They talk about the Christmas rose (and sometimes they actually say *Helleborus niger*—but why, when the common name sounds much better, the way common names do?); this plant, in bloom in December, is beautiful, but only in the way of a single clean plate found on a table many months after a large number of guests have eaten dinner there. Or people describe the barks of trees, in varying stages of peeling, and the moss or lichen growing on the barks of other trees, the precious, jewel-like sparkle of it at certain times of day, in certain kinds of light—and, you know, I like lichen and moss, but, really, to be reduced to admiring it because nothing else is there except brown bramble and some red berries and mist! It is willful, this admiration of the garden in winter, this assertion that the garden is then a beautiful place. Here is Miss Gertrude Jekyll (with whose writing I am so in love that I am always pleased to see a picture of her and realize how beautifully ugly she was, but never know what to make of her English habit of infantilizing and making cozy—a nice grouping of nut-bearing trees cannot remain so but must become The Nutwalk):

> A hard frost is upon us. The thermometer registered eighteen degrees last night, and though there was only one frosty night next before it, the ground is hard frozen. . . . How endlessly beautiful is woodland in winter! Today there is a thin mist; just enough to make a background of tender blue mystery three hundred yards away, and to show any defect in the grouping of near trees.

But this is not true at all, of course—not to me. I want to say to her (but I can't, she's dead), "This is just something you are saying, this is just something you are making up." I want to say that I am looking out my window, and the garden does not exist: it is lying underneath an expanse of snow, and there is a deep, thick mist slowly seeping out of the woods, and as I see this I do not feel enraptured by it. White is not a color at all (the snow is white, the mist suggests white); white only makes you feel the absence of color, and white makes you long for color, and white makes you understand that the space is blank and is waiting to be filled—with color.

It is best to accept what you have, and not go and take from other people the things that they have and you do not; and so I accept that I now live in a climate that has four seasons, one of which I do not fully appreciate—certainly not from a gardener's point of view. What I would really like is to have winter, but only outside the area that is my garden; my garden would be the West Indies, but only until spring. That is what I would really like. Since I cannot have it, I hope never to hear myself agreeing with this:

> I determined to bring life to my garden in winter—to make autumn join hands with spring. Winter was to be a season in its

own right, vital to the gardener who really wants to garden. I decided, like that innovative gardener, William Robinson, to banish the idea that "winter is a doleful time for gardens."

So says Rosemary Verey, in her book "The Garden in Winter." Not one idea or photograph in this book made me change my mind, and it is just the sort of thing to give pleasure a bad name. The effort to be put into finding beauty in a dry branch, a leafless tree, a clump of limp grass, the still unyielding earth is beyond me, and is not something I can summon naturally, without inner help.

One very cold night this winter, I had just had dinner with my friend Kristen in a dreary restaurant in Bennington (dreary only because it won't change the menu: year in, year out, it serves the same dishes, good-tasting dishes but always the same). Just as we were walking toward our cars, she pointed to a charred stalk, the remains of a purple cone flower (I had seen it when it was in bloom), and she said, "Oh, that's so great! You know, I have decided to plant only things that will look good when they are dead and it's cold in my garden."

Again, there was so much effort involved. I thought of the lilies in Albert's garden. Here is the reason I do not like those lilies. Years ago, when I was young, for a period of about a year I took a hallucinogenic drug at seven-day intervals. Near the end of the year, the hallucinogenic part of the drug ceased to have any effect; I experienced only the amphetamine part, which put my stomach in a taut and jittery state. This hallucinogenic drug was sometimes square, sometimes round; it fitted well in the middle of my tongue; it was glassy, sometimes yellow, sometimes orange—the exact texture and color of Albert's lilies. I never fail to see those flowers, their waxy texture, their psychedelic shades, without becoming aware of my stomach. At dinner with Kristen, I had been discussing how overwhelming is the beginning of winter, the middle of winter, the end of winter, and how much I missed my garden; and she mentioned seasonal mood shifts (those were her words, exactly) and the number of mood-modifiers available to the average person today. She spoke the word "Prozac." I had seen this drug; it was in the palm of a druggist's hand, being shown to me. It was two-toned: a slight shade of green and a smudged white—winter colors, from "nature's most sophisticated palette" (Rosemary Verey again). When Kristen and I parted, she was still in a state of admiration of the asleep and the dead, the remains of a fire by ice. At that moment, I was thinking, I want to be in a place where people don't see a landscape of things dead or asleep and desire it or move mountains to achieve its effect; by tomorrow, I want to be in a place that is the opposite of the one I am in now. At that moment I did not know if that place would be a modified mood or the West Indies.

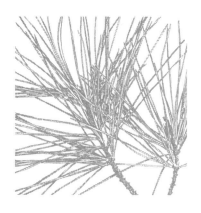

Matsuo Bashō

"Cold night" and other haiku

Matsuo Bashō, a seventeenth-century Japanese poet, took what had been a playful, lighthearted poetic form designed for a quick entertainment and transformed it into a literary art form. Instead of a mere game, the haiku in his hands became a poem that is able to express, in a very short capsule, the full range of human emotion and experience. He was able to make this transformation as part of his attempt to fuse literary craft with the search for spiritual truth as experienced in the natural world— a fusion he formed in his fuga, *his artist's way of life, within his exploration of Zen Buddhism.*

Though much of his life was reclusive, he formed his haiku during several journeys across Japan. Some of his winter poems depict strikingly lovely images set against a snowy landscape, but in most, winter is a time of loneliness, of hardship, of struggle to survive. Still, in his hands, haiku maintains its playfulness, so that the images, while stark, strike with a harsh delight.

Some of his winter poems depict strikingly lovely images set against a snowy landscape, but in most, winter is a time of loneliness, of hardship, of struggle to survive.

Cold night

the sound of a water jar
cracking on this icy night
as I lie awake

At the house of a person whose child had died

bending low—the joints,
the world, all upside down—
bamboo under the snow

---

to Kyoto
still half the sky to go—
snowy clouds

---

first winter shower—
the monkey also seems to want
a small raincoat

---

the winter garden—
thinning to a thread, the moon
and an insect's singing

a wintry gust—
cheeks painfully swollen,
the face of a man

somehow, in some way,
it has managed to survive—
pampas grass in the snow

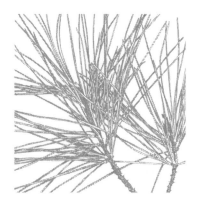

Barry Lopez

"ICE AND LIGHT"

In the Arctic, the summer is never long enough to take away the winter, warns Barry Lopez in his Arctic Dreams. *Lopez explores the connections between the landscape of the Arctic and its artistic, physiological, psychological, and biological manifestations. There he finds a world with a kind of purity and power that might be unique on earth, but it is at the same time both frightening and appealing.*

In this passage from "Ice and Light," Lopez begins by remarking on the contrast between the dark and light of the landscape, but he moves quickly to a depiction of the overwhelming cold of winter in the Arctic. It is so overwhelming, in fact, that it is almost unknowable.

> *I*t is the season that brings with it darkness and madness and oppression. It is pictured in Inuit art as a nightmare that threatens, in a supernatural sense. And oddest of all, it is a season that is still linked to beauty.

It is the season that makes rocks shatter and skin freeze. It is the season that brings with it darkness and madness and oppression. It is pictured in Inuit art as a nightmare that threatens, in a supernatural sense. And oddest of all, it is a season that is still linked to beauty.

ICE AND LIGHT

It is my habit when I travel to note resemblances, particularly of form and color. For example, that between the bones of a lemming and a strand of staghorn lichen next to it on the tundra. Or the sound of a native drum made from walrus intestine and its uncanny resemblance to the underwater voice of the walrus. Or between an object I have never seen before and objects I am familiar with—the head of an arctic hare's rib and the rainspout gorgons of cathedrals. Scoresby's observation is memorable; a pure contrast of black and white draws much in the Arctic together. Sunlit icebergs on a matte-dark sea are a very common example. But I also remembered this point when looking up to see arctic hares feeding on a shadowed hillside. Or any of the white summer birds against dark hills or soil—ivory gulls and tundra swans. Or the other way around—black guillemots flying over the white ice. Or any of the arctic birds in which the black-and-white pattern is so apparent—snowy owl, snow bunting, dovekie, common loon, snow goose. The black bowhead with its white chin patches. Walrus on an ice floe. Leads in the spring ice.

The startling contrast in these images became a reminder for me of the tendency to register only half of what is there in a harsh land, to ignore the other part, which is either difficult to reach or unsettling to think about. The dim-lit ocean beneath the ice, so difficult of access, remains unknown, as do the winter lives of many of the animals and plants. The ice life of the ribbon seal is known, but not its pelagic life. The beautiful throat-singing of the Eskimo, *kata-jak,* is heard by the winter visitor but not the shouts of a shaman bound by his helpers with walrus-hide cord and "traveling" in a trance. Caribou moving through the Ogilvie Mountains like wood smoke in a snowstorm, that image, but not the caribou cow killed by ravens in her birthing.

I would remember a flock of jet-black guillemots, streaking low over the white ice.

In the middle of summer, lying on my back on the warm tundra, I would think about the winter, because the summer by itself was so peaceful and I was trying to understand how the whole land-scape fit together. Winter, with its iron indifference, its terrible weight, explained the ecstasy of summer. The effects of winter were disquieting to contemplate. Not the cold, though that could make you whimper with pain; it could, they would say, make rocks give up and shatter. Not the cold but the oppression. The darkness that came down. The winter wind that picked up a boat in a village and pitchpoled it across the frozen beach, as if darkly mad. The oral literature of the Eskimo is full of nightmare images from the winter months, images of grotesque death, of savage beasts, of mutilation and pain. In the feeble light between the drawn-in houses of a winter village, you can hear the breathing of something with ice for a heart.

I remember a January in Fairbanks when the temperature stayed around minus 45°F for a week. Any bit of moisture in the air turned to crystals, creating an ice fog. It is haunting and beautiful to see the exhalations of a herd of caribou hanging over them like a cloud in that cold, or breath trailing behind a gliding snowy owl. But in Fairbanks, where the fog from furnaces and cars and wood fires was suspended just above the streets, it was oppressive. It blurred the edges of buildings and muffled the sound of the already obscure passing car. Snow as hard as concrete took the curbs away from the streets. In the witless gray light, huge ravens walked the alleys behind stores, tearing at bits of garbage. They hunkered on the tops of telephone poles in the white vapor, staring down, cawing that ear-splitting caw. I never felt anything so prehistoric.

Winter darkness shuts off the far view. The cold drives you deep into your clothing, muscles you back into your home. Even the mind retreats into itself.

In winter I try to remember the spring: light so brilliant the eyelid by itself is no protection. You sleep with a strip of felt tied over your eyes. (I would think of Winifred Petchey Marsh, wearing snow goggles with thin slits while she painted on the tundra at Eskimo Point, because sunglasses distorted the colors.) Of air so clear, a vista so open, you thought you would be able to see Iowa from the banks of the Colville, with just a little elevation. But in winter I would also dwell on darkness. A kind of darkness, for example, that afflicts the Kaminuriak caribou: excess killing at the hands of Eskimos, in modern times. Everyone is afraid to say something about it, for fear of being called a racist. It is easier to let the animals go than to confront that tenebrous region in ourselves. The darkness of politics, in the long hours, runs into the darkness of the land. Into anger.

I would think of the Eskimo. The darker side of the human spirit is not refined away by civilization. It is not something we are done with. Eskimo people, in my experience, have, still, a sober knowledge of their capacity for violence, but are reluctant to speak of it to whites because they have been taught that these are the emotions, the impulses, of primitives. We confuse the primitive with the inability to understand how a light bulb works. We confuse the primitive with being deranged. What is truly primitive in us and them, savage hungers, ethical dereliction, we try to pass over; or we leave them, alone, to be changed. They can humiliate you with a look that says they know better.

In the modern ironies of a remote village—satellite televising of game shows, a small boy wearing a Harvard sweatshirt, pasta for dinner with cloth napkins, after a sermon in the Baptist church about the scourge of Communism—even here, especially here, it is possible to catch a glimpse, usually in the preparation for a hunt, of the former power, the superhuman strength and unflinching intensity, of the *angakoq*. He is an intermediary with darkness. He has *qaumaneq,* the shaman light, the luminous fire, the inexplicable searchlight that enables him to see in the dark, literally and metaphorically. He reaches for the throat of darkness; that is the primitive, as primitive as an explosion of blood. Out hunting, in the welter of gore, of impetuous shooting, that heady mixture of joy and violence, sometimes it is possible for an outsider to feel the edge of the primitive. Unbridled, it is frightening. It also defeats starvation. And in its enthusiasm for the concrete events of life, it can defeat what weighs against the heart and soul.

Winter darkness brings on the extreme winter depression the Polar Eskimo call *perlerorneq*. According to the anthropologist Jean Malaurie, the word means to feel "the weight of life." To look ahead to all that must be accomplished and to retreat to the present feeling defeated, weary before starting, a core of anger, a miserable sadness. It is to be "sick of life," a man named Imina told Malaurie. The victim tears fitfully at his clothing. A woman begins aimlessly slashing at things in the iglu with her knife. A person runs half naked into the bitter freezing night, screaming out at the village, eating the shit of the dogs. Eventually the person is calmed by others in the family, with great compassion, and helped to sleep. *Perlerorneq*. Winter.

I would turn over a tiny Dorset mask, the anguished face, in my mind. I recall a day of errors, hunting seals in the ice of the Beaufort Sea. I felt whatever trouble we had had that day was due to my own failures of attitude, though this was self-indulgent thinking. I was skinning a bearded seal on a small ice cake with another man, in silence. The ocean—still as a pane of glass. One call only, from a loon. I thought how the ice under my feet *could suddenly melt*. I was standing on water over the water. My heart went into my neck. Later we ate. I ate the meat of the seal.

No summer is long enough to take away the winter. The winter always comes. You try to get a feeling for the proportions of a full life, one that confronts everything. An animal dies. You face two central, philosophical questions: What is death, and what is the nature of an animal? You fall asleep on the summer tundra in the streaming light. You awake to the sound of birds—plovers and Lapland longspurs. Inches from your eye, an intense cluster of Parisian blue flowers. A few inches farther a poppy nods under the weight of a bumblebee. Above, cumulus clouds as voluptuous as summer fruits. You roll over and embrace the earth.

A black guillemot flies over the white ice, and then disappears against the dark water.

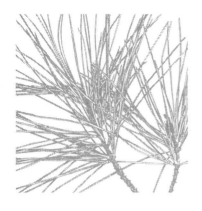

Kathleen Norris

FROM *THE CLOISTER WALK*

The frozen landscapes of Basho and Lopez provide a crucible for the soul that yearns for the life and heat of spring; it worries that perhaps these are lost forever. In her thoughts upon cold and winter, Kathleen Norris recognizes that winter is a season that leads one to contemplate endings and loss; some of her winter scenes occur in graveyards—an appropriate setting, she seems to suggest. And yet, her recognition of the meaning of the season enables her to make sense of the season and the experience that it affects. There is cold, and there is sorrow. It may be that there are demons dancing in the snow. And yet. . . .

> *In her thoughts upon cold and winter, Kathleen Norris recognizes that winter is a season that leads one to contemplate endings and loss.*

Kathleen Norris is a poet and essayist best known today for her books Dakota: A Spiritual Geography *and* The Cloister Walk. *In both works, Norris uses a specific place to focus her meditations of faith, grace, and the religious life—and the anomaly of such things in contemporary North America. In* The Cloister Walk, *from which the following selections are taken, she examines the Benedictine lifestyle and its meanings for an American at the turn of the century—something she could do only from the inside, so she became an oblate of Assumption Abbey in North Dakota, the state in which she lives. She organizes her book by using the Christian liturgical year, and much of her experience is affected by the seasonal nature of that organization.*

FEBRUARY 2: CANDLEMAS / PRESENTATION OF THE LORD

Today, the monks are doing something that seems futile, and a bit foolish. They are blessing candles, all the candles they'll use during worship for the coming year. It's good to think of the light hidden inside those new candles; walking to prayer each morning in the bitter cold, I know that the light comes earlier now. I can feel the change, the hours of daylight increasing. The ground has been covered by snow since Thanksgiving; in this climate, I'll seize hold of any bit of hope, even if it's monks saying prayers over candles. The reading from Karl Rahner, at morning prayer, came as a shock. To hear so esteemed a theologian cry out, "I have still to become a Christian" was humbling. The words have stayed with me all day. I wonder if one of the reasons I love the Benedictines so much is that they seldom make big noises about being Christians. Though they live with the Bible more intimately than most people, they don't thump on it, or with it, the way gorillas thump on their chests to remind anyone within earshot of who they are. Benedictines remind me more of the disciples of Jesus, who are revealed in the gospel accounts as people who were not afraid to admit their doubts, their needs, their lack of faith. "Lord, increase our faith," they say, "Teach us to pray." They kept getting the theology wrong, and Jesus, more or less patiently, kept trying to set them straight. Except for Peter, the disciples were not even certain who Jesus was: "Have I been with you all this time, and still you do not know me?" Jesus asks in the Gospel of John, not long before he's arrested and sentenced to death.

Maybe because it's the heart of winter, and the air is so cold that it hurts to breathe, the image of the sword from Luke's gospel comes to mind as I walk back home after vespers. We've heard it twice today, at morning prayer and at Mass. I wonder if Mary is the mother of *lectio,* because as she pondered her life and the life of her son, she kept Simeon's hard prophecy in her heart. So much that came easily in the fall has become a struggle this winter. I still walk to morning prayer—it seems necessary to do—but it requires more effort now. Still I know that it is nothing that I do that matters, but what I am, what I will become. Maybe Mary's story, and this feast, tell us that if the scriptures don't sometimes pierce us like a sword, we're not paying close enough attention.

TRIDUUM NOTES

On Holy Saturday, I walk up the hill to the cemetery and I meet old Fr. Gall walking stiffly toward me, dressed in a black suit, a narrow, European cut decades out of fashion. He twirls his walking stick and says, brightly, "Ah, you have come to visit those who are in heaven? You have come to seek the living among the dead!"

The air is full of the anticipation of snow, a howling wind. Words will not let me be: *in cold and silence you are born, from the womb of earth, the cloud of snow yet to fall.* And from somewhere in the liturgy: *What has been prepared for me?* Tonight I have a big responsibility; after the Service of Light, after the long story of the Exultet is sung—"This is the night, this is the night"—I will speak the first words of the Liturgy of the Word, the opening lines of Genesis: "In the beginning, God . . ."

My friend Columba and I share this first reading—here, they divide it between God and a narrator. Rehearsing in the abbey's chapter house, we had flipped a coin, and Columba won the part of God, which I didn't mind in the least. The narrator has better lines. Now, standing in the church full of people I can barely see, I say them slowly, as if I had all the time in the world. It is the creation of the world we are saying, and I'm surprised to find surprise in the lines: let there be . . . and there was, God waiting to see, and to call it good.

THE PARADOX OF THE PSALMS

There is much beauty in the psalms to stir up childlike wonder: the God who made whales to play with, who calls the stars by name, who asks us to drink from the stream of delight. Though as adults we want answers, we will sometimes settle for poetry and begin to see how it is possible to say, "My soul sings psalms to God unceasingly (Ps. 30:12), even if that means, in the words of one Benedictine nun, "I pray best in the dentist's chair."

The height and depth of praise urged on us in the psalms ("Let everything that lives and that breathes / give praise to the Lord" [Ps. 150:6]) can heighten our sense of marvel and awaken our capacity to appreciate the glories of this world. One Benedictine woman has told me of herself and another sister getting permission from their superior, in the days before Vatican II, to don army-surplus parkas and ski-patrol pants and go cross-country skiing in the early spring. Coming to a wooded hill, the women sank in waist-deep snow and discovered at their feet a patch of hypatia blossoms. "There'd been an early snow that fall," she said, "and those plants were still emerald green, with flower buds completely encased in ice. To me this was 'honey from the rock' [Ps. 81:16]. It was finding life where you least expect it."

Sometimes these people who live immersed, as all Benedictines do, in the poetry of the Psalter, are granted an experience that feels like a poem, in which familiar words that have become like old friends suddenly reveal their power to bridge the animal and human worlds, to unite the living and the dead. Psalm 42, like many psalms, moves the way our emotions do, in fits and starts: "Why are you cast down, my soul, / why groan within me? / Hope in the Lord, I will praise God still" (v. 5). But its true theme is a desire for the holy that, whatever form it takes, seems to be a part of the human condition, a desire easily forgotten in the pull and tug of daily life, where groans of despair can predominate. One sister wrote to me: "Some winters ago, when ice covered all the lands surrounding our priory, deer came close in search of food. We had difficulty keeping them from eating our trees and even the shrubs in our cemetery." Having been at the convent for many years, she had known most of the women buried there. One morning she woke to find that "each deer had selected a particular tombstone to lie behind, oblivious to us watching from the priory windows. The longing for God expressed at the beginning of Psalm 42, 'Like the deer that yearns / for running streams, / so my soul is yearning / for you, My God,' has stayed with me ever since."

FEBRUARY 10: SCHOLASTICA

One winter night, Benedict's sister, Scholastica, was awakened by a song bird. How can this be, she thought, and she looked out the window of her cell. Three naked men were dancing in the monastery garden by the light of the moon. One whistled like a bird and made her laugh. The men were fair to look at, Scholastica thought, but she knew she needed more rest before the first prayers of the day.

Kneeling by her bed, she closed her eyes and sleepily said a prayer for the men—if they were men—that they might find shelter, clothing, and rest for their dancing feet, and if (as she suspected) they were demons, that they might return to from whence they came.

When she awoke, her cell was filled with the scent of roses. Where the men had been dancing a rose bush had sprung up and was blooming in the snow. It bloomed all that winter, and it blooms to this day.

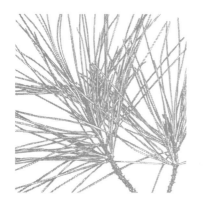

Jane Kenyon

"WHILE WE WERE ARGUING" AND "APPLE DROPPING INTO DEEP EARLY SNOW"

As Madeleine L'Engle reminded us, it is not only the physical deprivations of winter that engulf us, but even more destructively, the spiritual coldness that threatens our souls as we struggle against the loss of hope. Jane Kenyon,

poet and wife of the poet and essayist Donald Hall, chronicles such despair in sharp, precise images. Her poems link images to multilayered meaning and create the kind of vivid split moment that smacks of much beyond itself. So it is with "While We Were Arguing" and "Apple Dropping into Deep Early Snow," which link large, cosmic images—snow, a dark sky, the

> *As* Kenyon suggests in her final line, the desolation of winter may seem to gesture toward the silent emptiness of the world itself, "Lord, when did we see You?"

moon, shredding clouds, dusk, the damned—with small, particular images: tears on a sweater, cups of tea, shriveled fruit.

The argument between the couple comes with the first snow, and the shriveled fruit falls into a deepening snowdrift. In both cases, the narrator recognizes that something huge has happened in the universe: that small argu-

ments and shriveled fruit in wintertime are emblematic of something much, much larger. As Kenyon suggests in her final line, the desolation of winter may seem to gesture toward the silent emptiness of the world itself, "Lord, when did we see You?"

While We Were Arguing

The first snow fell—or should I say
it flew slantwise, so it seemed
to be the house
that moved so heedlessly through space.

Tears splashed and beaded on your sweater.
Then for long moments you did not speak.
No pleasure in the cups of tea I made
distractedly at four.

The sky grew dark. I heard the paper come
and went out. The moon looked down
between disintegrating clouds. I said
aloud: "You see, we have done harm."

Apple Dropping into Deep Early Snow

A jay settled on a branch, making it sway.
The one shriveled fruit that remained
gave way to the deepening drift below.
I happened to see it the moment it fell.
Dusk is eager and comes early. A car
creeps over the hill. Still in the dark I try
to tell if I am numbered with the damned,
who cry, outraged, Lord, when did we see You?

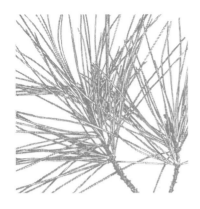

John Jerome

"November: Old Guys"

In Stone Work, *John Jerome, a writer from western Massachusetts, reflects upon what he calls "serious play"—the kind of good, hard work that is appropriate and important in itself, that smacks of inclination as well as necessity, and which allows the worker the opportunity to reflect on its meaning. The work he examines is moving a stone wall from the woods beside his farmhouse to a field so that he can see it. Organized around a single year, the work of moving the stones gives Jerome the opportunity to reflect on the meaning of life in a country, rather than urban, setting. He does this, like Jane Kenyon, by focusing on the particular.*

The question of permanence becomes acute for Jerome during the season of winter—a season that shows nothing is really permanent: all of life changes, all of life ends.

But Stone Work *is not nostalgic. The work is hard, unforgiving, and frustrating. The artistry shown by so many of the walls is elusive. The forces against him—gravity, frost, friction—all easily thwart him. There are temptations, too: he could build with the temporary in mind, rather than the eternal. But he does not. He recognizes that though the walls today are in the wrong places, marking fields that are no longer fields and are no longer owned within the same boundaries, still they are permanent. They are more than remnants.*

In this selection, "November: Old Guys," the question of permanence becomes acute for Jerome during the season of winter—a season that shows nothing is really permanent: all of life changes, all of life ends. Here, with winter setting in and the grinding tedium of the season bearing down, he reflects upon work and age, upon death and endurance, as winter sends him scurrying from work and into a world where things end and bring, with their endings, sorrow and the smell of carrion.

November: Old Guys

The woods go silver in November, almost transparent—and so, in some faltering, autumnal way, do I. The understory vegetation is gone now, the woods spare, a little gaunt, opened up to reveal the shape of the land. Snow comes and goes over a long succession of gray, thirty-five-degree days; with or without snow the loop stays slick, its trail underlain with sodden leaves, the footing treacherous. There's a weakness to the light, draining the woods of their dramatics. This morning we get a break, a bright sun and a whippy little north wind around the house, but in the woods all is calm. With four inches of crusty snow, the loop is a real slog: I break through and extricate myself again with every step. Halfway around, the dogs and I come across a patch of bloody snow where some predator has scored. Or I come across it; this time it's the dogs who don't pick it up, getting well past—downwind, to the south—before they do a twenty-yard double take and scamper comically back to investigate. I can't even feel a breeze, never mind smelling anything.

Down below, the new deck is almost finished—just in time to be buried under snow for the winter. We'd been trying since last spring to get a deck built on the west side of the house, a nicer one than my skills as a carpenter would allow. For this we hired Ed, the friend of a friend—somewhat nervously, never having seen his work—but a local building boom kept him from getting started until the fall. To reduce the cost, and to learn some carpentry, I volunteered as helper, full-time gofer, holder of the other end of boards. On the first day Ed produced a jackhammer and set me to work demolishing an old concrete stair—a new experience, running a jackhammer, and one that doesn't need repeating. The first few hours at it demonstrated that stone work had not made me as fit for hard labor as I had thought, and by nightfall I was doing some serious rethinking of my volunteer role, worried that I might not be physically able to continue. But over the next few days the aches began to go away, as I trained up for it, just as in athletics. I can still get in shape for work like this, I realized, I just don't want to.

With snow on the ground, work on the wall is out of the question. It's no fun when your hands are cold anyway, and I got enough of that finishing the deck, sticking out into the north wind like the prow of a ship. On many mornings there would be a rim of ice or a few inches of snow on the lumber. Ed would arrive at eight wearing long johns, bundled up in a hooded sweatshirt and down vest. I'd join him, similarly attired but also wearing gloves, which Ed disdained. This wasn't carpenter's machismo, but simple adaptation: he'd worked outdoors well into winter in the past, and would again, and there was no point in losing toughness painfully acquired. I once read of mountain-climbers who, in order to train their hands, skied through a winter without gloves, so I guess it can be done. Not by me.

Building the deck was real work all right, hammers and saws, all day every day, answering to Ed's schedule rather than my own. Just like a job. Demonstrating more eloquently than stone work had ever done what a dilettantish thing I was doing when I played around with my wall. What it required physically was pure stamina, to deal with the ongoing fatigue. By midafternoon in the November cold I'd be stumbling, no longer trusting myself to attempt anything that required more than the most fumbling efforts. Ed would go right on doing delicate or difficult work, maintaining a fine balance between the urge to get the job done and the patience to do it right. I couldn't maintain that balance and didn't really try. Didn't have to. Ed's helper, who wasn't much of a carpenter to start with, got steadily worse—stupider, and less ambitious—as the day wore on.

The weather finally got too damned cold for me, and I packed it in. All that remained was the very fine finish work anyway, which required a very fine patience (and none of my ham-handed skills), and I was pretty much reduced to standing around shivering while Ed fitted very fine wood into very fine joints. While I twitched nervously, brooding about the cost of the lumber, the cost of his time, the non-income-generating cost of my own. So I abandoned it to him—to his great relief, I'm sure—and came indoors. There were still a couple of chores that had to be done to get the place ready for winter, but otherwise, I decided, it was time for the great out-of-doors to start coming in shorter doses.

I bailed out of the deck project early in November and, knowing that at any moment winter would clang shut the door, set about battening down the place: putting the tractor up on blocks, hauling in lawn and garden stuff, winding hoses and draining faucets while the dark wind blew, getting the storm windows on and sealed. Bolting down hatches, reefing sails.

The shorter November's days become, in their shocking plunge into winter, the more obsessive I am about getting around the loop. Even while I was working with Ed, I'd wait for the moment he went home for lunch, then be off like a shot. After I quit and came inside, I'd work at my desk until I heard his truck leave, then bolt for the door—not having the chutzpah to stroll off into the woods while he was there doing honest labor.

I don't know why, but there's more carrion around in the late fall. Maybe the onset of cold weather kills off creatures too weak to make it through the winter, leaving them to rot instead of being sanitarily eaten by predators. (Willy suggests that the scavengers may have gone south, or into hibernation.) Anyway, it attracts the dogs. They stay with me on the trail only until they smell something interesting, which they then go find. Usually it is not carrion, and they smell it carefully and then return. If it is carrion, they roll in it first, decorating their withers, and come back prancing with joy and self-importance, trying to decorate me, too.

If I'm paying attention I can call them back before they get into the noisome stuff, but my mind wanders. Earlier this month Pawnee returned from one of these side trips with the silly grin that indicated she had a small treasure in her mouth—one that Molly or I should try to steal. It was the skull of some small mammal, a weasel or something, with enough flesh left on it to stink horribly. I got it away from her and put it well up out of reach in the crotch of a tree (breaking her heart and Molly's too, and ensuring a pilgrimage to that particular spot on every walk for the next several years). In the process I had to handle skull and dog, and by the time we got back to the house we both urgently needed a bath. I left parka and gloves outdoors, took Pawnee directly to the basement and bathed her, stripped and threw my clothes into the laundry, and took a shower myself.

It didn't really help, not enough. The smell—that awful, psychically terrorizing smell of death—kept hanging around for the rest of the day, in spite of anything I could do. It's been giving me the creeps ever since, that charnel-house aspect of death. I can't imagine why dogs are so attracted to it. The experts' explanations for this behavior are unsatisfactory. It makes me consider not taking the dogs with me into the woods for a while, at least until everything is covered by a sufficiently protective layer of snow.

Then, a day or two before my upcoming fifty-fifth birthday, one of our two old cats had a stroke, and began listing around the house, crashing into walls, unable to stand. These were *very* old cats, a mother and daughter. (The mother was born the summer of Robert Kennedy's assassination.) It was the daughter that had the stroke, and we knew immediately that she would have to be put down. The mother was already deaf, mostly blind, incontinent, had been for some time. The two were inseparable. It would be crueler, we realized, to leave the old mother alone than to go ahead and put her, too, out of her misery.

So on the morning of my birthday, we took them to the vet's and had the deed mercifully, quickly done, and brought the pathetic old bodies home, where, in a cold, sleety rain, I buried them. Deep. That, I announced, was the absolute guaranteed last goddamned outdoor chore of the year. Another couple of weeks and the ground would have been frozen and we couldn't have done it anyway. Those two old cats had been damned nuisances for years, and we eased them out of our lives (and theirs) with a sigh of relief. Matter-of-factly decided, matter-of-factly done. Except that we could barely speak to each other for about ten days, and would wait a whole two weeks after that before we got a new kitten.

The evening after the disposition of the cats, Willy came over—Liz was out of town—for a determinedly noncelebratory birthday dinner. We never mentioned the cats, or much of anything else, I'm afraid. Weird evening: he must have wondered what the hell was going on. Late fall may not be the best time of year for the dispatch of elderly animals.

A certain personal gloominess seems to set in in November anyway, starting, probably, when we go off daylight saving time at the end of October and lose one more hour out of days already grown depressingly short. I chose this period to haul an assortment of physical complaints off to the medical profession and was finally convinced, by experts, that what I thought was chronic tendinitis was in fact a mild, not particularly common form of arthritis. Not a tragedy, just a nuisance. Depressing. This is not the first time I've become depressed in the late fall. For a long time I regarded it as nothing more than an annual phobic reaction to the onset of the Christmas season—my fear of ceremony being surpassed only by an inborn panic at the threat of group activities.

I found reassurance, then, when the media began running their annual assortment of pop-science pieces about Seasonal Affective Disorder, or SAD. That's the trendy new scientific name for autumnal blues: an actual hormonal disturbance resulting from the shortening of the days. They've been talking about it for a few years now; medical science has finally come up with a disease for those of us who regularly find November more difficult than October, and December more difficult than November. We can begin to breathe a sigh of relief: thank God, it's real, it's hormones and not madness. *It's not our fault,* we shriek; they've finally jacked up our craziness and run a little physiology under it. (Are you willing to accept responsibility for your behavior, to vouch for its rationality from, say, November 15 to February 15 of last year? Think about it.)

November grinds darkly on, and the snow begins to get serious. I slog through it for as long as I can, but eventually it gets either too deep or too icy. When depth is the problem I can switch to skis or snowshoes, but this year, as often happens, we get freezing rain on top of snow, setting up such a glaze that skis or snowshoes can get no purchase. Ice skates would be more in order; to walk in ordinary boots is to ask for fractures. (Last year in these conditions I put on my skis at the back door, pushed off, fell instantly, and slid on my back the seventy-five yards down to the pond before I could stop. Had to take my skis off and virtually crawl back up to the house.) What I need are mountaineer's crampons.

I am determined not to give up the loop, not even long enough to wait for the next, softening snowfall. I am also determined, in some peculiarly crotchety way that I don't quite understand, not to buy a real set of crampons: too expensive, too formalized somehow, even if I knew where to get them. I decide instead to invent my own. I dig out an old pair of rubbers and push a handful of thumbtacks through the soles of each, from the inside out. I slip the rubbers over hiking boots, and set out. Perfect: like you've just stepped out of the rosin box, like gum-rubber soles on a freshly varnished gym floor. Very comfortable, stable, safe, you don't know you've got them on. I'm a genius.

Except that I gradually lose that reassuring traction, and when I finish the loop and take the rubbers off, the heads of the thumb-tacks pour out in my hand. Friction has broken off all the points. I need a heavier grade of tack. Nothing in the garage or the basement fits the bill, so I drive into town, to the hardware store. I browse the racks of brads and fasteners, considering carpet tacks versus uphol-stery tacks, roofing tacks, brads, big-headed nails, certain that just the right tack exists for my purposes, a vision of the perfect solution in my head. A salesperson offers assistance, but I am loath even to attempt an explanation of the peculiar specificity of my needs, and wave her off. Trying to get the physics right, I notice, can lead to a certain fussiness.

It is three-thirty on a gray November afternoon, the hardware store somnolent under flickering fluorescence. The quietness pene-trates my attention, and I look around. It's a large, modern store, and scattered here and there along the aisles are five or six old guys, picking through the racks of stuff. Must drive the sales force crazy, I think to myself, as my fingers flutter over the packages of tacks.

I describe this scene to Chris. "Right," she says. "Old guys: more and more intelligence focused on smaller and smaller problems."

Not intelligence—wisdom, says I. We old guys have much wis-dom to offer on subjects such as tacks.

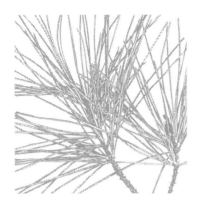

Robert Finch

"A Winter Burial"

Winter is a time of burial, and the metaphors so often attached to the natural world—"buried under feet of snow"—often seem to speak just as clearly and poignantly to the human experience. The naturalist and essayist Robert Finch finds this to be so in this short account of the winter burial of an older woman on Cape Cod. All burials, as John Donne pointed out, represent a loss to the whole, and though the essayist did not know this woman well, her death marks a kind of passing and is a powerful reminder of mortality. The reminder is particularly powerful when the natural world seems to join forces with human liturgies to spell ending, death, and burial.

As terrible as this irremediable emptiness of death is, an even deeper dread haunts us in winter. It is the fear that this time of barrenness, sterility, and loss will never reach its horizon but will stretch out into an unbearable eternity of ice—always winter, but never Christmas, as C. S. Lewis cast it in The Lion, the Witch, and the Wardrobe. *The conclusion of this essay speaks powerfully of this fear—and of the thwarted hope that may sometimes feed it.*

> *W*inter is a time of burial, and the metaphors so often attached to the natural world "buried under feet of snow"— often seem to speak just as clearly and poignantly to the human experience.

A WINTER BURIAL

In mid-March, about a week before the vernal equinox, there was a burial in the small church graveyard nearby. The deceased was a woman in her eighties, a native of the town and a neighbor of mine for several years. She had "not been well" this winter and had moved from the small old Cape where she had lived all her married and widowed life into her daughter's home down the street.

Two days earlier a pile of tarps and inverted rugs of AstroTurf had been deposited just inside the cemetery's wooden fence, in front of her husband's stone, which had been erected thirty years earlier. The following day I walked over and found that the grave had been dug and the concrete vault placed within it. Tarps covered the hole, the mound of dirt beside it, and the vault lid lying on the ground.

I stood there, on that bare, cedar-studded knoll, beneath the damp wind and grey skies of March, while wet flakes of snow fell on my head and shoulders and on nearly two hundred years of local graves surrounding me. I felt a strong sense of loss, though it was not personal in nature. True, I had known the deceased for nearly a decade, but it was only as a neighbor whom I had visited infrequently. She had shared many local stories and much neighborhood history with me, yet I had found her formal and reserved, difficult to warm to.

No, her death was, for me, more representative than individual. What I felt was a sense of fundamental change rather than personal loss—a deep change in the life and makeup of the neighborhood that had nothing to do with personal character. Until a few years ago, for instance, she had played a direct role in most of the infrequent burials that took place here. As one of the oldest residents in the area, she had been escorted to the cemetery each time by the funeral director to look over the proposed gravesite and pronounce it "clean," since, in her words, there were many "bones without stones and stones without bones." A strongly-rooted knowledge of place, I realized, was passing with her.

A night of wind and heavy rain left only a tattered and sodden blanket of the weekend's snow on the ground. The early redwings, singing in the nearby marsh, had been right after all. The burial service was scheduled for two o'clock that afternoon. During the morning, a truck from the funeral home roared unceremoniously up the road. Two young rough-shaven men got out and erected over the grave site a large green canopy, with canvas walls on the east and south sides as a protection against the expected prevailing winds.

At 1:30 I shaved, put on an overcoat, and walked over to the cemetery. The weather was still raw, grey, and wet. Several cars had already arrived, and soon the little triangle at the intersection of the two country roads was ringed with vehicles. The people, mostly older friends and neighbors, walked up the short cemetery road and, with canes and helping hands, negotiated the tall stone step at the opening in the fence and walked over to the canopied grave site. Some forty people in all came, including grandchildren from Florida, a town selectman, a farmer, the town archivist and the president of the local historical society, a landscaper, the rural mail carrier, and a retired lobsterman and his wife. Except for the grandchildren and the undertaker, few people there were under sixty.

The family and the most elderly of the mourners sat on folding chairs inside the canopy, while the rest of us stood, mostly bareheaded and silent, in the cold March wind for some twenty minutes, waiting for the last of the visitors to arrive. I was impressed by the number of mourners and by the cumulative years of friendship they represented, but even more by the organic fabric of personal ties visible in the assembly. Many of those here had played and gone to school as children with the deceased, and their families had intertwined over the years like the roots of catbriar growing down the bank. I realized that this was not just a gathering of friends, relatives, and acquaintances come to pay respects, but also a true community ritual, a witnessing of another of its own passing.

The canopy, from outside, appeared like a green proscenium, giving those seated within the air of participating in a curiously domestic scene, as if they were all visiting her in her sitting room, or at her bedside. The coffin—made of dark, massive, polished walnut—was raised on a bier and mounded with flowers (one basket had "GRAM" embroidered on a ribbon), so that it seemed larger than life, hiding, rather than emphasizing, the presence of an actual body within, as though she were already down in the earth with her husband. (I found myself musing, Would he be pleased to have company again after such long solitude? Or disturbed? Or perhaps, as Thornton Wilder suggests of the long dead in *Our Town,* merely temporarily inconvenienced and unremembering?)

The minister, indistinguishable from the other people in his heavy overcoat, read a few predictable verses from the New Testament, including that curious pronouncement of Christ's from the gospel of John: "In my Father's house are many mansions: if it were not so, I would have told you." Then why, I always think, why raise the doubt?

And that was all. The assembly quickly dispersed, many of them heading back to the daughter's house for some food and talk. As a casual acquaintance, I would not be going, but I went up to the daughter, a handsome, grey-haired woman in her late fifties with a gentle, sweet face. I said that I was glad to have known her mother and that I would miss her, which was true. She thanked me and said how much her mother had enjoyed some of my books.

There followed a long, awkward moment of silence as we stood facing one another. I knew I should have simply returned the thanks and withdrawn, but I felt the need to say something more, to connect a little more closely with the occasion. I clasped her hands and blurted out, "I'm glad to have known *you,* too!"

"Oh," she smiled sweetly, "we plan to be around for a while, I guess."

I started to stammer something about not meaning that, of course, but, instead, I gave an awkward chuckle and sidled away, having learned once again that you can't force belonging. As I did, an elderly woman with a cane came up to her, touched her arm, and said, "She didn't quite wait for spring, did she, dear?"

PART TWO

Winter As a Time to Be Scoured, and a Time to Succor the Scoured

INTRODUCTION

The relentless, pitiless winter weather highlights our frailty before the larger forces of the natural world, and it particularly highlights the vulnerability of those who are poor, dispossessed, or struggling on the outskirts of their culture and society. The writer of the Wakefield *Second Shepherds' Play* depicts the grim reality of being poor and cold on a winter's day:

> *Lord what these weathers are cold! And I am ill*
> > *happed;*
> *I am nearhand dold, so long have I napped;*
> *My legs they fold, my fingers are chapped.*
> *It is not as I would, for I am all lapped*
> *In sorrow:*
> *In storms and tempest,*
> *Now in the east, now in the west,*
> *Woe is him has never rest,*
> *Midday nor morrow!*

But the play does not leave the shepherd here. The winter season is for him and his companions a terrible time of trial, but it is precisely because they endure the trial well and fruitfully that, by the end of the play, though the season has not changed and the weather is still cold, they are now singing hymns of praise to God. The situation is mirrored in Christina Rossetti's well-known carol:

> *In the bleak midwinter,*
> *Frosty wind made moan,*
> *Earth stood hard as iron,*
> *Water like a stone.*
> *Snow had fallen, snow on snow*
> *Snow on snow,*
> *In the bleak midwinter,*
> *Long ago.*

The opening verse of the carol evokes winter as a time of desolation—it is cold, frozen, hard as iron, filled with snow, beset by a moaning wind. Yet, the next three verses of the carol are verses of joy and fulfillment, as the Christ child comes to earth because "heaven cannot hold him." Rossetti captures another vision of winter—a vision quite different from one of desolation. Yes, winter is hard and cold, but it is also a time within which is couched a quiet sense that we live through such a time by understanding our terrible vulnerability and by recognizing our need for something beyond the desolation.

And so we search around us for ways to beat back the darkness, the cold, the barrenness. In the Hindu faith, that darkness is represented in Deepawali, Hinduism's most important festival, which comes in early winter on Karthik Amavasya, the darkest night of the lunar year. To symbolize the beating back of the darkness, *deepas* (lamps) are lit to fill the emptiness with cheer and joy and to suggest the ultimate victory of goodness and justice and wisdom at a time when such victory seems far away. The lamps themselves represent detachment from this world, devotion to God, meditation, and spiritual wisdom—elements of the spiritual life that are hardly supported by a winter's landscape, it might seem. But with their light, they celebrate an individual and communal response to the darkness.

For this is a season that, in making us aware of our individual vulnerabilities, encourages a communal understanding; the winter, with its incipient danger and threat, reminds us of those most vulnerable to such threats. So it is entirely appropriate that for Orthodox Christians, one of the hallmarks of the winter feasts is the celebration of hospitality. An ode sung at Compline on the third day of the Prefeast of Christmas proclaims, "Come, O faithful, / Let us enjoy the Master's hospitality, / The banquet of immortality." For Christians, winter is the season in which God shows hospitality to humankind through the incarnation, but it is also the season in which we are enjoined to reflect that hospitality by opening hearts and hands to God and neighbor. "The most wise Lord comes to be born, / Receiving hospitality from His own creatures. / Let us also receive Him, / That this divine Child in the cave may make us His guests," sing Orthodox believers during Matins on the first day of the Prefeast.

The hospitality of God in the harshest of seasons is the theme with which the seventeenth-century preacher Lancelot Andrewes wrestles. He does not presume to know "why God, in the dispensations of the seasons, did so order, that at such a year of the world, such a month of the year, such a day of the month, this should fall out," but Andrewes does take the opportunity to "admire the high wisdom of God, in the dispensation of seasons; that now at this season, when we gather nothing, when nothing groweth to be gathered, there should be a gathering yet and a great one; nay, the greatest gathering that ever was or will be; and so by that means, the poorest and emptiest season in nature, become the fullest and richest in grace."

Seeing such hospitality in the time of winter, Andrewes argues, should lead us to a recognition of our own spiritual responsibilities. "For we also make it a season of gathering together; of neighbourly meetings and invitations, wherein we come together, and both ourselves have, and we make each other partakers of, what we have gathered, all the year before." And thus winter is turned around and becomes "the season of dispensation; in that we then dispense the blessings God hath sent us; and that is, in good house-keeping, and hospitality." In this sense, as Andrewes suggests, winter may in fact be called the season of fullness, for in dispensing hospitality in this season, we bring to ourselves and to others nothing short of a celebration of God's gifts. "There is more fulness in this season, than any other. And so it is the season of fulness then; for 'the hungry are then filled with good things'; then, of all the seasons of the year."

This is the kind of understanding suggested in another old carol, that of good King Wenceslas, who looks out from his time of feasting, sees the man laboring through the snow to gather winter fuel, and decides that he and his page will follow him to bring the feast that he himself is enjoying. Wenceslas realizes that the very act of hospitality is a way to turn aside the harshness of the winter season of the world, and of the soul, and to prepare for something quite different. "Mark my footsteps, my good page; / Tread thou in them boldly; / Thou shalt find the winter's rage / Freeze thy blood less coldly."

Ron Hansen

"WICKEDNESS"

Ron Hansen, known for his novels The Assassination of Jesse James by the Coward Robert Ford, Mariette in Ecstacy, Atticus, *and* Hitler's Niece, *assembles a collection of winter vignettes in "Wickedness." The title comes from a warning issued to a young easterner on her first trip out west: "Look out for the winters; weather in Nebraska can be the wickedest thing you ever saw." And indeed it is. As blizzards scour the countryside in 1888, Axel Hansen freezes into speech-lessness, Mathias Aachen shoots his entire family, and an Omaha cigar maker dies within fifty yards of his own home. The pitiless brutality of the cold penetrates—and even breaks—the warmest bonds of human companionship.*

> *For all its desolation, the wickedness of winter is not ironclad; it, too, must yield to the persistent human spirit.*

Yet, though a father forgets his love for his children, or finds it hopelessly perverted by the wicked cold, succoring warmth percolates up from unexpected sources. It arises like fragrant incense from the pigsty where Ainslie Classen warms his hands in the animals' pungent waste. It bubbles up from the boundless optimism of a seventeen-year-old heart, sustaining Addie Dillingham as she picks her way across the icy railway trestle toward Omaha. For all its desolation, the wickedness of winter is not ironclad; it too must yield to the persistent human spirit.

WICKEDNESS

In the year 1888, on the twelfth day of January, a pink sun was up just after seven and southeastern zephyrs of such soft temperature were sailing over the Great Plains that squatters walked their properties in high rubber boots and April jackets and some farmhands took off their Civil War greatcoats to rake silage into the cattle troughs. However, sheep that ate whatever they could the night before raised their heads away from food and sniffed the salt tang in the air. And all that morning streetcar mules were reported to be acting up, nipping each other, jingling the hitch rings, foolishly waggling their dark manes and necks as though beset by gnats and horseflies.

A Danish cattleman named Axel Hansen later said he was near the Snake River and tipping a teaspoon of saleratus into a yearling's mouth when he heard a faint groaning in the north that was like the noise of a high waterfall at a fair distance. Axel looked toward Dakota, and there half the sky was suddenly gray and black and indigo blue with great storm clouds that were seething up as high as the sun and wrangling toward him at horse speed. Weeds were being uprooted, sapling trees were bullwhipping, and the top inches of snow and prairie soil were being sucked up and stirred like the dirty flour that was called red dog. And then the onslaught hit him hard as furniture, flying him onto his back so that when Axel looked up, he seemed to be deep undersea and in icehouse cold. Eddying snow made it hard to breathe any way but sideways, and getting up to just his knees and hands seemed a great attainment. Although his sod house was but a quarter-mile away, it took Axel four hours to get there. Half his face was frozen gray and hard as weatherboarding so the cattleman was speechless until nightfall, and then Axel Hansen simply told his wife, That was not pleasant.

Ainslie Classen was hopelessly lost in the whiteness and tilting low under the jamming gale when his right elbow jarred against a joist of his pigsty. He walked around the sty by skating his sore red hands along the upright shiplap and then squeezed inside through the slops trough. The pigs scampered over to him, seeking his protection, and Ainslie put himself among them, getting down in their stink and their body heat, socking them away only when they ganged up or when two or three presumed he was food. Hurt was nailing into his finger joints until he thought to work his hands into the pigs' hot wastes, then smeared some onto his skin. The pigs grunted around him and intelligently snuffled at his body with their pink and tender noses, and Ainslie thought, *You are not me but I am you,* and Ainslie Classen got through the night without shame or injury.

Whereas a Hartington woman took two steps out her door and disappeared until the snow sank away in April and raised her body up from her garden patch.

An Omaha cigar maker got off the Leavenworth Street trolley that night, fifty yards from his own home and five yards from another's. The completeness of the blizzard so puzzled him that the cigar maker tramped up and down the block more than twenty times and then slept against a lamppost and died.

A cattle inspector froze to death getting up on his quarter horse. The next morning he was still tilting the saddle with his upright weight, one cowboy boot just inside the iced stirrup, one bear-paw mitten over the horn and reins. His quarter horse apparently kept waiting for him to complete his mount, and then the quarter horse died too.

A Chicago boy visiting his brother for the holidays was going to a neighbor's farm to borrow a scoop shovel when the night train of blizzard raged in and overwhelmed him. His tracks showed the boy mistakenly slanted past the sod house he'd just come from, and then tilted forward with perhaps the vain hope of running into some shop or shed or railway depot. His body was found four days later and twenty-seven miles from home.

A forty-year-old wife sought out her husband in the open range land near O'Neill and days later was found standing up in her muskrat coat and black bandanna, her scarf-wrapped hands tightly clenching the top strand of rabbit wire that was keeping her upright, her blue eyes still open but cloudily bottled by a half inch of ice, her jaw unhinged as though she'd died yelling out a name.

The one A.M. report from the Chief Signal Officer in Washington, D.C., had said Kansas and Nebraska could expect "fair weather, followed by snow, brisk to high southerly winds gradually diminishing in force, becoming westerly and warmer, followed by colder."

Even at six o'clock that evening, there was no heat in Mathias Aachen's house, and the seven Aachen children were in whatever stockings and clothing they owned as they put their hands on a Hay-burner stove that was no warmer than soap. When a jar of apricots burst open that night and the iced orange syrup did not ooze out, Aachen's wife told the children, You ought now to get under your covers. While the seven were crying and crowding onto their dirty floor mattresses, she rang the green tent cloth along the iron wire dividing the house and slid underneath horse blankets in Mathias Aachen's gray wool trousers and her own gray dress and a ghastly muskrat coat that in hot weather gave birth to insects.

Aachen said, Every one of us will be dying of cold before morning. Freezing here. In Nebraska.

His wife just lay there, saying nothing.

Aachen later said he sat up bodingly until shortly after one A.M., when the house temperature was so exceedingly cold that a gray suede of ice was on the teapot and his pretty girls were whimpering in their sleep. You are not meant to stay here, Aachen thought, and tilted hot candle wax into his right ear and then his left, until he could only hear his body drumming blood. And then Aachen got his Navy Colt and kissed his wife and killed her. And then walked under the green tent cloth and killed his seven children, stopping twice to capture a scuttling boy and stopping once more to reload.

Addie Dillingham was seventeen and irresistible that January day of the great blizzard, a beautiful English girl in an hourglass dress and an ankle-length otter-skin coat that was sculpted brazenly to display a womanly bosom and bustle. She had gently agreed to join an upperclassman at the Nebraska School of Medicine on a journey across the green ice of the Missouri River to Iowa, where there was a party at the Masonic Temple in order to celebrate the final linking of Omaha and Council Bluffs. The medical student was Repler Hitchcock of Council Bluffs—a good companion, a Republican, and an Episcopalian—who yearned to practice electro-therapeutics in Cuernavaca, Mexico. He paid for their three-course luncheon at the Paxton Hotel and then the couple strolled down Douglas Street with four hundred other partygoers, who got into cutters and one-horse open sleighs just underneath the iron legs and girders of what would eventually be called the Ak-Sar-Ben Bridge. At a cap-pistol shot the party jerked away from Nebraska and there were champagne toasts and cheers and yahooing, but gradually the party scattered and Addie could only hear the iron shoes of the plowhorse and the racing sleigh hushing across the shaded window glass of river, like those tropical flowers shaped like saucers and cups that slide across the green silk of a pond of their own accord.

At the Masonic Temple there were coconut macaroons and hot syllabub made with cider and brandy, and quadrille dancing on a puncheon floor to songs like the "Butterfly Whirl" and "Cheater Swing" and "The Girl I Left Behind Me." Although the day was getting dark and there was talk about a great snowstorm roistering outside, Addie insisted on staying out on the dance floor until only twenty people remained and the quadrille caller had put away his violin and his sister's cello. Addie smiled and said, Oh what fun! as Repler tidily helped her into her mother's otter-skin coat and then escorted her out into a grand empire of snow that Addie thought was thrilling. And then, although the world by then was wrathfully meaning everything it said, she walked alone to the railroad depot at Ninth and Broadway so she could take the one-stop train called The Dummy across to Omaha.

Addie sipped hot cocoa as she passed sixty minutes up close to the railroad depot's coal stoker oven and some other partygoers sang of Good King Wenceslaus over a parlor organ. And then an old yardman who was sheeped in snow trudged through the high drifts by the door and announced that no more trains would be going out until morning.

Half the couples stranded there had family in Council Bluffs and decided to stay overnight, but the idea of traipsing back to Repler's house and sleeping in his sister's trundle bed seemed squalid to Addie, and she decided to walk the iron railway trestle across to Omaha.

Addie was a half hour away from the Iowa railway yard and up on the tracks over the great Missouri before she had second thoughts. White hatchings and tracings of snow flew at her horizontally. Wind had rippled snow up against the southern girders so that the high white skin was pleated and patterned like oyster shell. Every creosote tie was tented with snow that angled down into dark troughs that Addie could fit a leg through. Everything else was night sky and mystery, and the world she knew had disappeared. And yet she walked out onto the trestle, teetering over to a catwalk and side-stepping along it in high-button shoes, forty feet above the ice, her left hand taking the yield from one guy wire as her right hand sought out another. Yelling winds were yanking at her, and the iron trestle was swaying enough to tilt her over into nothingness, as though Addie Dillingham were a playground game it was just inventing. Halfway across, her gray tam-o'-shanter was snagged out just far enough into space that she could follow its spider-drop into the night, but she only stared at the great river that was lying there moon-white with snow and intractable. Wishing for her jump.

Years later Addie thought that she got to Nebraska and did not give up and was not overfrightened because she was seventeen and could do no wrong, and accidents and dying seemed a government you could vote against, a mother you could ignore. She said she panicked at one jolt of wind and sank down to her knees up there and briefly touched her forehead to iron that hurt her skin like teeth, but when she got up again, she could see the ink-black stitching of the woods just east of Omaha and the shanties on timber piers just above the Missouri River's jagged stacks of ice. And she grinned as she thought how she would look to a vagrant down there plying his way along a rope in order to assay his trotlines for gar and catfish and then, perhaps, appraising the night as if he'd heard a crazy woman screaming in a faraway hospital room. And she'd be jauntily up there on the iron trestle like a new star you could wish on, and as joyous as the last high notes of "The Girl I Left Behind Me."

William Cooper

FROM CONCIO HYEMALIS. A WINTER SERMON

The eighteenth-century Boston minister William Cooper sees a link between the particulars of human life and the universal, perhaps cosmic, world. For Cooper, winter is a warning, a natural sign that causes us to recognize how much sorrow and hardship are part of our lives. Winter makes us withdraw from the world; it pinches, disables, tempts us to neglect our duties, and threatens us with an inward cold—suggesting a loss of love for God and others. Yet winter also nudges us toward God, for in the bitterest cold life continues, and we edge slowly but surely toward the coming of spring.

In the end, Cooper holds out the vision of a heavenly place where there is no need for seasons—where, in fact, winter, with its sorrow and hardship, will be forever dispelled. "The better country is the heavenly," he writes, "for

> *W*inter makes us withdraw from the world; it pinches, disables, tempts us to neglect our duties, and threatens us with an inward cold—suggesting a loss of love for God and others. Yet winter also nudges us toward God, for in the bitterest cold life continues, and we edge slowly but surely toward the coming of spring.

there will be no uncomfortable changes or vicissitudes." This is the tension that Cooper sets out: winter is a time of hardship, but also a time when God preserves. Winter is the lowest point of the seasonal cycle, but evidence too of God's sustaining hand. Humanity faces the winter of pinches and with-drawal, but also the possibility of a heavenly country of eternal summer.

FROM *CONCIO HYEMALIS. A WINTER SERMON*

The changes and extremities of the weather are the matter of our daily observation, and the subject of our common talk, and serve perhaps oftener than any one thing to open our conversation when we meet together: but how seldom do we think and speak of these things after a religious manner.

The Psalmist was not so inobservant and irreligious as this. He adores the God of Israel as the God of nature: that God from whom all the powers of nature are deriv'd, and on whom they depend, and who produceth all the changes of the seasons, particularly of the winter season. "He sendeth forth his commandment upon earth, his word runneth very swiftly. He giveth snow like wool; he scattereth the hoar frost like ashes. He casteth forth his ice like morsels: Who can stand before his cold? He sendeth out his word and melteth them: He causeth his wind to blow, and the waters flow."

This is a lively and beautiful description of the winter season, which succeeds the summer. How is the face of the earth then changed? The gay and pleasant flowers are withered, the fruits for delight and necessity are gathered in, and the creatures that us'd to feed and play in the verdant pastures and meadows are hous'd; and nothing to be seen abroad but snow, frost, and ice, which are [en]gendered by the cold which we now feel, until the temper of the air is alter'd, by the return of the sun, and the blowing of warmer winds, by which the frost, snow, and ice, are presently dissolv'd, and the face of the earth happily renew'd.

As we have felt, and seen the effects of the cold in the weeks past, in a degree beyond what is usual, I shall endeavor to make a religious improvement of it, in a short discourse this morning, from that part of the text which has been read, "Who can stand before His cold?" . . .

No creature can, as the degree of it is sometimes increas'd. The beasts cannot; then they go into dens, and remain in their close places. And then the strongest and fiercest of them are more easily conquer'd. And men can stand before it less than the most of the brute creatures. They are now forc'd to put on their double clothing, and to retire into their houses, and to their firesides; and all little eno' when the cold is in extremity. Many that have been expos'd to it when the degree of it has not been beyond what is common among us, have lost not only their limbs, but their lives by it. And God could easily increase it to such a degree, that all our defenses shou'd not be sufficient to secure us from being mortally pierced with it, to the stopping the circulations of the fluids of the body, and therewith the breath of life.

And so I come to see what good Use may be made of this winter meditation; to show you how the cold we feel may be improv'd to the ends of devotion and practice. And in this part of the discourse I must still be short, because we can't stand long before His cold.

Let us reflect now, think, and say,

The Lord is great in power! He makes the sons of men to know this, if indeed they will know it, in his changing of the seasons. The effect of cold particularly, which is freezing; whereby the breadth of the waters is straitened; the rivers that spread themselves, and flow'd with a great deal of strength and liberty, are suddenly arrested, congeal'd, and bound up, so as to become a strong bridge for men to walk and ride on to the opposite shore.

Wisdom, as well as might is His! His wisdom appears in the variety of His works. Everything is beautiful in its season; and there is a beauty in every season of the year. God has for wise ends appointed the succession of summer and winter. The fruitfulness of the earth, and the health of man, are consulted hereby. The cold of the winter purifies the air; and generally cold countries are the most healthful and long liv'd. And the snow, produc'd by the cold, not only waters the earth, but cherishes it, and makes it to bring forth. Some of the most beneficial fruits of the earth, are our winter grain, produc'd by God's blessing on the cold and snow.

We shou'd be patient under the cold, since 'tis God's cold. When our bodies are pinched by it at any time, and our hands seal'd up, in its disabling us for our work and business; or we are put to extraordinary expense to guard ourselves against it; let us bear these and such inconveniences arising from the cold without murmuring or fretting. . . .

Let us learn our obligation to thankfulness, for warm houses, clothes, and beds; for comfortable food and fuel, to relieve us against the rigor of the cold!

And it deserves a particular thankful notice, that God has spar'd our habitations to us in this extreme season that has pass'd over us; that fire has not broken out in this large town, in which there are such a vast number of fires kept every day, and so many careless and vicious inhabitants, at a time when the water in the docks and in many of our pumps is frozen, and men cou'd not stand long before the cold to put out a fire. This, I say, is a wonder of undeserved mercy, for which we are indebted to a kind and watchful providence.

We shou'd likewise be thankful to God who has carried us thus far thro' the difficulties of the present hard winter, and thro' all the winters of the years of our lives. If his visitation had not constantly preserv'd our spirits, his cold had been too hard for us, notwithstanding all the reliefs against it, with which we are provided. The aged among us have been carried thro' many a winter. The years of your lives contain some scores of winters; and tho' it may be of a tender and weakly constitution, yet having obtain'd help of God you continue to this day.

Let us beware of the temptations of the season; and not make the cold an unjust pretence to neglect any of our duties. . . . The usual exercises of religion should still go on. The cold should not keep us out of our closets, nor chill our devotions there. It shou'd not keep us from the house of God. . . . Next to the love of God we shou'd keep up a warm love to our neighbour. . . . Therefore the colder the season is, the warmer shou'd our charity be; for then the needs of the poor are greatly increased. Blessed be God that this excellent grace is so warm in many of you that hear me, whereby the bowels of the poor members of Christ are refreshed! But what thanks shou'd we render to God for those at a distance from us, who are so enriched by Him to all bountifulness, both to the brethren at home, and to strangers abroad, that their charities are diffused like the kind rays of the morning sun?

Lastly, the better country is the heavenly: For there will be no uncomfortable changes or vicissitudes. There nothing will molest or disquiet us. The sun will not smite us, nor the cold pierce us. . . .

There we shall dwell under the direct beams of the glorious sun of righteousness, and be always enlivened and warmed by him. Here we must shorten our devotions sometimes, because we can't stand long before his cold; there we shall serve him day and night in his temple, without any thing to impede us, and go no more out. Our now weak bodies will then be powerful ones, never weary, never need any of those refreshments which now we can't do long without; they will be able to keep pace with our souls in the service of God, and the devotions of them will be ever warm and lively, like those of their companions the angels, whom he makes a flame of fire.

O! how shou'd the inconveniences of the present world make us long for that, and hasten to it as fast as we can; where we shall bid an eternal farewell to winter, and enter upon an everlasting spring of heavenly joys and consolations, without any mixture or alloy.

Jim dale Huot-Vickery

"CLOSING THE CIRCLE"

Jim dale Huot-Vickery's "Closing the Circle" is a work that comes out of living in a remote cabin in Minnesota's Boundary Waters. Here in the wilderness of the north, where winter grapples the land for seven months of the year, Huot-Vickery finds a world both still and eager, both beautiful and harrowing. It is a place of solitude and isolation, but it is also a place whose winter provides for an exploration of the meaning of that solitude. Here, winter is the crucible of the search for the self.

In a place where winter is so harsh and so long, the question of vulnerability is a very real one; the season shows in dramatic fashion how frail life may be. In this chapter, Huot-Vickery watches for two deer, hoping for their survival despite the freezing cold nights, the lack of food, and the work of the wolves. The search for those two deer, the hope amid the despair, the strong sense of his place in the circle of the world—all of these contribute to Huot-Vickery's sense of the meaning of the winter event.

If winter is to remind us of vulnerability, Huot-Vickery suggests, then that notion should be understood and even embraced, not particularly feared or even particularly overcome. Winter is what it is, and as such it takes its place in our own cycles of spiritual despair, slow renewal, and growth.

> The question of vulnerability is a very real one; the season shows in dramatic fashion how frail life may be.

CLOSING THE CIRCLE

Stars: 15°F: Barometer Steady

> Had a dream of a bunch of eagle feathers under water. They were attached to each other, and had red ribbons.
>
> Other feathers—smaller ones—fringed the eagle feathers, all running parallel, like a blanket or shield of feathers.
>
> The feathers were in a flowing river.
>
> —journal, Hocoka, Winter

The circle of Hocoka tightened and closed, I suppose, on a starry winter night when I howled with the wolves. Inevitably the snows had come, again and again, deepening, astounding even old men and women of many winters. By March the snow-depth approached the all-time record of 122 inches, almost double the winter average, almost three feet more snow than what deer, wolf, and people were used to.

It was winter 1995–96.

It was my thirteenth winter at Hocoka.

There'd be days of ten inches of snow, then a few inches, then a blizzard dumping two more feet. Or just a foot, then another foot a week later. Tree branches broke. Roofs in Ely collapsed. Sheds at remote cabins crumbled. Bitter cold followed snowfall after snow-fall. All life cringed when the thermometer bottomed-out at minus 60°F: 92°F colder than ice on puddles.

The effect of so much snow and cold intensified over time.

Slowly, yet inexorably, the wolves stopped ranging except on roads. Never had I seen the wolf patterns so disrupted. Usually a pack would pass through Hocoka about every three weeks: often along Rainbow Ridge and the smaller ridge behind the cabin. They seemed to drive deer through the woods of these ridges out onto the lake where, with a wolf coming from two directions, a deer might make a fatal mistake. This changed as the snow became too deep for the wolves to travel in without bounding. It cost too much to jump. Hence the wolves shrank back to what avenues were open: the plowed corridors of people and their packed trails.

There was a trail into my place, granting entry, but the deep snow beyond Hocoka made for a dead end.

The deer, meanwhile, began to starve.

I saw it in their ribs, their flanks, their growing lethargy.

While out walking a road one afternoon, for example, I came across a fawn that ran away from me and disappeared around a bend in the road. When I rounded the bend moments later, the fawn was curled up, exhausted, on the plowed edge of the road. At first I didn't realize what it was until, getting closer, the skinny fawn stood, ran another thirty feet, then plopped down on the roadside. The snowbanks on the side of the road were five feet high, or more, and although deer tracks led over the top into the woods the small fawn no longer had the strength to leap up and over the barrier.

Just as I thought of turning around, the fawn scrambled up the snowbank. I could see, as I walked by, it didn't go far but merely collapsed on the other side of the bank.

Head up, ears swiveling, it marked my passage.

The fawn was likely going to die.

Deer biologist John J. Ozoga put it this way in *Whitetail Winter:*

"Death from malnutrition is an insidious, pathetically slow process. Fat depletion and physical weakening progress with nearly undetectable signs, until it's too late for recovery. In the final stages, however, a deer's coat roughens, its hip bones show, and hollows appear in its flanks. The starving animal spends most of its time bedded down, in a curled head-to-tail position to minimize body surface exposure. It adopts a lethargic, uncaring attitude, no longer bounding away, flag waving, as danger nears. Small deer, especially, stand hump-backed, their front legs spread slightly, back legs close together, and hold their head up at a 45 degree angle. Deer so weakened become easy prey for predators—a sudden and merciful fate compared to a lingering death from starvation."[1]

Maybe so.

Maybe not.

I soon saw another deer, though, who might have agreed with Ozoga. I was down on the lake near a rock point, fetching water, when a buck walked around the corner. He stopped broadside twenty feet in front of me. The buck was not a regular visitor to Hocoka nor did I know who he was. It was clear, however, he was exhausted. His hip bones and ribs showed. His head hung low. Each step was heavy and slow. Most significantly, perhaps, when the buck saw me he did not run. Did not move or flinch.

Just stood there.

Spare energy, at this point for anything but standing, simply wasn't available anymore.

For me, living as I did, chores multiplied as the severity of winter progressed.

There was twice as much snow to shovel off roofs, deck, and paths as during a normal winter. There was more sledding and handling of firewood. Getting water required snowshoes instead of mukluks on a packed trail. I needed a shovel more often to get at the wooden waterhole cover, and there was more-than-average chiseling of ice followed by a delicate slog with buckets uphill to the cabin.

Mornings were colder to awaken to (with, sometimes, ice in water and slop buckets . . . getting thicker during the coldest spells). The cabin took longer to heat and, some nights, I'd need to rise to an alarm clock to feed the stove, meaning less deep sleep. Even trails had to be packed with snowshoes more often and sometimes that didn't do much good.

I'd slip off the packed snowshoe trail, either stumbling on my snowshoes or, risking mere boots, hitting the trail's unseen edge, losing balance, and falling sideways or forwards. My arm couldn't reach through the deep snow all the way down to the ground for support so I'd wallow, flounder, kind of swim in snow until I scrambled upright.

Falling and getting up used a lot of energy.

Once, seven times from car to cabin.

I'd laugh, I'd curse, I'd keep going.

But I could feel the drain.

Losing weight, burning energy to stay warm or do chores, I'd eat all the time—bananas, apples, cheese, fig newtons, pizzas, beef jerky, gorp, granola, crackers, peanut butter: anything edible—eating for energy, eating for heat, yet still losing ground like the deer out my cabin windows.

Bad head trips didn't help:

Winter's seasonal, post-rangering unemployment.

The beautiful young woman of soulful aspiration who step-laddered through me—too old now—and left a trail of bizarrely slammed doors.

Memories of Chris, Rip, my mother's cremation: ghosts all around on long, isolated nights.

It wore on a man.

Even a canoe expedition from northeastern Minnesota's Quetico-Superior to Hudson Bay hounded me. For years I'd wanted to flow like a feather on the waters of my life, the rains and snows of my years, and of Hocoka, downstream to the sea. But I had always put it off. I'd return to rangering: to duty, responsibility, obligations, paycheck, the challenges of Lake Superior, and the potentials of human companionship. There were bills to pay. Money to make. Primary partners to nurture. Alleged security. There were countless excuses for postponing a canoe journey that wouldn't go away, that was preposterous in scope, yet that called for some unknown soulful purpose for five years, ten, forever: most powerfully at critical personal junctures.

But never had I gone.

There were always too many bridges to burn. Too much at risk.

Would I *ever* embrace my quest for the sea or was it all just talk on the deck?

Maybe, as I grew older, I lacked the guts to go.

My soul felt stifled.

The head trips, the physical drain of deep snow and persistent sub-zero cold, the penetrating presence of a season civilization insulates itself against: it all reminded me of how the great naturalist Richard Nelson remarked that the earth's core is winter.

Even the universe is winter.

"Life is only something taken for a moment," he wrote in *The Island Within*,[2] "rubbed warm and held back from the chill. . . . Winter waits and finds all life. In the end, each of us stares through the dark eyes of winter."

A March night came when I heard wolves howling so I stepped out on the cabin deck beneath winter's stars.

I'd seen no sign of wolves for six weeks and missed their wild presence. Everything, it seemed, had been building to a head: all the winters, the cold and darkness, the starving deer, the inexorable loneliness of living on the edge: even the wolves were gone. Perhaps now, however, as winter's snowpack crusted over and provided better footing, the wolves were heading back into the hinterlands.

It was good to hear the wolves again.

They were howling toward the southwest, toward the lake the Ojibwe once called Kawasachong from the mist and foam of its adjacent waterfalls, while other wolves howled from the east. Likely one split pack.

I howled back.

Silence.

I howled again and the wolves joined in.

Deep, chesty bawls rose into the night through a flurry of high, excited yapping. There were moments of silence then a lone, distant howl, more howls coming from the other direction, my own rising wail, then more howling yet. Deep. Chesty. Songs drawn-out, falling, fading. Barks. Yipping. Then the deep howl again: summoning, announcing: crying out against the wintry night of all time.

Feel it the land speaking *do you hear-feel it?*

And I felt, more than knew, why the land-through-wolves was

howling. Felt why. Felt what the deep pool of silent knowledge, the voice of all primordial time, was singing.

It rose through my spirit like a wave passing onward, onward, into the infinite light of stars.

The howling.

Winter warming but the howling here.

Life worn out.

Life, sometimes, worn to death.

I awoke later from a restless sleep in the middle of the night. Very unusual for me to have insomnia. Tossed and turned.

Something happening?

Darkness filled the cabin.

I listened carefully.

Silence.

I refused to get up, as I had two nights earlier, to light lamps at 4:30 in the morning to start my day.

Why, though, the waking? Why the waking?

The first thing I saw the next morning, as I lay in bed looking out the window, was a bald eagle.

I jumped up and looked more closely.

Circling with the eagle, beneath cloudy sky, were ravens: all swooping and gliding above the cove where, *Oh no,* a deer carcass was sprawled on the snow.

Soon I was on snowshoes and, with staff, shuffling toward the deer. The snow was crusty above a layer of slush. Wolf tracks converged from several directions. *They'd come.* Flecks of fur. Deer shit. Then the deer, a yearling, twisted and mangled. Eyes gone. Rib cage red with blood. A rear haunch was ripped open and eaten.

I squatted near the yearling—one of Princess's? Solo's?—and smoked some tobacco, saluting the four directions in honor of the whitetail's short life, its hard winter struggle, and its final terror with wolves.

It was easy to understand the wolves, of course. I'd howled with them, sensed their need, and knew, like people, they had to kill to live. Still, the death, like the yearling that died at my own hand four years earlier, saddened me.

Death seemed the hunter, life-heart the prey, with soul cut by sensitivity to a tragic but necessary violence.

I'm too soft . . . too soft, I thought while snowshoeing back to the cabin. *She was right. Too damn sentimental. Feeling death like a hoof's blow yet loving enough to feel.*

A cursed blessing. A blessed curse.

Two more bald eagles joined the first one—circling 'round, screeching—as I phoned a friend, canceled her visit to Hocoka, and left the cabin for a walk out to the road.

Should not the dead yearling, eagles, and ravens be left alone?

Even as the scavengers celebrated, there was grief in the air.

There would be no gawkers this hour.

The eagles were gone when I returned although Renard was walking on crusted snow along the cove's shore.

Ravens spotted the fox, set up a racket of alarmed calls, then a lone raven flew over to Renard to swoop in circles around his head: buzzing him, harassing him: *ka-roke, ka-roke:* then land on white snow. Renard, having found shelter in brush behind a shoreline pine, came back out onto the lake and walked toward the raven, getting close, until both raven and fox knew when close was too much.

The raven leapt and flew.

Renard ran into the woods.

Later, at twilight, the hour of power, Renard crossed the cove to the dead deer and ate.

Snow began to fall.

There was no sign of Princess and her fawns, Pan and Saut, the next day. This began to concern me.

They had been daily visitors to Hocoka and, over the years, I'd become particularly fond of Princess. I named her for her slanted, Oriental eyes, and their almost sovereign expression, yet I could have named her Patience instead. She would often stand patiently by the deck and look at the cabin door or, if I was outside splitting firewood, she'd watch me until she seemed to stare me down.

I'd have to say something endearing to her or, as she likely preferred, get corn.

The last few times I'd seen Princess, shortly before the yearling was killed, she seemed nervous. Different somehow. One day she held up a leg several times and shook it as if it was sprained or annoyed her. Later I noticed her eyelids had begun to twitch which, of course, I assumed was involuntary. Half-wink twitches. She'd look away then back at me as if she knew something I didn't, suspected something, or perhaps sensed the coming presence of a force evoking violent shift.

Maybe, now, it was one of *her* fawns, possibly Saut, that was dead on the ice.

I'd gone back to the carcass after watching an immature eagle circle and soar above it, get driven off by harassing ravens, then fly back to the deer, land, and feed. By the time I got there, all that was left of the yearling was its head, skinny legs, fur, and spine gnawed clean to bone.

But where, meanwhile, was Princess or, for that matter, Solo?

I decided to look for them.

I skied to the far end of the lake, seeing old wolf tracks along the shoreline all the way. In one of the last coves, I found a piece of fur that looked like the foot-long end of a wolf's tail. I could see where bone or cartilage had ripped through and free.

Had a wolf tried to escape another wolf who bit its tail, hung on, or gave it a yank?

The next day, still searching for sign of Princess and Solo, I skied around the north end of Pine Island where, at its northern-most point, I noticed tufts of deer fur along the shore. There was discolored snow and a stained, well-used trail leading up into the woods.

I took off my skis and followed the trail into a grove, no, grave, of white pines where I found the body of a large doe. It was spread out, ribs showing, in trampled snow of wolf tracks, fur, blood, and viscera. Above the dead whitetail was a large white pine beneath which the doe had bedded.

Had she been surprised by the wolves? I wondered. *Or had she chosen to make this spot her last stand—tired of winter, no place to run, so be it?*

I looked closely at the doe's face.

She might have been Princess but it was hard to tell. Her face was too disfigured. Ravens and eagles had gone quickly for the eyes.

Two days later, a Monday, beneath overcast sky and as temperatures nudged above freezing, I awoke to another wolf-killed deer.

Saw it first thing, like the other one, straight out the bedroom window.

Down near the cove's water hole.

Enough, I thought, rolling out of bed to put my mukluks on. *Enough.* I'd slept in socks and sweater so that, at least, was taken care of. *Tired.* I put on pants, a wool shirt—*Tired of the killing*—and made a cup of coffee.

My next task was loud and clear.

Two immature bald eagles, adult-sized but brown with flecks of white, and a flock of ravens (black, black, black) fed on the freshly killed deer *Which one this time?* as I finished my coffee then hiked down to the cove to disturb the congregation. My turn. The eagles and ravens flew off. I paid my respects to the deer, a yearling doe, Pang, and decided to move her. She was too visible from the cabin, suggested more than I wanted to bear every time I glanced outside, and her remains—fur, bones, scat, along with raven and eagle shit—would settle into the ice too close to my waterhole.

Maybe contaminate it.

Right or wrong, I grabbed a leg and slid the deer to the nearest shore, scrambled through a knee-deep snowdrift, and left the stiff carcass beneath a small cedar.

Ravens found the deer by afternoon.

An eagle also returned. It perched near the top of a dead red pine along the slope of Rainbow Ridge. There, not dropping to feed, it posted a gold-eye watch on Hocoka's wild world.

"Admit it, Jim dale."

Dirk Hanson, an Ely friend and author, was challenging me after listening to some of my stories about the deer, wolves, and related fallout of the most brutal winter on record.

"Admit it. You're drawn to the dark side."

"Huh," I said, thinking:

Not so much drawn as found *there.*

Renard came by again the evening I found the last yearling. He hadn't located the new carcass yet so worked on my attention until I tossed him a chunk of suet.

Such eyes on that fox: golden, quizzical, finding mine in what seemed intelligent recognition: a pooling in those eyes of wildness, some glint of acknowledgment I couldn't quite grasp.

Could he see clear through me?

How little or much, really, did Renard know?

Were there reasons deeper than suet for why he was at my door? And why, as day ended and darkness settled, he curled up nearby to sleep?

How could I ever know this except to catch some winter sign of certainty?

Two bad dreams came back-to-back as the fuzzy light of comet Hyakutaki, visible only once every ten thousand years, passed the stars of Ursa Major with its Big Dipper.

In the first dream I was walking a grassy field with a friend and saw a lion coming toward us at an angle. It had a thick, shaggy mane that rippled and shone as the lion approached over the rolling hills. Yet as the lion got closer I saw it was a cougar. My friend and I lay down in the grass, face to the earth, as the cougar came closer. I glanced up and it was upon us.

The cougar bit into my thigh and started lifting me as I fought back.

Soon I was walking away from the grassy fields and down into a wooded area of red pines and cabin. My friend's dog, Buckwheat, was there; he, too, was scratched, bitten, mangled up. I held him and coaxed him to strength. My own wounds hurt but wouldn't be fatal. People milled around like ghosts.

Three nights later, after wolves had returned to feed on the deer beneath the shoreline cedar, and as snow fell, I dreamt of black bears attacking me. At least three bears coming, charging, across the cabin deck. One large bear stood threateningly at the cabin door.

I shot it with my rifle.

If the gifts brought to people by bears in event or dream are strength, introspection, and self-knowledge, as some people believe they are,[3] then I lost my chance.

If, however, the message was that being unaware of my limits, throwing caution to the wind in certain settings, can be dangerous, then I got the point.

I also sensed—fighting the cougar, shooting the bear—that perhaps I needed to fight back with more force in my life. Somehow resist the hostile forces of death swirling around me and, by now, within me.

Clearly, contact had been made at Hocoka and there was blood on the tracks.

But how fight back?

By embracing life more indomitably? More impeccably? By letting the spiritual warrior surface?

Winter, I could see, doesn't just come after the body. It fully challenges and, for those who survive, strengthens the soul.

By March 24, a little over a week since I'd howled with the wolves and they'd swept through Hocoka, 1 knew of at least six dead deer within a half-mile of the cabin.

Princess and Solo were still missing.

There was a dead doe and yearling at the far northeastern tip of the lake. There was the dead doe on Pine Island,[4] possibly Princess. There were two dead yearlings on, and along, the cove below the cabin. And there was another yearling—in Lund's Cove to the west—that had partially settled into meltwater where, cold weather returning, it froze in solid ice.

A fox had gnawed exposed bone.

It seemed there were deer carcasses everywhere.

Certainly, I thought, *deer feel pain, shock, and terror when they're killed.*

This wasn't anthropomorphic, some kind of human emotion cast onto the Bambis of the world.

Why else do they bawl out when they're ripped into?

Pain hurts. Life wants more life. And life prefers life joyful.

The terror of losing life, the beautiful terror, so that other life might live, could send a shudder right through me.

Nights came, some with moonlight, and I'd glance out cabin windows looking for the usual silhouettes of winter deer.

There were none.

One more deer carcass surfaced to shock me.

Deer number seven.

It was late winter, bordering on spring, and the snow was melting fast. Trails were high-ridged and treacherous, caving at the sides. A full moon, haunting, had passed. Fresh snow had fallen. Then, as days grew warmer, patches of meltwater formed aquamarine puddles of all sizes on the lake. Four eagles, perhaps those I'd seen circling each other high against a haloed sky, fed off the yearling carcass by the cove cedar. I'd started watching those eagles through binoculars: one eagle gliding through thick snowflakes along the face of Rainbow Ridge, another settling into clear water of a lake puddle where—perfectly reflected—its legs sent ripples toward bordering snow, and yet another eagle that perched atop a rock bluff's white pine.

The pine overlooked a lake landing where I kept stacks of firewood: the exact same landing, I recalled, where Chris and I—thirteen years earlier—had first found the draw leading up to Hocoka.

It was there I found the last deer carcass.

I was fetching a load of firewood when I sensed something strange, looked up, and saw the dead deer. It was hanging upside down in a fallen balsam fir on the steep slope of the bluff. Completely gutted. Rib cage and spine showed. The deer's head and legs were still attached to the skeleton. It spooked me. I felt nauseous, almost as if, with spring coming, the mangled and skeletal deer had emerged from melting snow on top the prone fir to dangle grotesquely in front of my eyes. It was a reminder, perhaps, one final sign, of all the dead deer that had come before, but this time the carcass hung in branches *above* me, could fall on me, as it baked in late-winter sunshine.

That deer could have been in those branches under snow for a month and I'd gathered my firewood nearby oblivious to its fate.

Had the deer died of starvation during a blizzard only to be dragged by wolves over the edge of the bluff?

Had it leapt down the bluff toward safety only to get caught in deep snow and the fallen fir's branches, where it struggled until exhausted then died before a burying blizzard?

It made me sick to think this might have happened as I lived my little life, well-fed, and stove-side.

Daylight, now, fading fast.

I returned to the carcass the next morning, a Sunday, as warm sunshine softened night's snow crust.

I brought a rope. Surely I had to move the deer.

I climbed the bluff from the back side, thinking I could get at the deer from above, and found tufts of deer fur scattered in needle duff beneath the white pine where the eagle had perched. That angle didn't work so I scrambled down below then slogged through knee-deep snow up to the deer. I tied the rope to a leg and slid the deer—hoping it wouldn't come apart—out of the fir branches, down the slope, then along the lakeshore to a thicket of alders beneath a cliff. I positioned the body as respectfully as I could and covered it with sticks and birchbark.

Stepping back out onto the lake, kneeling, resting in sun, I smoked tobacco in honor of another whitetail's spirit.

"The deer spoke to me."

A friend, a neighbor, was soon telling me of her dream.

In it, a starving deer had appeared to her. Part of its side was missing and its ribs showed. The deer asked her to break boughs off cedar trees so it could eat.

"I was so frightened by a talking deer," she said, "that I ran away."

Inevitably, and as I had after I shot the yearling four years earlier, I skied to the far end of the lake, visited its small island, then turned around and headed home.

Circles. Always circles.

The sun was bright on the undulating patterns of wind-packed snow. Otter tracks stitched together the lake's northernmost islands as paw marks and belly slides scrawled a wild script.

Better glide than me, I thought.

Blue sky.

White snow.

More deer.

This time they were alive and standing among pines of a ridge above me. I skied closer. One of the deer, looking down at me, stood erect and alone in the open of a snowy ridgetop. So beautiful. Solo? Princess? I slid to a stop, looked closer at that deer on ancient bedrock, *Nope, neither,* then leaned on my ski poles and—couldn't help it—just bowed my head.

Bowed, after all, to the wild beauty.

Bowed to the weight of passing winter.

Bowed to my life with whitetails and wolves.

I looked back up.

"Belle wâwashkeshi," I called as the deer began to slip away.

The rear doe stopped and turned at the sound of my voice. "Beautiful deer," I called once more.

And the light again, crystallizing, that blue sky, the shining brightness, the pines, half-moon, and whitetails, all the comings and goings, the deaths and struggles and coming sun. Such a long trail whitetails had walked: the seemingly infinite time: the wolves and winters: the Ojibwe and other peoples hungering for their meat and skin. Countless whitetail generations had come and gone, year after year, flowing with the wolves across the face of the land.

It was the way of the wolf: the way of the deer.

Call it magic and mystery like critter man Denny Olson. Call it the pulse of the Quetico-Superior, or call it Sigurd F. Olson's singing wilderness.

It was all of this and more.

Death in the white crystal light.

Life in the white crystal night.

Such a vision of terrible beauty.

Tears came to my eyes as I turned—recognizing my gift, my witnessed power, my moment of grace—to face sunshine on snow.

Let it sing, I thought skiing home. *Let it all sing.*

*Let the snow and ice and darkness, the winds and shadows, the deer bleats and wolf howls, the grunts and snorts and bawls, the fox barks and raven calls, the countless crystals and brilliant moons, the dreams and loves and enduring life: let the winter sign sing—*You took me—*let it sing on and on and on à la belle étoiles, beneath the beautiful stars.*

Let it sing.

Then they came back.

The day arrived, about a month after the wolves had killed at least seven of Hocoka's deer, when Princess sashayed up the slope from the lake as if she'd been gone an hour. I'd seen Ruff again, who looked healthy and strong, and Dusty, who had also returned to Hocoka, but Princess's appearance understandably came as a surprise.

With her were Pan and Saut, her two fawns.

And my heart soared like an eagle.

Two days later, precisely thirty-six days since I'd last seen her, Solo showed up. She, too, looked nonchalant. No cuts, no scratches, no broken bones.

The little tramp.

"Belle wâwashkeshi," was all I could say.

She, too, had been missing since the wolves had so visibly passed through. After being at Hocoka every day all winter, nay, most days every winter for ten years, then suddenly disappearing for five weeks in the wake of wolves, who *wouldn't* have assumed she was a goner?

Part wolf by April Fool's day, perhaps, or part eagle and fox.

"Welcome back," I said, restraining my joy. "Make yourself at home."

And suddenly I knew, beyond doubt, what I was going to do.

I looked at Solo, the melting snow, and the rotting lake ice of Otter beyond. It would be another three weeks before that thick ice was gone but I'd already seen crows and, at night, could hear gulls partying it up in open water beneath Kawasachong's falls. Loons flew by daily, checking ice conditions. And that very day, just before Solo appeared, I had heard the song of spring's first robin.

The winter of all winters was ending.

It was time, soon, to get going.

It was time to start packing.

It was time to varnish paddles and prepare the canoe.

Another circle needed closing.

Or was a new circle, ever so delicately, beginning to open and flower?

When the snow finished melting and rivers ran high, sure thing, I would flow with the spirit of winter's living and dead—honoring Solo's kind, the wolf's kind, my kind—all the way to the sea.

Po Chü-yi

"Bitter Cold, Living in the Village"

The harshness of winter tests not only the resources of the self but those of the community as well. We are reminded of the particular vulnerability of the poor in the spare, simple lines of the ninth-century Chinese poet Po Chü-yi, who recounts the suffering of snowbound villagers. He minutely details the fragile resources—homespun cloth and brambles—that barely sustain nine families against the brutal cold, in marked contrast to the "ample warmth" enjoyed by the tenth.

The harshness of winter tests not only the resources of the self but those of the community as well.

Yet such physical suffering also compels a searching self-analysis. "I ask myself what kind of man am I," the narrator concludes. Although the poem ends here, we hear in that final line the promise of renewed compassion.

Bitter Cold, Living in the Village

In the twelfth month of this Eighth Year,
On the fifth day, a heavy snow fell.
Bamboos and cypress all perished from the freeze.
How much worse for people without warm clothes!

As I looked around the village,
Of ten families, eight or nine were in need.
The north wind was sharper than the sword,
And homespun cloth could hardly cover one's body.
Only brambles were burnt for firewood,
And sadly people sat at night to wait for dawn.

From this I know that when winter is harsh,
The farmers suffer most.
Looking at myself, during these days—
How I'd shut tight the gate of my thatched hall,
Cover myself with fur, wool, and silk,
Sitting or lying down, I had ample warmth.
I was lucky to be spared cold or hunger,
Neither did I have to labor in the field.

Thinking of that, how can I not feel ashamed?
I ask myself what kind of man am I.

Donald Hall

"WINTER"

Donald Hall, essayist, poet, writer of short fiction and children's books, has centered much of his work on his grandfather's farm in New Hampshire. This is most particularly true of Seasons at Eagle Pond, *a collection of four ruminative pieces from which "Winter" is taken; in each of these essays, Hall explores the effects of the season on the spirit. It is telling that he begins the collection with "Winter" and sees in the season the need for all of us to prepare against the onset of the cold—to prepare, in essence, for survival.*

On a farm, this means bringing in the wood, cleaning out the wood stove, canning. Yet one need not see in winter a kind of devastating darkness, but instead a time when we can wrap ourselves in the security of our heat, when we can celebrate the ways in which we have staved off our vulnerabilities.

> *One need not see in winter a kind of devastating darkness, but instead a time when we can wrap ourselves in the security of our heat, when we can celebrate the ways in which we have staved off our vulnerabilities.*

In this sense, the chores of winter—taking care of the animals, bringing in the wood, gathering the sap for maple syrup—are all ways to overcome vulnerability: physical, economic, and spiritual. Winter, Hall suggests, becomes a time when we can come to understand who we are, when we can recognize that spring and summer are on the way. But we also need to understand that winter is what makes them as sweet as maple syrup.

WINTER

In New Hampshire we know ourselves by Winter—in snow, in cold, in darkness. For some of us the first true snow begins it; for others Winter begins with the first bruising assault of zero weather. There is yet another sort, light-lovers, for whom Winter begins with dark's onset in mid-August. If we wake as we ought to at 5:30, we begin waking in darkness, and dawn turns throaty with the ululations of photophiliacs, noctophobics, some of whom are fanatical enough to begin lamentation late in the month of June—when dawn arrives at 4:32 A.M. and the day before it arrived at 4:31:30. On June 22 my wife Jane exchanges postcards of commiseration with a fellow in Michigan who is another amorist of light. Fortunately this mountain has an upside as well as a downside. When in January daylight lasts half a minute longer every day, Jane's faint green leaves take on color; she leans south toward Kearsarge and the low, brief but lengthening pale Winter sun. An observer can spy the faint buds that will burst into snowdrops and daffodils in April, tulips in May.

Some of us, on the other hand, are darkness-lovers. We do not dislike the early and late daylight of June, whippoorwill's graytime, but we cherish the gradually increasing dark of November, which we wrap around ourselves in the prosperous warmth of woodstove, oil, electric blanket, storm window, and insulation. We are partly tuber, partly bear. Inside our warmth we fold ourselves in the dark and its cold—around us, outside us, safely away from us; we tuck ourselves up in the long sleep and comfort of cold's opposite, warming ourselves by thought of the cold, lighting ourselves by darkness's idea. Or we are Persephone gone underground again, cozy in the amenities of Hell. Sheltered between stove and electric light, we hollow islands of safety within the cold and dark. As light grows less each day, our fur grows thicker. By December 22 we are cozy as a cat hunkered under a Glenwood.

Often October has shown one snow flurry, sometimes even September. For that matter, it once snowed in New Hampshire every month of the year. In 1816 it snowed and froze in June, in July, in August—the Poverty Year, season of continuous Winter, when farmers planted over and over again, over and over again ripped out frozen shoots of corn and pumpkin. An 1815 volcanic eruption in Indonesia did it—though at the time our preachers thought the source more local and divine wrath explicit.

Winter starts in November, whatever the calendar says, with gray of granite, with russet and brown of used leaves. In November stillness our stonewalls wait, attentive, and gaunt revenant trunks of maple and oak settle down for Winter's stasis, which annually mimics and presages death for each of us and for the planet. November's palette, Braque's analytic cubism, squared with fieldstones, interrupts itself briefly with the bright-flapped caps of deer hunters and their orange jackets. Always it is modified by the black-green fir, enduring, hinting at permanence. Serious snow begins one November afternoon. South of us Mount Kearsarge gradually disappears into white gauzy cloud, vanishing mountain, weather-sign for all of us to its north. For one hundred and eighty years the people of this house have looked south at dawn's light and again at sunset to tell the coming weather, reliable in 1803 when the first builder put in the south windows and reliable still. When Kearsarge disappears the storm comes closer. Birds gather at the feeder, squabbling, gobbling their weight. When they are full they look for shelter, and we do the same, or at least we bring wood from the shed to stack beside the old Glenwoods and the new Jøtul.

Every year the first snow sets me dreaming. By March it will only bring the grumps, but November snow is revenance, a dreamy restitution of childhood or even infancy. Tighten the door and settle a cloth snake against the breeze from the door's bottom; make sure the storms are firmly shut; add logs to the stove and widen the draft. Sit in a chair looking south into blue twilight that arrives earlier every day—as the sky flakes and densens, as the first clear flakes float past the porch's wood to light on dirt of the driveway and on brown frozen grass or dry stalks of the flower border. They seem tentative and awkward at first, then in a hastening host a whole brief army falls, white militia paratrooping out of the close sky over various textures, making them one. Snow is white and gray, part and whole, infinitely various yet infinitely repetitious, soft and hard, frozen and melting, a creaking underfoot and a soundlessness. But first of all it is the reversion of many into one. It is substance, almost the idea of substance, that turns grass, driveway, hayfield, old garden, log pile, Saab, watering trough, collapsed barn, and stonewall into the one white.

We finish early in November the task of preparing the house for snow—tacking poly over the low clapboards, raking leaves against the foundations as high as we can rake them. When the first real snow arrives, no dusting half inch but a solid foot, we complete the insulation, for it is snow that keeps us warm. After a neighbor's four-wheel-drive pick-up, plough bolted in front, swoops clean our U-shaped driveway, and after we dig out the mailbox for Bert's rural delivery, it is time to heap the snow over leaves and against poly, around the house, on all sides of the house, against the granite foundation stones. Arctic winds halt before this white guard. When bright noon melts inches of snow away from the house, reflecting heat from the snowy clapboard, it leaves cracks of cold air for us to fill when new snow falls all Winter long.

But November, although it begins Winter, is only Winter's approach, with little snow and with cold that announces itself only to increase. The calendar's Winter begins at the solstice, Advent's event: the birth of the child who rises from Winter to die and rise again in Spring. November is Autumn's burial, and the smoke of victims sacrificed is thanks for harvest and magic as we go into ourselves like maples for Winter's bearsleep. We make transition by way of feast and anticipatory snow, toward the long, white, hard hundred days, the true Winter of our annual deaths. We wait for December to feel the *cold,* I mean COLD, for longer than a week, but now we are ready for snow.

The first big snow accumulates one night. Kearsarge may disappear at noon, and darkness start early. In teatime twilight, big flakes slowly, as if hesitant, reel past the empty trees like small white leaves, star-shaped and infrequent. By bedtime, driveway and lawn turn shaggy with the first cover. It is good to go to bed early in Winter, and tonight as we sleep our dreams take punctuation from the thudding of snowploughs as they roll and bluster up and down Route 4, shaking the house yet comforting our sleep: Someone takes care, the solitary captains in their great snowships breasting through vast whiteness, cleaving it sideways into gutter drifts. If we stir as they thump past, we watch revolving yellow lights flash through our windows and reflect on the ceiling. We roll over and fall back into protected sleep. In a house full of pets we sleep not alone, for the snowploughs that reassure us frighten our dog like thunder or rifle-fire; cats crawl between our warm bodies under warmer electric blankets.

When we become aware, by the ploughs' repeated patrols, that the first deep snow accumulates, when the first intense and almost unbreakable sleep finishes and we climb to the frangible second storey of the night's house, I pull myself out of bed at two or three in the morning to inspect the true oncoming of Winter's work. I walk through the dark house from one vantage to another—parlor window that looks west toward pond, kitchen from which I look toward Kearsarge, dining room that gives on the north and, if I twist, back to the slopes of Ragged Mountain rising east above us. The night's flaking air breaks black sky into white flecks, silent and pervasive, shuttering the day's vista. This snow fills the air and the eyes, the way on Spring nights peepers fill the ears. Everywhere I look, limited by snow-limits, cold dewy whiteness takes everything into itself. Beside the covered woodshed, side by side, I see the shapes of two small cars rounded and smooth like enormous loaves of dead-white bread. Where the woodpile waits for final stacking in the shed, a mound rises with irregular sticks fagging out of it. Up on the hill the great cowbarn labors under a two-foot layer of snow, its unpainted vertical boards a dark upright shadow in all the whiteness, like the hemlocks above it on Ragged's hill. Although snowploughs keep Route 4 passable, they do not yet scrape to the macadam: In the darkness the highway is as white as the hayfields on either side. Down the road the white cottage disappears against the white field, its green shutters a patch of vacancy in the whiteness. In the stillness of two A.M., in a silent unlit moment with no ploughs thudding, I regard a landscape reverted to other years by the same snow, and I might be my great-grandfather gazing from the same windows in 1885. Or it might be his mother's eyes I gaze from, born on a Wilmot hill in 1789. Or maybe I look, centuries earlier, from the eyes of a Penacook wintering over the pond.

But now the snowplough's thunder signals itself, and I watch the revolving yellow light reflect upward into white prodigious air, and hear the great bruising barge roar and rumble past the house as a steel prow swooshes high waves of whiteness up and over the gutter almost to the front of the house, and buries the mailbox.

One year the first great snow came Christmas Eve after the family had struggled to bed. When we lit the tree in the morning, the day past the windows was thick and dark, and as we opened our presents the snow deepened in yard and hayfield outside, and on Christmas Day, all day, the great ploughs of state and town kept Route 4 clear. Snow stopped at three in the afternoon, and when Forrest rolled in to plough the driveway in the early blue twilight, Jane heaped slices of turkey between homemade bread to comfort him in his cab as he drove over the countryside digging people out.

The next morning was cold, thirty below, cold enough to notice. January in fact is the coldest month, although many would argue for February. Usually our cold is dry and does not penetrate so much as damp cold. December of 1975, our first full Winter here,

I tried starting the Plymouth one morning with normal confidence in the old six and without coldweather precautions; I flooded it. When I looked at the thermometer I was astonished to find it seventeen degrees below zero, for my face and forehead had not warned me that it was *cold*. I had recently spent my winters in Michigan's damp cold; Ann Arbor's occasional zero felt harsher than New Hampshire's common twenty below.

Later that Winter we did not complain of mildness. In January of 1976, morning after morning was thirty below; one morning on the porch the thermometer read thirty-eight degrees under—a temperature we did not equal until 1984. My grandmother had just died at ninety-seven, and she had spent most of her late Winters going south to Connecticut. The house had grown unaccustomed to Winter, the old heavy wooden storm windows broken, no central heat, and no insulation. Jane and I had never lived without central heat. Now we had a parlor Glenwood stove for heating, two kerosene burners in the kitchen, and on occasion an electric oven with the door open. This twelve-room house, in January of 1976, dwindled to a one-room house with a kitchen sometimes habitable. Working at the dining room table twenty feet from the living room's Glenwood I felt chilly. At the time we were too excited or triumphant to complain: We were camping out; we were earning our stripes. The next summer we added aluminum combination storms and screens together with some insulation; we added two more woodstoves, one for each study, so that we could each work despite the Winter. (My grandparents survived with only two woodstoves because they bustled around all day; in our work we sit on our duffs and require extra stoves.) When February came we learned we had passed our initiation, for it had been the coldest January since New Hampshire started keeping records more than a hundred years earlier. In all my grandmother's ninety-seven Januarys she had not known so cold a month.

My grandfather Wesley Wells worked all day without any heat except for the bodies of his cows. While he sat at morning and evening between two great steaming black and white Holstein hulks, pulling the pale thin tonnage of blue milk from their cud-chewing bodies, he kept warm. Other chores were cold. I can remember him, on my Winter visits to the farm as a boy, scurrying into the house for a warm-up between his outdoor tasks, rubbing his hands together, opening the drafts of one of the woodstoves and looming over it for a moment. Early and late, he moved among cold sheds and unheated barns. In the cowbarn, he fed the cattle hay, grain, and ensilage, and provided his horse Riley with oats and hay and water. He let the Holsteins loose to wander stiff-legged to the old cement watering trough next to the milk room, from which he first removed a layer of ice. Their muzzles dipped one by one into the near-freezing water. And he fed the sheep in sheepbarn and sheepyard. From the sheep's trough he scooped water for the hens who lived next door to the sheep, and he carried feed for his hens from the grainshed beside the cowbarn.

He would start these chores early, most days of deep Winter, rising at four-thirty, perhaps three hours before the sun, to do half the daily chores of feeding and watering, of milking and readying milk for the milktruck, because the special daily chores of Winter were the year's hardest, the pains of minus twenty exacerbated by hard labor. To chop wood for next year's stove, the farmer stalked with his ax into his woodlot after chores and breakfast, and often marched far enough so that he carried with him his bread and but-ter, meat, pie, and thermos of coffee for dinner. Setting out with a great ax, usually working alone, the farmer chopped a tree down, trimmed branches, cut the trunk into four-foot sections, and stacked it. Later he would hitch oxen to the sledge and fetch the cordwood downhill to the barnyard for cutting to stove-length pieces and for splitting. Maybe ten cord of a Winter for the house—more for the sugaring in March.

In January he harvested another Winter crop, the crop that people forget when they think of the needs of an old farm—the harvest of ice, cut in great oblongs two or three feet thick from Eagle Pond, ox-sledded up to the icehouse in back of the cowbarn's watering trough, packed against warm weather, six months hence.

Each Winter the farmer waited for a cold stretch, augering through the pond ice to check its thickness. Then he cut checkerboard squares with an ice saw. He kept himself heavily mittened not only against cold and wind rattling over the open desert lake, but also against the inevitable clasp of near-frozen water. A crew of them—neighbors cooperated to fetch ice—sawed and grappled, lifted and hauled, hard work and cold work. In the icehouse they stacked layers of ice, thickly insulated with sawdust, to last from the earliest warmth of April through hot spells of June and the long Summer hay days of July and August through Autumn with its Indian Summer, until the pond froze again. In the hot months my grandfather brought one chunk a day downhill from the icehouse, great square balanced with ice tongs on his shoulder, to the toolshed behind the kitchen where my grandmother kept her icebox, drip drip. Most ice went to cool the milk, hot from the udders of Holsteins, so that it would not spoil overnight in Summer. July and August, I was amazed every time we dug through the wet sawdust in the cool shade of the icehouse to find cold Winter again—packed silvery slab of Eagle Pond preserved against Summer, just as we hayed to preserve Summer's grass for the Winter cattle. On the hottest days when we returned sweaty from haying, my grandfather cracked off a little triangle of ice for me to suck on. Every January when he dug down in the icehouse to bury his crop of new ice, he found old ice underneath. After all, you never wanted to find yourself all out; some years, there might be hot days even in November when you would require a touch of ice. One long hot Autumn he found at the bottom of the icehouse, farther than he ever remembered digging, a small coffin-shaped remnant from times past, ice that might have been five years old, he told me, maybe older.

And my grandfather told me how, in the state of Maine especially, in the old days, sailing ships loaded ice and sawdust in Winter and sailed this cargo-transient mineral, annual and reproducible reverse-coal tonnage—down the East Coast to unload its cool for the South, which never otherwise saw a piece of ice: ice by the ton for coastal cities like Charleston, South Carolina. Sometimes they sailed all the way to the West Indies with their perishable glossy cargo: Maine ice for the juleps of Charleston, northern January cooling Jamaica's rum.

By tradition, the hard snow and heavy cold of January take a vacation for the eldritch out-of-time phenomenon of January thaw. Sometimes the January thaw comes in February, sometimes it never arrives at all, and on the rarest occasions it starts early and lasts all Winter. Mostly the January thaw lives up to its name. Some strange day, after a week when we dress in the black of twenty below, we notice that we do not back up to the fire as we change our clothing. Extraordinary. Or at midday we pick up the mail in our shirt-sleeves, balmy at forty-two degrees. (It is commonplace to observe that a temperature which felt Arctic late in August feels tropical in mid-January.) Icicles drip, snow slides off the south roof in midday sun, and mud takes over the driveway. Snow melts deeply away from clapboard and poly. Or the January thaw comes with warm rain ("If this was snow we'd have twelve feet. . ."), and if warm rain pours for three January days, as I have known it to do, Ragged's melt floods our driveway, snow vanishes from all hayfields, and water drowns the black ice of Eagle Pond. Our small universe confuses itself with false Spring. Bears wake perplexed and wander looking for deer corpses or compost heaps, thinking that it's time to get on with it. I remember fetching the newspaper one morning at five-thirty (I pick up the *Globe* outside a store that does not open for customers, slug-abeds, until six o'clock) on the third day of a warm rain. Chugging through deep mud in my outboard Nissan, I pulled up at the wet porch to see a huge white cat rooting about in perennials beside the walk, a white pussycat with black spots. . . . Oh, no. I remained in the front seat quietly reading the paper, careful not to make a startling sound or otherwise appear rude until the skunk wandered away.

Until we replaced rotten sills three years ago, a family of skunks lived in our rootcellar every Winter. We never saw them but we found their scat; we found the holes by which they entered and exited. Of course we confirmed their presence by another sense. In the Spring they sometimes quarreled, possibly over the correct time and place for love, and we could hear them arguing and discovered that skunks used on each other their special skunk equipment: Once a year in February or March we needed to throw all windows open. On one occasion, Ann Arbor friends visited in March, dear friends notable for an immaculate house in a culture of unspotted houses. When we brought them home with their skis from the airport, we opened the door to discover that our rootcellar family had suffered domestic disagreement. We opened all downstairs windows although it was fifteen below; as we prepared to take our friends up to their bedroom, where the air would be purer, we opened the hallway door to discover a dead rat on the carpet, courtesy of a guardian cat. Welcome to the country.

January thaw is dazzling but it lasts only a moment. If this were January in England we would expect crocuses and snowdrops soon; here we know enough to expect replacement battalions of snow's troopers following on coldness that freezes the melt, covering it with foot upon foot of furry whiteness and moon-coldness. We return to the satisfactions of Winter, maybe even to the deliverance and delirium of a full moon. In New Hampshire the full moon is remarkable all year long because we suffer relatively little from garbage-air and less from background light. The great cloudless night of the full moon is werewolf time, glory of silver-pale hauntedness whenever it happens but most beautiful in Winter. I set the internal alarm, maybe three or four nights in a row, and wander, self-made ghost, through pale rooms in the pewter light while the moon magnifies itself in bright hayfields and reflects upward, a sun from middle earth, onto shadowy low ceilings. High sailing above, higher than it has a right to, bigger, the February full moon, huge disc of cold, rides and slides among tatters of cloud. My breathing speeds, my pulse quickens; for half an hour I wander, pulled like a tide through the still house in the salty half light, more asleep than awake, asleep not in house or nightshirt but in moon, moon, moon. . . . What old animal awakens and stretches inside the marrow of the bones? What howls? What circles, sniffing for prey?

It's no Winter without an ice storm. When Robert Frost gazed at bowed-over birch trees and tried to think that boys had bent them playing, he knew better: "Ice-storms do that." They do that and a lot more, trimming disease and weakness out of the tree—the old tree's friend, as pneumonia used to be the old man's. Some of us provide life-support systems for our precious shrubs, boarding them over against the ice, for the ice storm takes the young or unlucky branch or birch as well as the rotten or feeble. One February morning we look out our windows over yards and fields littered with kindling, small twigs and great branches. We look out at a world turned into one diamond, ten thousand carats in the line of sight, twice as many facets. What a dazzle of spinning refracted light, spiderwebs of cold brilliance attacking our eyeballs! All Winter we wear sunglasses to drive, more than we do in Summer, and never so much as after an ice storm, with its painful glaze reflecting from maple and birch, granite boulder and stonewall, turning electric wires into bright silver filaments. The snow itself takes on a crust of ice, like the finish of a clay pot, that carries our weight and sends us swooping and sliding. It's worth your life to go for the mail. Until sand and salt redeem the highway, Route 4 is quiet. We cancel the appointment with the dentist, stay home, and marvel at the altered universe, knowing that midday sun will strip ice from tree and roof and restore our ordinary white Winter world.

Another inescapable attribute of Winter, increasing in years of affluence, is the ski people, cold counterpart to the Summer folks who fill New Hampshire's Julys and Augusts. Now the roads north from Boston are as dense on a February Friday as they are on a July, and late Sunday afternoon, southbound Interstate 93 backs up miles from the tollbooth. On innumerable Toyotas pairs of skis ride north and south every Winter weekend; at Christmas vacation and school holidays every hotel room fills all week with families of flatlanders.

They wait in line at the tows, resplendent in the costumes of money, booted and coifed in bright petrochemical armor. They ride, they swoop, they fall, they drink whiskey, and the bonesetter takes no holiday on a New Hampshire February weekend, and the renter of crutches earns time and a half. Now that cross-country rivals downhill, the ski people grow older and more various. Tourism, which rivals the yard sale as the major north country industry, brings Massachusetts and New York money to fatten purses in the cold country. In the fashionable areas—much of Vermont and Waterville Valley in New Hampshire's White Mountains—restaurants and boutiques, cute-shops and quiche-cafes buzz like Winter's blackflies.

Few natives ski, though some have always done, and in our attic there are wide heavy wooden skis from the time of the Great War on which my mother and her sisters traipsed all Winter, largely doing cross-country but perfectly willing to slide down a hill. Old-timers remember the horse-as-ski-tow, pulling adventurers uphill.

The motorcycle roar of snowmachines, from a distance indistinguishable from chainsaws, interrupts the downy quiet of mid-week evenings, as kids roar along disused railroad tracks and over the surface of frozen lakes. Older folks, men mostly, park their bob-houses on frozen Winter lakes, saw holes through the ice, light a fire, warm themselves with a pint of whiskey, and fish for the wormless perch of Winter. Like deer hunting in November, this fishing is not mere sport; it fills the freezers of shacks, trailers, and extended farm-houses. On Eagle Pond we count six or a dozen bobhouses each Winter, laboriously translated by pick-up and slipped across the ice to a lucky spot. After the labor of cordwood and ice in the old days, as the Winter ended, followed the great chore of maplesugaring. It still arrives, though without so much labor. Usually it comes in one stretch of March, but on occasion the conditions for sap turn right for two weeks in February, go wrong for twenty days, then right themselves again—a split season for sugaring. Right conditions are warm days when snow melts followed by cold nights when it freezes.

Nowadays people suction sap from the sugarbush with miles of plastic tubing. In the old time, syrupers pounded the spigot into the tree—several of them in a good-sized three-hundred-year-old maple—and hung a bucket from each for the sap to drip into. My grandfather trudged from tree to tree every day, wearing a wooden yoke across his shoulders; long pails hung from the ends of it, narrow on top and wide on bottom, for collecting sap from each bucket. He emptied these yoke pails into a great receptacle sledged by an ox—oxen were especially useful in the Winter, slow but unbothered by snow—and when he filled this great sledge kettle, his ox pulled it to a funnel and pipe whence the sap flowed downhill to a storage tank behind the saphouse. Gathering sap was a third of the work, or maybe a quarter. There was cordwood to cut, to burn under the trays boiling the sap down. Someone tended the fire day and night, watched and tested the sap on its delicate journey to syrup. In 1913 my grandfather corked five hundred gallons at a dollar a gallon, big money in 1913, with the help of his father-in-law Ben Keneston, cousin Freeman, and Anson the hired man. Remember that it takes about forty gallons of sap, boiled down, to make a gallon of syrup.

Not only the cash was sweet. To maplesyrup and maplesugar my grandfather and grandmother added honey from the beehive beside the barn and the hollyhocks; they grew and produced their own sweetening. But big money from syrup bought land and paid taxes. Often their tax was little or nothing, for in the old days many farmers paid their taxes by doing road work—scraping and rolling the dirt roads, filling in with hardpan, and in Winter rolling down the snow of the road to make it fit for the runners of sleighs, taking on a mile of Wilmot's Grafton Turnpike.

March was always the month for blizzards. Still is. It is the time when we all tell ourselves: *We've had enough of Winter.* Old folks come back from Florida and Hilton Head; younger ones, fed up, head off for a week where the weather performs like May or June in New Hampshire. Every morning the *Globe* measures a word from

Florida: *baseball.* . . . In New Hampshire, tantalizing melt is overwhelmed by four feet of snow, drifts to twelve feet. . . . We comfort each other, when we use the form of complaint for our boasting, that even if we lost the old outhouse yesterday or the '53 Buick that the chickens use for Summer roosting, what comes quick in March goes quick in March, and three or four days from now it'll melt to reveal the lost Atlantis of the family barnyard. Then three or four days later we wake to another four feet.

In the 1940s, the old people still bragged about the great blizzard of '88. My Connecticut grandfather and my New Hampshire one, who shared little, shared the blizzard of '88: a great watershed for bragging or for telling lies about. And in the 1980s I still ask old people what they remember that *their* old people told them about '88, much as the '88ers themselves asked their old-timers about the Poverty Year of 1816. Paul Fenton told me a story he heard as a boy, not about '88 but just about "the big snows we used to have, back in the old days." It seems that a bunch went out after a heavy snow, dragging the roads with the help of oxen so that people could use their sleighs and sledges, when one of the oxen slipped and got stuck, couldn't move at all, got a hoof caught in something. . . . Well, they dug down, dug around, trying to free the ox's hoof, and what do you know. . . . That ox had stuck its foot into a chimney!

Now, the blue snow of 1933 is *not* a lie. I am sure of it because of the way Ansel Powers tells me about it, because his wife Edna confirms it, because Les Ford from Potter Place, who has never been known to collaborate on a story, remembers it just as well and tells the same stories. It may be hard to believe, *but it was blue.* You stuck a shovel in it and it was *blue,* blue as that sky, blue as a bachelor's-button. It fell in April, a late snow, and it fell fast. Les remembers that he'd been to a dance at Danbury, and when he went to bed at midnight, the sky was clear and full of stars; when he woke up in the morning, there it was. The snowploughs were disassembled for Summer; the road agent had to start up the old dozer and go patrol the road with it to clear a way for Model T's—and a few shiny Model A's. Sam Duby, the same blacksmith who made the first snowploughs in Andover, woke up at two or three in the morning and had to do something, you know. Well, the outhouse was across the road in the barn and he went out to the end of the porch and it was snowing to beat the band and he just dropped a load right there. . . . He's the only one who saw it snow; the rest of us went to bed under stars, woke up to the sun shining on three feet of blue snow.

In *The Voyage of the Beagle* Charles Darwin wrote about finding red snow, *Protococcus nivalis,* on the Peuquenes Ridge in Chile in 1835. "A little rubbed on paper gives it a faint rose tinge mingled with a little brick-red." When he examined it later, Darwin found "microscopical plants." As far as I know, no one took our blue snow into a laboratory.

Of course it snows in April every year, most often white, but you cannot call it Winter anymore. Snow sticks around, in the north shade, most years until early in May, but it is ragged and dirty stuff, and we overlook it as we gaze in hopeful amazement at this year's crop of daffodils. Every year the earlier daffodils fill with snow, bright yellow spilling out white crystals, outraged optimism overcome by fact, emblem of corny desolation. And the worst storm I have driven through, after ten New Hampshire Winters, occurred a few years back on the ninth day of May.

But annual aberration aside, March is the end of Winter, and the transition to Spring is April's melt. One year not long ago we had an open Winter, with very little snow, *no* snow we all said; we exaggerated a little, for we had an inch here and an inch there. The Winter was not only dry but mild, which was a good thing, for an open Winter with cold weather destroys flowers and bushes and even trees, since snow is our great insulator. As it was, in our open Winter we suffered one cold patch—twenty below for a week—and in the Spring that followed, and in the Summer, we discovered winterkill: A few rosebushes and old lilacs, plants and bulbs that had survived for decades, didn't make it that year. When Spring came without a melt, when mild days softened with buttery air and the protected daffodils rose blowing yellow trumpets, we felt uneasy. All of us knew: Lacking the pains of Winter, we did not deserve the rapture and the respite of Spring.

Our annual melt is the wild, messy, glorious loosening of everything tight. It is gravity's ecstasy, as water seeks its own level on every level, and the noise of water running fills day and night. Down Ragged Mountain the streams rush, cutting through ice and snow, peeling away Winter's cold layers: rush, trickle, rush. Busy water moves all day and all night, never tired, cutting away the corrupt detritus of Winter; fingers of bare earth extend down hillsides; south sides of trees extend bare patches, farther every day; root-pattern rivulets, melting, gather downhill to form brief streams; dirt roads slog and driveways turn swamps.

Then it dries; last snow melts; trees bud green; soft air turns. Who can believe in Winter now?

All of us. We know that Winter has only retreated, waiting. When the bear comes out of its Winter sleep, Winter itself goes into hibernation, sleeping off the balmy months of peeper-sing until the red leaf wakes it again and the white season returns with the New Hampshire Winter by which we know ourselves.

PART THREE

Winter As a Time of
Shoring Ourselves Up

INTRODUCTION

In a landscape that is frozen and bleak, there is certainly a sense of hardship. But if winter is emblematic of hardship, loss, and endings, so too is it a time that calls with a clarion voice to make conscious provision for such a period in life. One such provision is the spiritual gift of hospitality, certainly. Another is the recognition of the role of scouring and hardship in our lives. And there are other, very practical preparations. Winter is the time when the wood is brought in from the outside shed, when the canned goods have been stored, when the tree boughs have been set around the foundations and extra inches of insulation have been added. It is the time when coats and mittens and hats are recovered, when shovels are leaned by the back door, when car batteries are checked and windows shut tight against the frost.

Despite the preparation, the warmth, the security of home, winter is still hardship. But there is also the very real sense, suggested by Donald Hall, that underneath the bleakness lies the seed of new life. Is all this preparation for mere survival? Perhaps—but if so, then winter is merely the season to get through, a transient sort of thing with no purpose other than to be gotten past. But if spring follows, perhaps winter is more. Perhaps winter is the time to shore up so that the fertile ground will be there when the snow is gone and the spring has come.

This is what the sound of the rivulet from under the snow reminds us of, that green patch that breaks through in the warm and sunny spot, the surprising tracks, the barked trees—the sense that life after all is surviving, even thriving in a frozen world. Here is the rhythmic role of the season creating the space, or world, or conditions in which the soul can begin anew. Here is the possibility of finding a new and unexpected hope, as in Jane Kenyon's "Depression in Winter."

There comes a little space between the south
side of a boulder
and the snow that fills the woods around it.
Sun heats the stone, reveals
a crescent of bare ground: brown ferns,
and tufts of needles like red hair,
acorns, a patch of moss, bright green. . . .

I sank with every step up to my knees,
throwing myself forward with a violence
of effort, greedy for unhappiness—
until by accident I found the stone,
with its secret porch of heat and light,
where something small could luxuriate, then
turned back down my path, chastened and calm.

One of the most striking evocations of the harshness of winter and the life that throbs beneath the icy sheen appears in Lancelot Andrewes's meditation on the journey of the wise men to worship the Christ child born in Bethlehem. "It was no summer progress," he tells us. "A cold coming they had of it, at this time of the year; just the worst time of the year, to take a journey, and specially a long journey in. The ways deep; the weather sharp; the days short; the sun farthest off, in *solstitio brumali*, 'the very dead of winter.' . . . And these difficulties they overcame, of a wearisome, irksome, trouble-some, dangerous, unseasonable journey; and for all this, they came." Andrewes then compares the speed of the Magi during the winter season with our own momentum to worship. "Our fashion is, to see and see again, before we stir a foot; specially, if it be to the worship of Christ. Come such a journey, at such a time? No; but fairly have put it off to the spring of the year, till the days longer, and the ways fairer, and the weather warmer; till better travelling to Christ. Our Epiphany would, sure, have fallen in Easter-week at the soonest."

Andrewes's sense of the incongruity of winter's exigencies and its spiritual meaning of the advent of a great hope was shared by Father Alexander Schmemann, dean of Saint Vladimir's Seminary in Crestwood, New York, who died on December 13, 1983. During his years as a teacher and priest, he coined the term "Winter Pascha" to describe the feasts celebrated during the Christmas and Epiphany seasons by Orthodox believers. He linked those feasts to the feast of Easter, and heightened that linking by recognizing that the time of festive birth is celebrated during a season marked by cold and darkness. Then, when he himself learned that he had can-cer, Father Schmemann undertook his own personal Winter Pascha as he completed what his wife later called "the feast of Father's dying." It was fitting, he said, to confirm by God's grace and power all he had proclaimed throughout his life. This joyful acceptance of adversity exemplifies the scouring force winter brings into our lives and the remarkable beauty it may create through pain.

But shoring against the harshness of winter and spiritual bar-renness need not be a retreat as much as it is a careful preparation, as well as a sense that here is the time to wait, here is the time to watch. As Kathleen Norris trudges through the frozen downtown streets, a canticle of praise for, among other things, winter comes to her mind: here is waiting. As Jane Kenyon says goodbye to her flow-ers and vegetables, she accepts their need, and hers, for the dormant winter season: here is watching.

In the second century B.C.E., Antiochus, the king of Syria, conquered the land of Judea. He entered Jerusalem and came to the holy Temple, which he pillaged—stealing, among other things, the menorah from the altar. When the winter solstice came, he had the Temple rededicated to pagan gods. Three years later, Judah the Maccabee led a small rebellion against Antiochus, against odds so formidable as to be almost laughable. But Judah and his people retook Jerusalem, and so came to the Temple again; they found the menorah, filled it with what was left of the sacred oil, and lit it—on another winter solstice. And though there was only enough oil for a single day, the flames burned in the oil for eight days—a miracle of holy light in the darkness.

Here too is watching.

Kathleen Norris

"Weather Report: February 10"

In Dakota: A Spiritual Geography, *Kathleen Norris explores the ramifications of living in a region that most people in North America consider to be remote, sparsely populated, and unattractive. It is a world of snow and ice, of terrible cold—a place, Norris suggests, that acts as a crucible for the soul and that tends to keep the riffraff away. It is a land more ocean than earth, rolling and untamable. But in this land, Norris finds a kind of peace that brings gratitude and acceptance. It is a place where silence and quiet can be, and where the soul can come to learn and appreciate the beauties of that silence.*

> *A* place where silence and quiet can *be*, and where the soul can come to learn and appreciate the beauties of that silence.

In this short selection, that quiet, even when it comes in frigid cold, leads to a surprising contemplation. Here, Norris finds that even in cold, one can bless the Lord.

WEATHER REPORT: FEBRUARY 10

I walk downtown, wearing a good many of the clothes I own, keeping my head down and breathing through several thicknesses of a wool scarf. A day so cold it hurts to breathe; dry enough to freeze spit. Kids crack it on the sidewalk.

Walking with care, snow barely covering the patches of ice, I begin to recall a canticle or a psalm—I can't remember which—and my body keeps time:

> *Cold and chill, bless the Lord*
> *Dew and rain, bless the Lord*
> *Frost and chill, bless the Lord*
> *Ice and snow, bless the Lord*
> *Nights and days, bless the Lord*
> *Light and darkness, bless the Lord.*

Another line comes to mind: "at the breath of God's mouth the waters flow." Spring seems far off, impossible, but it is coming. Already there is dusk instead of darkness at five in the afternoon; already hope is stirring at the edges of the day.

John Updike

"THE COLD"

John Updike's short essay "The Cold," originally printed in the Brazilian newspaper Folha de S. Paulo, *argues that winter shows us that the universe does not love us. It is an active agent, he suggests—a thing that we prepare against, an absence that feels like a presence with its threat, with its numbing quality. It creates whole worlds of dirt, of specialized clothing, even of vocabulary. To escape from it, he concludes, is to be reminded of our need to be grateful for a civilization that has erected shelters against the cold.*

And yet beneath this sense of cold's enormity is an equally strong sense of its ability to make us sensitive to one another, to ourselves, to our world. We come to the fireplace where all the family members have gathered. We come to drink coffee to warm ourselves and to be with others. We greet the snowbound stranger with affection and companionship in a kind of mutual distress. Cold is itself a companion, but it leads to other kinds of companionships and to other kinds of growth as well.

> *B*eneath this sense of cold's enormity is an equally strong sense of its ability to make us sensitive to one another, to ourselves, to our world.

THE COLD

A Brazilian once told me, before I was setting out to visit his fabulous country, "Americans don't understand inflation, and Brazilians don't understand the cold." Now, I hear, there is no more inflation in Brazil; but there is still plenty of cold in North America. Recent temperatures in New England have been around zero Fahrenheit; in parts of the Midwest they have been thirty and forty degrees below zero; and even in Florida, where perpetual summer is supposed to reign, temperatures have gone below freezing, to the peril of oranges, strawberries, and alligators.

Cold is an absence, an absence of heat, and yet it feels like a presence—a vigorous, hostilely active presence in the air that presses upon your naked face and that makes your fingers and toes ache within their mittens and boots. Cold is always *working*, it seems— busy freezing water in the ponds and rivers, knitting intricate six-sided snowflakes by the billions, finding cracks around the walls and windows of your house, forcing furnaces in the cellar to roar away. Cold fights you—it doesn't want your automobile engine to ignite in the morning, and once your car is on the highway it clogs its path with snow and slush. A whole secondary world of dirt, of sand and salt, is called into being by the cold, and an expensive and troublesome array of wearing apparel—mufflers, earmuffs, wool-lined boots and gloves, parkas, leggings, long underwear, and knitted face-masks. If for some of these items words do not exist in Brazilian Portuguese, be grateful.

These thick and clumsy items of winter wear complicate every social gathering with their extra bulk. Because of them a special room in restaurants and theatres and schools exists, a room called, though almost no one wears cloaks any more, the cloakroom. When I was a schoolchild, the cloakroom was a narrow and exciting transitional chamber where the concept of undressing stirred a certain rowdiness; there was a powerful semi-sexual smell to the cloakroom, of wet wool and snow-chilled rubber that I have never forgotten. For adults, the tip to the cloakroom attendant adds one more expense to an already expensive evening on the town. I once was in Russia in late November, and pitied the little grandmotherly women who tottered back and forth under the heaps of heavy coats entrusted to their care by opera-goers.

In Brazil, the skin is beneath the clothes, and, often, not very far beneath—the naked self and the dressed self do not pose a dramatic dichotomy. In a winter climate, there is a multiplicity of wraps—a padded, furry armor is peeled away, indoors, to reveal a butterfly clad in less ponderous clothes, somewhat as the well-to-do women of Arabia and Iran gaily strip off, in the homes of their friends, the drab garbs of purdah to reveal flashing Paris fashions. Thus, duplicity is created. The cold, in seeking to freeze the body, makes one, puritanically, seethingly aware of it, as each limb and body part struggles to keep warm in its dark place of concealment.

The cold generates a whole code of shelter and warmth: the fireplace hearth was, before central heating, the center of the house, the place where all the family members gathered. The burning, crackling log fire still signals hospitality and festivity, and ancient ceremonies of alcohol and caffeine consumption revolve about the notion of "warming up." A sense of oneself as a brave and resourceful survivor attends the dweller in a cold climate. With the camaraderie of soldiers on dangerous missions, muffled strangers greet each other on the snowbound, windswept street. Cold challenges the blood; it sets the cheeks to tingling and the brain to percolating. By making the indoors cozy, it encourages intellectual activity. On the map of Europe, the statistics for readership go down as the latitude becomes southerly; a warm climate invites citizens outdoors, to the sidewalk cafe, the promenade, the brain-lulling beach. I like winter because it locks me indoors with my books, my word processor, and my clear and brittle thoughts.

There is a visual poetry that goes with the cold. Ferns and stars of frost mysteriously appear on the windows and take their place in a child's mythology, along with icicles, snowmen, snowballs, and Santa Claus in his gliding sleigh. Snowsuits, which were dark wool outfits in my own childhood, have become, in the age of Dacron

and Gore-Tex, wonderfully bright and gaudy, so that children clustered at a bus stop on a cold morning look like a pack of little cir-
cus clowns. (Adolescents—girls as well as boys—display their
bravado in dressing as skimpily as possible, in sneakers and cotton
T-shirts, and in my college days at Harvard it was a mark of shame
to venture forth on even the coldest day wearing any coat heavier
than a sports jacket, with shirt, tie, and khaki pants.) A wealth of
special sports equipment—sleds, ice skates, skis, snowboards—
emerges to harvest fun from the cold. The drama of snowplows,
working all night to heave up great white mounds along the road-
ways, adds to the excitement, and television weathermen,
pompously padding their predictions with all manner of computer
graphics, work up an almost hysterical excitement as another winter
storm approaches. The sight of the world made new and fantastic by
a sparkling fresh snowfall repays many days of numbing discomfort.
And nature, even when locked most deeply in the cold's embrace,
gives off signs of persistent activity—chirping birds, swelling buds,
the tracks of fox and deer.

The cold has the philosophical value of reminding men that
the universe does not love us. Cold as absolute as the black tomb
rules space; sunshine is a local condition, and the moon hangs in the
sky to illustrate that matter is usually inanimate. Most of the body's
caloric intake is consumed in its effort to maintain body temperature. The cold is our ancient companion; prehistoric men developed
their art and technology on the edge of ice-age glaciers. To return
back indoors after exposure to the bitter, inimical, implacable cold is
to experience gratitude for the shelters of civilization, for the islands
of warmth that life creates.

Vidyākara

FROM THE *TREASURY*
OF *WELL-TURNED VERSE*

This eleventh-century anthology of Sanskrit poetry depicts the deprivations of winter through short, sharply etched physical descriptions. The Indian landscape turns harsh and foreboding; the rural folk withdraw indoors. But walls and fires prove weak defenses against the aggressive cold. An old woman, reduced to the mere outlines of her body—back, hands, thighs, and elbows—hunches over an ineffectual warming pan. We too feel chilled, desiccated, parched, and weary. Is there no way, we ask, to combat this cold? The answer points us away from flimsy shelters and dying embers to the source of living warmth. To hold another's body, to share even a pillow of straw, is to keep winter's chill at bay. Indeed, it is to turn the banished cold into an ally against the loneliness that threatens us all. Winter, we discover, breaks down barriers and nudges us toward one another. In its cold embrace we find the warm companionship for which our hearts long.

> *I*s there no way, we ask, to combat this cold? The answer points us away from flimsy shelters and dying embers to the source of living warmth.

The moon bears likeness
to a frightened woman's face;
the sun's weak glow
is like a bankrupt's order.
The dung fire is as gentle
as a new bride's wrath,
the winter wind as cruel
as a hypocrite's embrace.

With rags upon her back, holding her hands
over the chaff fire placed between her fire-scarred
thighs
and pressing her shivering elbows to her sides,
the old woman leaves the house now
neither day nor night.

The peasant and his wife
sleep in a grass hut at the corner of the field
with coverlet and pillow made of barley straw.
The frost avoids their slumbers,
a boundary being drawn to its advance
by the warmth emitted from the wife's plump breasts.

Annie Dillard

FROM *THE WRITING LIFE*

In The Writing Life, *Annie Dillard chronicles the difficulties—practical and spiritual—of crafting words. But Dillard, who always speaks about more than what is on the surface of her language, is also writing about the craft of learning how to live. The frustrations, the joys, the odd pleasures, the panics, the passions—all these elements that are part of the writing life are part of all our lives. At least, Dillard suggests, they should be.*

In this selection from The Writing Life, *Dillard must front elemental cold as she lives in a cabin on Puget Sound in order to finish a book she has been working on. It is a single room, heated with a woodstove. For most of us, the notion of heat from a woodstove is rather charming, but for Dillard it is absolutely necessary—and particularly difficult. She learns, however, as she crafts the written word, that there is also craft in splitting a piece of wood and that, perhaps, these arts may not be all that different. The expert woodcutter aims past the chunk of alder, past that piece of wood to the cutting block. So, too, the writer—and the human being—looks beyond what is immediate to an end that can only be intuited, or perhaps grasped by faith.*

> *For most of us, the notion of heat from a wood stove is rather charming, but for Dillard it is absolutely necessary— and particularly difficult.*

FROM *THE WRITING LIFE*

Once, in order to finish a book I was writing and yet not live in the same room with it, I begged a cabin to use as a study. I finished the book there, wrote some other things, and learned to split wood. All this was on a remote and sparsely populated island on Haro Strait, where I moved when I left Virginia. The island was in northern Puget Sound, Washington State, across the water from Canadian islands.

The cabin was a single small room near the water. Its walls were shrunken planks, not insulated; in January, February, and March, it was cold. There were two small metal beds in the room, two cupboards, some shelves over a little counter, a wood stove, and a table under a window, where I wrote. The window looked out on a bit of sandflat overgrown with thick, varicolored mosses; there were a few small firs where the sandflat met the cobble beach; and there was the water: Puget Sound, and all the sky over it and all the other wild islands in the distance under the sky. It was very grand. But you get used to it. I don't much care where I work. I don't notice things. The door used to blow open and startle me witless. I did, however, notice the cold.

I tried to heat the cabin with the wood stove and a kerosene heater, but I never was warm. I used to work wearing a wool cap, long wool tights, sweaters, a down jacket, and a scarf. I was too lazy to stick a damper in the wood stove chimney; I kept putting off the task for a warm day. Thoreau said that his firewood warmed him twice—because he labored to cut his own. Mine froze me twice, for the same reason. After I learned to split wood, in a manner I am shortly to relate—after I learned to split wood, I stepped out into the brute northeaster and split just enough alder to last me through working hours, which was not enough splitting to warm me. Then I came in and kindled a fire in the stove, all the heat of which vanished up the chimney.

At first, in the good old days, I did not know how to split wood. I set a chunk of alder on the chopping block and harassed it, at enormous exertion, into tiny wedges that flew all over the sand-flat and lost themselves. What I did was less like splitting wood than chipping flints. After a few whacks my alder chunk still stood serene and unmoved, its base untouched, its tip a thorn. And then I actually tried to turn the sorry thing over and balance it on its wee head while I tried to chop its feet off before it fell over. God save us.

All this was a very warm process. I removed my down jacket, my wool hat and scarf. Alas, those early wood-splitting days, when I truly warmed myself, didn't last long. I lost the knack.

I did not know it at the time, but during those first weeks when I attacked my wood every morning, I was collecting a crowd—or what passed on the island for a crowd. At the sound of my ax, Doe and Bob—real islanders, proper, wood-splitting islanders—paused in their activities and mustered, unseen, across the sandflat, under the firs. They were watching me (oh, the idleness) try to split wood. It must have been a largely silent comedy. Later, when they confessed, and I railed at them, Bob said innocently that the single remark he had ever permitted himself had been, "I love to watch Annie split wood."

One night, while all this had been going on, I had a dream in which I was given to understand, by the powers that be, how to split wood. You aim, said the dream—of course!—at the chopping block. It is true. You aim at the chopping block, not at the wood; then you split the wood, instead of chipping it. You cannot do the job cleanly unless you treat the wood as the transparent means to an end, by aiming past it. But then, alas, you easily split your day's wood in a few minutes, in the freezing cold, without working up any heat; then you utterly forfeit your only chance of getting warm.

The knack of splitting wood was the only useful thing I had ever learned from any dream, and my attitude toward the powers that be was not entirely grateful. The island comedy was over; everybody had to go back to work; and I never did get warm.

Patricia Hampl

FROM *A ROMANTIC EDUCATION*

Patricia Hampl, a poet and essayist who grew up and still lives in St. Paul–Minneapolis, calls her hometown the "coldest metropolitan area in the world." In her memoir A Romantic Education, *she recalls the sense of civic pride her family felt in surviving the long, bitter winter—and her own childish impatience when its interminable months stretched into April and then into May. "I didn't personally hate the winter; I hated that there didn't seem to be anything but the winter."*

But even as a child she felt the tug of winter's enchantments, sensed the incubation of desires and dreams that invited the Muse to share her nights. The silent, private winter, "more like a country than a season," nurtured in Hampl a love for words and a longing to set them down on papery blank whiteness. Reading, writing, traveling into the dream that is more piercing, and more accurate, than reality—these too are gifts that winter offers.

> The silent, private winter, "more like a country than a season," nurtured in Hampl a love for words and a longing to set them down on papery blank whiteness.

FROM *A ROMANTIC EDUCATION*

We were not really the Midwest, my father explained; that would be Iowa or Nebraska, Kansas—hopeless places. We were the Upper Midwest, as the weatherman said, elevating us above the dreary mean. My father pointed with derision at the cars with Iowa license plates, hauling boats on trailers behind them, as we passed them on Highway 200 going north. "Will you look at that," he said. "Those Iowa people have to lug that boat all the way up here." My brother and I looked at the dummies in the Iowa car as we passed. "They're crazy to get to the water, they'll even fish in the middle of the day," he said, as if the Iowa Bedouins were so water mad that a school of walleye could toy with them in the noon heat, while my father coolly appeared at dawn and twilight to make the easy Minnesota-savvy kill. He pointed out to us, over and over, the folly of the Iowans and their pathetic pursuit of standing water.

Our supremacy came from our weather, and the history of our weather: the glacier had given us these beautiful clear lakes, my father explained. The glacier receded and—Paradise, with lakes. And as if the single great historical event, the glacier, had been enshrined as a symbol, in my family we were not to speak against the winter. Our cold was our pride. We watched the *Today Show* weather report and a shiver—not of cold but entirely of civic pride—ran through us as, week after week, some aching Minnesota town came in with the lowest temperature in the country. We did not delight in the admittance of Alaska, our icy rival, into the Union. We said nothing against it, but it was understood that it didn't really count, it had an unfair advantage which caused us to ignore it. "Didn't Alaska belong to Russia?" my mother said. "I mean, isn't it strictly speaking part of Siberia?"

Much better to think of International Falls, the Minnesota border town known on the *Today Show* and elsewhere as "the Nation's Ice Box." We took pride in our wretched weather ("St. Paul–Minneapolis is the coldest metropolitan area in the world," my mother read to us from the paper) the way a small nation does in its national art, as if the ice cube, our symbol, were the supreme artifact of civilization. And like a small nation, we hardly cared among ourselves that the myths and legends, the peculiar rites of the land, were unknown and undervalued elsewhere, as long as we could edify ourselves again and again with the stunning statistics that constituted our sense of ourselves: the weather, the god-awful winters, which were our civic, practically our cultural, identity. I didn't personally hate the winter; I hated that there didn't seem to be anything *but* the winter.

The cold was our pride, the snow was our beauty. It fell and fell, lacing day and night together in a milky haze, making everything quieter as it fell, so that winter seemed to partake of religion in a way no other season did, hushed, solemn. It was snowing and it was silent. Good-bye, good-bye, we are leaving you forever: this was the farewell we sent to the nation on the *Today Show* weather report. Or perhaps we were the ones being left behind, sealed up in our ice cube for winter as the rest of the world's cities had their more tasteful dabs of cold, and then went on to spring. "Even Moscow! Even Leningrad!" my mother read to us from the newspaper, "can't begin to touch us."

"If you stepped outside right now without any clothes on," my brother said one day when we had not been allowed to go skating because the temperature was 25° below zero, "you'd be dead in three minutes." He sounded happy, the Minnesota pride in the abysmal statistic—which, for all I knew, he had made up on the spot. We looked out the dining room window to the forbidden world. The brilliant, mean glare from the mounds of snow had no mercy on the eye and was a mockery of the meaning of sun. "You'd be *stiff*. Like frozen hamburger," he said. "Or a frozen plucked chicken," regarding me and finding a better simile. "And when you thawed out, you'd turn green." The pleasure of being horrified, standing there by the hot radiator with my ghoulish brother.

We shared the pride of isolation, the curious glamour of hermits. More than any other thing I can name, the winter made me want to write. The inwardness of the season (winter is *quiet*) and its austerity were abiding climatic analogues of the solitude I automatically associated with creativity. "Minneapolis—a great book town," I once overheard a book salesman say with relish. And what else was there to do in the winter? Stay inside and read. Or write. Stay inside and dream. Stay inside and look, safely, outside. The Muse might as well be invited—who else would venture out?

The withdrawn aloofness of what had been, recently, leafy and harmless, now had a lunar beauty that was so strange and minimal it had to be foreign. But it was ours, our measure of danger and therefore our bit of glamour and importance. Or perhaps the relation between the winter and writing, which I felt, was a negative one: maybe I hated the season and wanted to cover up the whiteness; a blank page was the only winter I could transform. That's how little I understand winter, how it can bewitch its inhabitants (for it is more like a country than a season, a thing to which one belongs), so they cannot say and don't know whether they love the winter or hate it. And we always said "*the* winter," not simple "winter," as if for us the season had a presence that amounted to a permanent residence among us.

Spring didn't exist. I read about it in books that I read curled up on my grandmother's horsehair sofa, the English springs of the Brontës, full of brave early flowers and all that English reawakening of life:

> Spring drew on, she was indeed already come; the frosts of winter had ceased; its snows were melted, its cutting winds ameliorated . . . a greenness grew over those brown beds, which, freshening daily, suggested the thought that Hope traversed them at night, and left each morning brighter traces of her steps. Flowers peeped out amongst the leaves; snow-drops, crocuses, purple auriculas, the golden-eye pansies.

Jane Eyre's April. Sometimes in St. Paul it snowed in May, once, definitely, in June. We skipped spring and plunged right into summer, maybe to get warmed up. "Don't plant until after the fifteenth of May," my father warned his customers at the greenhouse. They didn't always listen. "I told her," he would say at the dinner table, giving us the news of Mrs. Beauchamp's punishment by the season, as if her folly in planting her geraniums and petunias before May 15 and the result ("she lost a couple of hundred dollars there") were a working lesson in the effects of hubris in daily life. "I told her not before May fifteenth. I said, the twentieth would be better—in fact, why not just wait till June. What's the rush?" My father allied himself with winter and therefore could always feel righteous.

By April my brother and I were charmed no longer, but my mother and father were loyal. April 10, snowing a blizzard, and my mother, looking out the window, said mildly, "Well, at least we get a change of the seasons." She and my father shook their heads over the appalling uniformity of the weather in places like Florida and California.

The winter and the conundrum of wealth (the hill) became attached in my mind, became related in an unapproachable coldness. This may be because of the story I read by F. Scott Fitzgerald titled "Winter Dreams," which affected me strongly. The story is set in St. Paul. It is about wanting what the rich have—specifically, it is about Dexter Green wanting Judy Jones, the daughter of a rich man, with all her golden, buffaloing beauty. To begin with, I was overpowered by living—for the first time—in the setting of a story, of fiction, a state of mind and life I sought and expected to find only on English moors and in other inaccessible places like New England. But here, as I walked home from school, was "the avenue" where "the dwellings of the rich loomed up . . . somnolent, gorgeous, drenched with the splendor of the damp moonlight." Summit Avenue, the hill, nearby.

The story hardly takes place in winter. Winter happens, for the most part, off-stage. The romance, the action, the betrayal—are all part of the summer and the long days at the lake. But the story's title is apt. For it is the dream of Dexter Green, with his self-mocking springish name, whose mother, we're told, "was a Bohemian of the peasant class" who had "talked broken English to the end of her days," this dream of beauty and possession is the winter thing, the longing, the vast desiring for the world and for the light that comes only from long winter and its deep burial in a provincial city where, because there is wealth and winter, there are dreams—of beauty and beyond.

I realized and I believed that winter light was, precisely, dream light. The gauzy winter light of a snowy day is the light of dreams because it is easy on the eye, and allows the sleeper to watch the dream's action, to look long and relaxed, without the eye being transfixed by darts of brightness. You wake from such dreams with no desire to analyze or understand the dream's meaning—the dream itself is enough, to have dreamed it. Winter dreams of this sort grow and grow, the eye steady, dilating, creating its tableaux and then succumbing to them, perhaps dangerously, as Dexter Green succumbs to Judy Jones, the beautiful rich girl. Judy Jones betrays Dexter not simply by dumping him but, many years later when he no longer lives in "the Midwestern city" and has lost track of her, she betrays him again, more devastatingly. He hears, from a business acquaintance (he has become rich, a New Yorker, himself), that gorgeous Judy Jones has faded, is a drab figure, a wife who stays home with the kids: her husband runs around. She betrays Dexter then by ceasing finally to be reckless and unusual—beautiful, in a word—as the dream of loveliness must always be. The dream, not the woman, causes his real sorrow. He could sustain the loss of her, but not of the dream she was: that was himself. The dream of this kind happens in the light of winter, the silent, private season. These are the dreams of "the beauty that must die." And then dies.

Jane Kenyon

"SEASON OF CHANGE AND LOSS" AND "GOOD-BY AND KEEP COLD"

The grave necessity of winter is nowhere more apparent than in Jane Kenyon's meditations on her garden. In "Season of Change and Loss," she reminds us that the coming of winter is the coming of death, or rather, the coming of the many little deaths we call goodbyes. Goodbye to bare feet and naked flesh; goodbye to basil and songbirds; goodbye to the light. We feel ourselves descending into winter, our souls as fragile as the lush, spendthrift, doomed grass of the late autumn. Yet winter has its own revelations: landscapes shorn of their green tresses emerge with startling clarity; books once again resume their rightful priority; hats and gloves collect on top of the fridge. And if we bury our losses in sleep, these little "hellos" keep alive the promise of the sparrow's wakening call.

In "Good-by and Keep Cold," Kenyon casts her end-of-the-year chores as the act of preparing her garden for bed—tucking in the perennial

> *Our souls endure the cold sleep of winter, their colors subdued to the dull browns of late November, taking on faith that warm life—small and insignificant as earthworms—still stirs at their core.*

*plants, adjusting the brown coverlet of mulch and manure, waiting for winter
to pull up its chilly sheets. Yet all this loving, maternal attention ensures not
that the plants stay warm but that they remain cold, locked into the deep,
silent frost that will preserve their lives until the springtime revels begin. So
too, Kenyon intimates, our souls endure the cold sleep of winter, their colors
subdued to the dull browns of late November, taking on faith that warm
life—small and insignificant as earthworms—still stirs at their core.*

Season of Change and Loss

All Saints' and All Souls' have circled around again: All Saints', a celebration of the lives of the Christian saints and martyrs, and All
Souls', a remembrance of the souls of ordinary believers through all
time.

Maybe your faith does not mark these days, or maybe you
belong to no religious persuasion, or your persuasion is to have no
persuasion, but you recognize the season "When yellow leaves, or
none, or few, do hang / Upon those boughs which shake against the
cold, / Bare ruin'd choirs, where late the sweet birds sang."

You may already have left the hose to drain down some sloping place in the yard, planted a few bulbs, raked a few leaves. Possibly you've pulled down the winter sashes on the storm windows
and noticed the increasingly strident calling of crickets from the
grass. The autumn sun can't dry the dew from the lawn, even on the
brightest afternoon. The grass is lush, spendthrift, doomed.

A few small, unharvested green tomatoes dangle from black-
ened plants, having frozen modestly in their pots on the porch. The
smell of them is pungent, close to the smell of edible food but a little off. Rainwater in the ashtray on the garden table freezes by night
and thaws again by day.

Acorns drop from the oaks with a sound like rain, acorns this
year small but plentiful. They've come down without their tops so
that we miss the childish pleasure of whistling on their caps. Geese

fly over in sweet disorder, controlled chaos, one leader pulling the string for a while, then another emerging to take the leader's place. The dog looks up to see where the commotion is coming from.

Good-bye to flesh. Turtlenecks and woolens come out of drawers and garment bags smelling of naphthalene, and the resumption of sober activities in public places, and love in a cold climate. Good-bye to getting the paper barefoot, or nipping out to the kitchen garden for a handful of basil or chervil. The basket on top of the fridge fills with odd hats and gloves, and our sandals withdraw discreetly to the back of the closet.

Little deaths. Somewhere in the psyche all these changes and losses register as death. What shall we do against it? One might bake a pie, as Joyce Maynard has been doing all summer against the big kind of death—the death of her mother. "Comfort me with apples. . . . " Just now there are many kinds: Macouns, Spartans, Gravensteins, Empires, Paula Reds, Baldwins, Northern Spies. It is a fine thing to build a pie, a bulwark against autumnal entropy.

Another defense against reality is to confront it—to admit the pervasiveness of change and loss and replacement. We are in fact like the grass that flourishes and withers, just as the psalmist says. Gardening teaches this lesson over and over, but some of us are slow to learn. We can only acknowledge the mystery, and go on planting burgundy lilies.

Walking. Something else to do besides baking pies and planting bulbs. The bugs are gone, and the deer hunt hasn't started in earnest. We're free to notice the multitude of drying vines and grasses, mushrooms and puffballs, like the one that's growing faster than a shopping mall in the backyard. The dog's afraid of it.

Leaves come down around us, and the profile of the land emerges again, coming clear as a thought. Now we see ledges and stone walls that had been obscured by ferns and brush all summer. Now we see architecture; some of us see bones.

At twilight the sedges are purple, and, as if to compensate for the loss of day, the sunsets become more resplendent than ever. These are the skies through which, my Methodist grandmother used to tell me, Jesus will come a second time into the world, trailing clouds of glory, to judge the quick and the dead.

Certainly diminishing light contributes to our sense of loss. Not for nothing that Christmas and Chanukah—celebrations of light's triumph over darkness—come when the sky is indigo by 4:30. Even before the stores have finished touting Halloween—All Hallows' Eve is a variant name for All Saints'—I begin to string sets of small white lights on the larger houseplants in the parlor.

No more mowing after supper in the buttery light. We come inside, where the evenings are long and silent. Baseball is dead; even Commissioner Giamatti is dead. There are books, the consolations of philosophy. There's one last cricket in the window well, sounding half-convinced, and a spider I brought in unintentionally with the geraniums, who lives in the general area of the sink.

My plan is to live like the bears: to turn the compost a few more times, prowl around a little longer and then go to sleep until the white-throated sparrow, with its coarse and cheerful song, calls me out of the dark.

GOOD-BY AND KEEP COLD

The gloomiest garden chore I can think of is preparing the perennial beds for winter. The golden days of autumn—when chrysanthemums and asters still bloom, and a cricket or two still chirp in the long, lush grass that needs mowing one more time—those apple-fragrant days are gone, replaced by days when the ground never softens, but remains gray and buff and dry and hard—the ruts in the frozen drive seemingly turn to stone.

By now the mower is back in the barn, empty of gas and of life's noisy possibilities; I cover it with a tarp against bat droppings. Garden tools lean in the dark shed, everything idle, the raking and transplanting done. Our revels now are ended.

In October we cut the flower stalks to the ground and cart away the refuse. The undiseased stalks we pitch onto the compost pile; those flecked with mildew or black spot go over the edge of the ravine behind the barn—the horticultural equivalent of an automotive graveyard, the end of the line. Asparagus stalks rattle with the dryness of bamboo when I cut them down, a mournful sound. We gather up armfuls of long, straplike leaves of Siberian iris; moist, reddish peony stalks; woody hollyhock stems, taller than I am. We lay bare the crowns of the plants, and let them freeze deliberately.

Now that the ground is hard, perennials locked into the earth, it's time to mulch the long beds with chopped-up leaves and a top dressing of manure. Over it all we put cut boughs of pine to keep the brown coverlet in place, to keep the ground frozen, not to keep it warm, so that a mild spell won't tempt the plants into growth, only to be killed by the next cold weather. My red-haired step-daughter, Philippa, who majored in plant science, explained to me that the alternate freezing and thawing of plant cells, expansion and contraction, bursts the cells, producing what we call winterkill. Robert Frost wrote:

> *No orchard's the worse for the wintriest storm:*
> *But one thing about it, it mustn't get warm.*
> *"How often already you've had to be told,*
> *Keep cold, young orchard, good-by and keep cold.*

Now the last leaves are down, except for the thick, dark leaves of the oak and ghostly beech leaves that click in the breeze, and we're reduced to a subtler show of color—brown, gray, and buff, perhaps a little purple in the distance, and the black-green of moss, hemlock, and fir. To my eye these hues are more beautiful than the garish early autumn with its orange leaves—orange, the color of madness—and leaves the color of blood. Let hot life retire, grow still: November's colors are those of the soul.

Thanksgiving, with its reliable bounty, its reunions, its hours of perfumed air, is over, and the raking, the planting of bulbs, and the digging of root crops are finished for the year. The freezer and pantry shelves are as full as they are going to be: What we have done, we have done; and what we have left undone, we have left undone.

Silence and darkness grow apace, broken only by the crack of a hunter's gun in the woods. Songbirds abandon us so gradually that, until the day when we hear no birdsong at all but the scolding of a jay, we haven't fully realized that we are bereft—as after a death. Even the sun has gone off somewhere. By teatime the parlor is as black as the inside of a cupboard.

Reading after supper on the couch, I let my mind wander to the compost pile, bulging with leaves and stalks. I've turned it a few times since October, but the pile's hard surface no longer yields to the fork. Even the earthworms have retreated from the cold and closed the door behind them. There's an oven warm at the pile's center, but you have to take that on faith. Now we all come in, having put the garden to bed, and we wait for winter to pull a chilly sheet over its head.

Henry David Thoreau

"THE POND IN WINTER"

For Henry David Thoreau, living at Walden Pond for two years and two months, all of life was lived on at least two levels. There was, first, the immediate presence of Walden Pond, an ever-changing natural glory. In this selection, for example, Thoreau is struck by the beauty of the pond as well as by its usefulness for catching fish, cutting ice, and even surveying. But at the same time, the winter and the ice on Walden suggest larger meanings about how we live our lives, about the glory of the ordinary, about the permanence of purity and beauty.

The winter and the ice on Walden suggest larger meanings about how we live our lives, about the glory of the ordinary, about the permanence of purity and beauty.

THE POND IN WINTER

After a still winter night I awoke with the impression that some question had been put to me, which I had been endeavoring in vain to answer in my sleep, as what—how—when—where? But there was dawning Nature, in whom all creatures live, looking in at my broad windows with serene and satisfied face, and no question on *her* lips. I awoke to an answered question, to Nature and daylight. The snow lying deep on the earth dotted with young pines, and the very slope of the hill on which my house is placed, seemed to say, Forward! Nature puts no question and answers none which we mortals ask. She has long ago taken her resolution. 'O Prince, our eyes contemplate with admiration and transmit to the soul the wonderful and varied spectacle of this universe. The night veils without doubt a part of this glorious creation; but day comes to reveal to us this great work, which extends from earth even into the plains of the ether.'

Then to my morning work. First I take an axe and pail and go in search of water, if that be not a dream. After a cold and snowy night it needed a divining-rod to find it. Every winter the liquid and trembling surface of the pond, which was so sensitive to every breath, and reflected every light and shadow, becomes solid to the depth of a foot or a foot and a half, so that it will support the heaviest teams, and perchance the snow covers it to an equal depth, and it is not to be distinguished from any level field. Like the marmots in the surrounding hills, it closes its eyelids and becomes dormant for three months or more. Standing on the snow-covered plain, as if in a pasture amid the hills, I cut my way first through a foot of snow, and then a foot of ice, and open a window under my feet, where, kneeling to drink, I look down into the quiet parlor of the fishes, pervaded by a softened light as through a window of ground glass, with its bright sanded floor the same as in summer; there a perennial waveless serenity reigns as in the amber twilight sky, corresponding to the cool and even temperament of the inhabitants. Heaven is under our feet as well as over our heads.

Early in the morning, while all things are crisp with frost, men come with fishing-reels and slender lunch, and let down their fine lines through the snowy field to take pickerel and perch; wild men, who instinctively follow other fashions and trust other authorities than their townsmen, and by their goings and comings stitch towns together in parts where else they would be ripped. They sit and eat their luncheon in stout fear-naughts on the dry oak leaves on the shore, as wise in natural lore as the citizen is in artificial. They never consulted with books, and know and can tell much less than they have done. The things which they practice are said not yet to be known. Here is one fishing for pickerel with grown perch for bait. You look into his pail with wonder as into a summer pond, as if he kept summer locked up at home, or knew where she had retreated. How, pray, did he get these in midwinter? Oh, he got worms out of rotten logs since the ground froze, and so—he caught them. His life itself passes deeper in nature than the studies of the naturalist penetrate; himself a subject for the naturalist. The latter raises the moss and bark gently with his knife in search of insects; the former lays open logs to their core with his axe, and moss and bark fly far and wide. He gets his living by barking trees. Such a man has some right to fish, and I love to see nature carried out in him. The perch swallows the grub-worm, the pickerel swallows the perch, and the fisherman swallows the pickerel; and so all the chinks in the scale of being are filled.

When I strolled around the pond in misty weather I was sometimes amused by the primitive mode which some ruder fisherman had adopted. He would perhaps have placed alder branches over the narrow holes in the ice, which were four or five rods apart and an equal distance from the shore, and having fastened the end of the line to a stick to prevent its being pulled through, have passed the slack line over a twig of the alder, a foot or more above the ice, and tied a dry oak leaf to it, which, being pulled down, would show when he had a bite. These alders loomed through the mist at regular intervals as you walked half way round the pond.

Ah, the pickerel of Walden! when I see them lying on the ice, or in the well which the fisherman cuts in the ice, making a little hole to admit the water, I am always surprised by their rare beauty, as if they were fabulous fishes, they are so foreign to the streets, even to the woods, foreign as Arabia to our Concord life. They possess a quite dazzling and transcendent beauty which separates them by a wide interval from the cadaverous cod and haddock whose fame is trumpeted in our streets. They are not green like the pines, nor gray like the stones, nor blue like the sky; but they have, to my eyes, if possible, yet rarer colors, like flowers and precious stones, as if they were the pearls, the animalized *nuclei* or crystals of the Walden water. They, of course, are Walden all over and all through; are themselves small Waldens in the animal kingdom, Waldenses. It is surprising that they are caught here—that in this deep and capacious spring, far beneath the rattling teams and chaises and tinkling sleighs that travel the Walden road, this great gold and emerald fish swims. I never chanced to see its kind in any market; it would be the cynosure of all eyes there. Easily, with a few convulsive quirks, they give up their watery ghosts, like a mortal translated before his time to the thin air of heaven.

As I was desirous to recover the long lost bottom of Walden Pond, I surveyed it carefully, before the ice broke up, early in '46, with compass and chain and sounding line. There have been many stories told about the bottom, or rather no bottom, of this pond, which certainly had no foundation for themselves. It is remarkable how long men will believe in the bottomlessness of a pond without taking the trouble to sound it. I have visited two such Bottomless Ponds in one walk in this neighborhood. Many have believed that Walden reached quite through to the other side of the globe. Some who have lain flat on the ice for a long time, looking down through the illusive medium, perchance with watery eyes into the bargain, and driven to hasty conclusions by the fear of catching cold in their breasts, have seen vast holes 'into which a load of hay might be driven,' if there were anybody to drive it, the undoubted source of the Styx and entrance to the Infernal Regions from these parts. Others have gone down from the village with a 'fifty-six' and a wagon load of inch rope, but yet have failed to find any bottom; for while the 'fifty-six' was resting by the way, they were paying out the rope in the vain attempt to fathom their truly immeasurable capacity for marvellousness. But I can assure my readers that Walden has a reasonably tight bottom at a not unreasonable, though at an unusual, depth. I fathomed it easily with a cod-line and a stone weighing about a pound and a half, and could tell accurately when the stone left the bottom, by having to pull so much harder before the water got underneath to help me. The greatest depth was exactly one hundred and two feet; to which may be added the five feet which it has risen since, making one hundred and seven. This is a remarkable depth for so small an area; yet not an inch of it can be spared by the imagination. What if all ponds were shallow? Would it not react on the minds of men? I am thankful that this pond was made deep and pure for a symbol. While men believe in the infinite some ponds will be thought to be bottomless.

A factory-owner, hearing what depth I had found, thought that it could not be true, for, judging from his acquaintance with dams, sand would not lie at so steep an angle. But the deepest ponds are not so deep in proportion to their area as most suppose, and, if drained, would not leave very remarkable valleys. They are not like cups between the hills; for this one, which is so unusually deep for its area, appears in a vertical section through its centre not deeper than a shallow plate. Most ponds, emptied, would leave a meadow no more hollow than we frequently see. William Gilpin, who is so admirable in all that relates to landscapes, and usually so correct, standing at the head of Loch Fyne, in Scotland, which he describes as 'a bay of salt water, sixty or seventy fathoms deep, four miles in breadth,' and about fifty miles long, surrounded by mountains, observes, 'If we could have seen it immediately after the diluvian crash, or whatever convulsion of nature occasioned it, before the waters gushed in, what a horrid chasm must it have appeared!

So high as heaved the tumid hills, so low
Down sunk a hollow bottom broad and deep,
Capacious bed of waters—.'

But if, using the shortest diameter of Loch Fyne, we apply these proportions to Walden, which, as we have seen, appears already in a vertical section only like a shallow plate, it will appear four times as shallow. So much for the *increased* horrors of the chasm of Loch Fyne when emptied. No doubt many a smiling valley with its stretching cornfields occupies exactly such a 'horrid chasm,' from which the waters have receded, though it requires the insight and the far sight of the geologist to convince the unsuspecting inhabitants of this fact. Often an inquisitive eye may detect the shores of a primitive lake in the low horizon hills, and no subsequent elevation of the plain has been necessary to conceal their history. But it is easiest, as they who work on the highways know, to find the hollows by the puddles after a shower. The amount of it is, the imagination, give it the least license, dives deeper and soars higher than Nature goes. So, probably, the depth of the ocean will be found to be very inconsiderable compared with its breadth.

As I sounded through the ice I could determine the shape of the bottom with greater accuracy than is possible in surveying harbors which do not freeze over, and I was surprised at its general regularity. In the deepest part there are several acres more level than almost any field which is exposed to the sun, wind, and plow. In one instance, on a line arbitrarily chosen, the depth did not vary more than one foot in thirty rods; and generally, near the middle, I could calculate the variation for each one hundred feet in any direction beforehand within three or four inches. Some are accustomed to speak of deep and dangerous holes even in quiet sandy ponds like this, but the effect of water under these circumstances is to level all inequalities. The regularity of the bottom and its conformity to the shores and the range of the neighboring hills were so perfect that a distant promontory betrayed itself in the soundings quite across the pond, and its direction could be determined by observing the opposite shore. Cape becomes bar, and plain shoal, and valley and gorge deep water and channel.

When I had mapped the pond by the scale of ten rods to an inch, and put down the soundings, more than a hundred in all, I observed this remarkable coincidence. Having noticed that the number indicating the greatest depth was apparently in the centre of the map, I laid a rule on the map lengthwise, and then breadthwise, and found, to my surprise, that the line of greatest length intersected the line of greatest breadth *exactly* at the point of greatest depth, notwithstanding that the middle is so nearly level, the outline of the pond far from regular, and the extreme length and breadth were got by measuring into the coves; and I said to myself, Who knows but this hint would conduct to the deepest part of the ocean as well as of a pond or puddle? Is not this the rule also for the height of mountains, regarded as the opposite of valleys? We know that a hill is not highest at its narrowest part.

Of five coves, three, or all which had been sounded, were observed to have a bar quite across their mouths and deeper water within, so that the bay tended to be an expansion of water within the land not only horizontally but vertically, and to form a basin or independent pond, the direction of the two capes showing the course of the bar. Every harbor on the sea-coast, also, has its bar at its entrance. In proportion as the mouth of the cove was wider compared with its length, the water over the bar was deeper compared with that in the basin. Given, then, the length and breadth of the cove, and the character of the surrounding shore, and you have almost elements enough to make out a formula for all cases.

In order to see how nearly I could guess, with this experience, at the deepest point in a pond, by observing the outlines of a surface and the character of its shores alone, I made a plan of White Pond, which contains about forty-one acres, and, like this, has no island in it, nor any visible inlet or outlet; and as the line of greatest breadth fell very near the line of least breadth, where two opposite capes approached each other and two opposite bays receded, I ventured to mark a point a short distance from the latter line, but still on the line of greatest length, as the deepest. The deepest part was found to be within one hundred feet of this, still farther in the direction to which I had inclined, and was only one foot deeper, namely, sixty feet. Of course, a stream running through, or an island in the pond, would make the problem much more complicated.

If we knew all the laws of Nature, we should need only one fact, or the description of one actual phenomenon, to infer all the particular results at that point. Now we know only a few laws, and our result is vitiated, not, of course, by any confusion or irregularity in Nature, but by our ignorance of essential elements in the calculation. Our notions of law and harmony are commonly confined to those instances which we detect; but the harmony which results from a far greater number of seemingly conflicting, but really concurring, laws, which we have not detected, is still more wonderful. The particular laws are as our points of view, as, to the traveller, a mountain outline varies with every step, and it has an infinite number of profiles, though absolutely but one form. Even when cleft or bored through it is not comprehended in its entireness.

What I have observed of the pond is no less true in ethics. It is the law of average. Such a rule of the two diameters not only guides us toward the sun in the system and the heart in man, but draw lines through the length and breadth of the aggregate of a man's particular daily behaviors and waves of life into his coves and inlets, and where they intersect will be the height or depth of his character. Perhaps we need only to know how his shores trend and his adjacent country or circumstances, to infer his depth and concealed bottom. If he is surrounded by mountainous circumstances, an Achillean shore, whose peaks overshadow and are reflected in his bosom, they suggest a corresponding depth in him. But a low and smooth shore proves him shallow on that side. In our bodies, a bold projecting brow falls off to and indicates a corresponding depth of thought. Also there is a bar across the entrance of our every cove, or particular inclination; each is our harbor for a season, in which we are detained and partially landlocked. These inclinations are not whimsical usually, but their form, size, and direction are determined by the promontories of the shore, the ancient axes of elevation. When this bar is gradually increased by storms, tides, or currents, or there is a subsidence of the waters, so that it reaches to the surface, that which was at first but an inclination in the shore in which a thought was harbored becomes an individual lake, cut off from the ocean, wherein the thought secures its own conditions—changes, perhaps, from salt to fresh, becomes a sweet sea, dead sea, or a marsh. At the advent of each individual into this life, may we not suppose that such a bar has risen to the surface somewhere? It is true, we are such poor navigators that our thoughts, for the most part, stand off and on upon a harborless coast, are conversant only with the bights of the bays of poesy, or steer for the public ports of entry, and go into the dry docks of science, where they merely refit for this world, and no natural currents concur to individualize them.

As for the inlet or outlet of Walden, I have not discovered any but rain and snow and evaporation, though perhaps, with a thermometer and a line, such places may be found, for where the water flows into the pond it will probably be coldest in summer and warmest in winter. When the ice-men were at work here in '46–7, the cakes sent to the shore were one day rejected by those who were stacking them up there, not being thick enough to lie side by side with the rest; and the cutters thus discovered that the ice over a small space was two or three inches thinner than elsewhere, which made them think that there was an inlet there. They also showed me in another place what they thought was a 'leach-hole,' through which the pond leaked out under a hill into a neighboring meadow, pushing me out on a cake of ice to see it. It was a small cavity under ten feet of water; but I think that I can warrant the pond not to need soldering till they find a worse leak than that. One has suggested, that if such a 'leach-hole' should be found, its connection with the meadow, if any existed, might be proved by conveying some colored powder or sawdust to the mouth of the hole, and then putting a strainer over the spring in the meadow, which would catch some of the particles carried through by the current.

While I was surveying, the ice, which was sixteen inches thick, undulated under a slight wind like water. It is well known that a level cannot be used on ice. At one rod from the shore its greatest fluctuation, when observed by means of a level on land directed toward a graduated staff on the ice, was three quarters of an inch, though the ice appeared firmly attached to the shore. It was probably greater in the middle. Who knows but if our instruments were delicate enough we might detect an undulation in the crust of the earth? When two legs of my level were on the shore and the third on the ice, and the sights were directed over the latter, a rise or fall of the ice of an almost infinitesimal amount made a difference of several feet on a tree across the pond. When I began to cut holes for sounding there were three or four inches of water on the ice under a deep snow which had sunk it thus far; but the water began immediately to run into these holes, and continued to run for two days in deep streams, which wore away the ice on every side, and contributed essentially, if not mainly, to dry the surface of the pond; for, as the water ran in, it raised and floated the ice. This was somewhat like cutting a hole in the bottom of a ship to let the water out. When such holes freeze, and a rain succeeds, and finally a new freezing forms a fresh smooth ice over all, it is beautifully mottled internally by dark figures, shaped somewhat like a spider's web, what you may call ice rosettes, produced by the channels worn by the water flowing from all sides to a centre. Sometimes, also, when the ice was covered with shallow puddles, I saw a double shadow of myself, one standing on the head of the other, one on the ice, the other on the trees or hillside.

While yet it is cold January, and snow and ice are thick and solid, the prudent landlord comes from the village to get ice to cool his summer drink; impressively, even pathetically, wise, to foresee the heat and thirst of July now in January—wearing a thick coat and mittens! when so many things are not provided for. It may be that he lays up no treasures in this world which will cool his summer drink in the next. He cuts and saws the solid pond, unroofs the house of fishes, and carts off their very element and air, held fast by chains and stakes like corded wood, through the favoring winter air, to wintry cellars, to underlie the summer there. It looks like solidified azure, as, far off, it is drawn through the streets. These ice-cutters are a merry race, full of jest and sport, and when I went among them they were wont to invite me to saw pit-fashion with them, I standing underneath.

In the winter of '46–7 there came a hundred men of Hyperborean extraction swoop down on to our pond one morning, with many carloads of ungainly-looking farming tools—sleds, plows, drill-barrows, turf-knives, spades, saws, rakes, and each man was armed with a double-pointed pike-staff, such as is not described in the New England Farmer or the Cultivator. I did not know whether they had come to sow a crop of winter rye, or some other kind of grain recently introduced from Iceland. As I saw no manure, I judged that they meant to skim the land, as I had done, thinking the soil was deep and had lain fallow long enough. They said that a gentleman farmer, who was behind the scenes, wanted to double his money, which, as I understood, amounted to half a million already; but in order to cover each one of his dollars with another, he took off the only coat, ay, the skin itself, of Walden Pond in the midst of a hard winter. They went to work at once, plowing, harrowing, rolling, furrowing, in admirable order, as if they were bent on making this a model farm; but when I was looking sharp to see what kind of seed they dropped into the furrow, a gang of fellows by my side suddenly began to hook up the virgin mould itself, with a peculiar jerk, clean down to the sand, or rather the water—for it was a very springy soil—indeed all the *terra firma* there was—and haul it away on sleds, and then I guessed that they must be cutting peat in a bog. So they came and went every day, with a peculiar shriek from the locomotive, from and to some point of the polar regions, as it seemed to me, like a flock of arctic snowbirds. But sometimes Squaw Walden had her revenge, and a hired man, walking behind his team, slipped through a crack in the ground down toward Tartarus, and he who was so brave before suddenly became but the ninth part of a man, almost gave up his animal heat, and was glad to take refuge in my house, and acknowledged that there was some virtue in a stove; or sometimes the frozen soil took a piece of steel out of a plowshare, or a plow got set in the furrow and had to be cut out.

To speak literally, a hundred Irishmen, with Yankee overseers, came from Cambridge every day to get out the ice. They divided it into cakes by methods too well known to require description, and these, being sledded to the shore, were rapidly hauled off on to an ice platform, and raised by grappling irons and block and tackle, worked by horses, on to a stack, as surely as so many barrels of flour, and there placed evenly side by side, and row upon row, as if they formed the solid base of an obelisk designed to pierce the clouds. They told me that in a good day they could get out a thousand tons, which was the yield of about one acre. Deep ruts and 'cradle-holes' were worn in the ice, as on *terra firma,* by the passage of the sleds over the same track, and the horses invariably ate their oats out of cakes of ice hollowed out like buckets. They stacked up the cakes thus in the open air in a pile thirty-five feet high on one side and six or seven rods square, putting hay between the outside layers to exclude the air; for when the wind, though never so cold, finds a passage through, it will wear large cavities, leaving slight supports or studs only here and there, and finally topple it down. At first it looked like a vast blue fort or Valhalla; but when they began to tuck the coarse meadow hay into the crevices, and this became covered with rime and icicles, it looked like a venerable moss-grown and hoary ruin, built of azure-tinted marble, the abode of Winter, that old man we see in the almanac—his shanty, as if he had a design to estivate with us. They calculated that not twenty-five per cent of this would reach its destination, and that two or three per cent would be wasted in the cars. However, a still greater part of this heap had a different destiny from what was intended; for, either because the ice was found not to keep so well as was expected, containing more air than usual, or for some other reason, it never got to market. This heap, made in the winter of '46–7 and estimated to contain ten thousand tons, was finally covered with hay and boards; and though it was unroofed the following July, and a part of it carried off, the rest remaining exposed to the sun, it stood over that summer and the next winter, and was not quite melted till September, 1848. Thus the pond recovered the greater part.

Like the water, the Walden ice, seen near at hand, has a green tint, but at a distance is beautifully blue, and you can easily tell it from the white ice of the river, or the merely greenish ice of some ponds, a quarter of a mile off. Sometimes one of those great cakes slips from the iceman's sled into the village street, and lies there for a week like a great emerald, an object of interest to all passers. I have noticed that a portion of Walden which in the state of water was green will often, when frozen, appear from the same point of view blue. So the hollows about this pond will, sometimes, in the winter, be filled with a greenish water somewhat like its own, but the next day will have frozen blue. Perhaps the blue color of water and ice is due to the light and air they contain, and the most transparent is the bluest. Ice is an interesting subject for contemplation. They told me that they had some in the icehouses at Fresh Pond five years old which was as good as ever. Why is it that a bucket of water soon becomes putrid, but frozen remains sweet forever? It is commonly said that this is the difference between the affections and the intellect.

Thus for sixteen days I saw from my window a hundred men at work like busy husbandmen, with teams and horses and apparently all the implements of farming, such a picture as we see on the first page of the almanac; and as often as I looked out I was reminded of the fable of the lark and the reapers, or the parable of the sower, and the like; and now they are all gone, and in thirty days more, probably, I shall look from the same window on the pure sea-green Walden water there, reflecting the clouds and the trees, and sending up its evaporations in solitude, and no traces will appear that a man has ever stood there. Perhaps I shall hear a solitary loon laugh as he dives and plumes himself, or shall see a lonely fisher in his boat, like a floating leaf, beholding his form reflected in the waves, where lately a hundred men securely labored.

Thus it appears that the sweltering inhabitants of Charleston and New Orleans, of Madras and Bombay and Calcutta, drink at my well. In the morning I bathe my intellect in the stupendous and cosmogonal philosophy of the Bhagvat-Geeta, since whose composition years of the gods have elapsed, and in comparison with which our modern world and its literature seem puny and trivial; and I doubt if that philosophy is not to be referred to a previous state of existence, so remote is its sublimity from our conceptions. I lay down the book and go to my well for water, and lo! there I meet the servant of the Bramin, priest of Brahma and Vishnu and Indra, who still sits in his temple on the Ganges reading the Vedas, or dwells at the root of a tree with his crust and water jug. I meet his servant come to draw water for his master, and our buckets as it were grate together in the same well. The pure Walden water is mingled with the sacred water of the Ganges. With favoring winds it is wafted past the site of the fabulous islands of Atlantis and the Hesperides, makes the periplus of Hanno, and, floating by Temate and Tidore and the mouth of the Persian Gulf, melts in the tropic gales of the Indian seas, and is landed in ports of which Alexander only heard the names.

PART FOUR

Winter As a Time of
Purity and Praise

INTRODUCTION

In October 1802, Dorothy Wordsworth sat down to write in her journal. "It is a pleasure to the real lover of Nature," she wrote, "to give winter all the glory he can, for summer *will* make its own way, and speak its own praises." It will indeed. "Glory" is not often a word associated with winter, and when the very word "winter" conjures up images of freezing desolation and barrenness, the word "glory" seems particularly inappropriate. Slush, mud, shoveling, cold, mittens, frostbite, shoveling, dying car batteries, black ice and slippery roads, frost heaves, shoveling, ice under the shingles, shoveling some more—little glory here. Cold, as John Updike pictures it, is the adversary from which to escape.

Yet the stillness of winter and the sharp clarity of its images evoke outbursts of praise, as in these lines from the ninth-century poet Liu Zongyuan:

> *A thousand mountains. Flying birds vanish.*
> *Ten thousand paths. Human traces erased.*
> *One boat, bamboo hat, bark cape—an old man.*
> *Alone with his hook. Cold river. Snow.*

Winter's sheer physical beauty, its immensity and ineffability tug at our imaginations. Patricia Hampl feels it in the streetlights of St.

Paul, which "throw their buttery rounds on the heaped snowbanks and seem to promise not light but warmth. Their frail yellow," she continues, "always reminded me of snow, even in summer, for the little blobs of light seemed to need the greater radiance of the rounded snow to *be* streetlights at all. Their charm was their ineffectual streetlighting, their inability to do the job. They led, in their evenly spaced formations down Summit and the other smaller streets, from darkness to darkness, sentinels of the night, not its illumination."

And yet winter also illuminates; it brightens and lightens the world it covers. God asks Job, "Have you entered into the treasures of the snow?" The Psalmist asks the Lord to wash him so that he "shall be whiter than snow." The Eastern Orthodox prayer book celebrates the feast of Epiphany—a feast that focuses on the union of creation and the work of Christ—by praising God for granting "the baptismal garment of snowy whiteness by water and Spirit." To see ice crystals hovering in perfectly blue air, to walk on a moonlit night through a field of freshly fallen snow, to mark the tracery of a snowflake, to slide or ski or skate or roll on ice and snow, to stand under a crow sending a dusting of snow down from a hemlock tree—there is glory here.

Recognizing the glory in winter is a spiritual gift, and, as Lancelot Andrewes points out, the seasons are established for spiritual, not merely physical, needs. "But, are there seasons for the things on earth and their fulness, and are there not also seasons for the things in Heaven, and for the filling of them? All, for the relief of the bodily wants here below; none, for the supply of spiritual necessities above? All, for the body, and never a season for the soul?"

All the great liturgies recognize the spaciousness within which we live our humble and perhaps frantic daily lives. Indeed, perhaps it is their main function to wipe the sleep from our eyes so that we may catch a glimpse of true reality and recognize that spaciousness. The *Amidah,* the Eighteen Benedictions that anchor the Jewish liturgy, conjoins the intensely inward motion of quiet prayer with an almost unbearably expansive vision of the cosmos, stretching back into history, forward into the future, and upward to the heavens, stretching our eyes beyond present circumstances to acknowledge the providential care of God—as in the New Moon blessing, which recognizes and celebrates the establishment of the natural order of the seasons and the passing of time. And it is an order that is played out in the universe and is reflected even in the life of the individual:

> Blessed art thou, Lord our God, King of the universe, who didst create the heavens by thy command, and all their host by thy mere word. Thou hast subjected them to fixed laws and time, so that they might not deviate from their set function. They are glad and happy to do the will of their Creator, the true Author, whose achievement is truth. . . . Blessed art thou, O Lord, who renewest the months.

In this sense, winter is about the fulfillment of appointed yearly rounds; it points not to harshness but to the benevolence and power of its creator.

Here too is a glory.

FROM THE DAILY *HALLEL*
(HALLEL SHEB'KHOL YOM)

In Jewish liturgy, the Daily Hallel *are the last six songs in the Book of Psalms: Psalms 145–150. They are psalms of praise, the last five of which begin with "Halleluyah!" In this tradition, the snow and wintry ice too come from God's hand, just as is suggested in William Cooper's sermon. But in this translation, taken from* My People's Prayer Book Volume 3—*P'sukei D'Zimrah* (Morning Psalms) *(Jewish Lights), the emphasis is on the participation of winter in all the affairs of creation.*

> *The* only appropriate human response to frost and cold, suggest the psalms, is one of praise.

The only appropriate human response to frost and cold, suggest the psalms, is one of praise.

PSALM 147

Halleluyah. It is good to sing to our God and it is pleasant; praise is beautiful. Adonai rebuilds Jerusalem; He will gather the dispersed among Israel. The One who heals the brokenhearted will repair their sorrow. The One who counts the stars will give each a name. Great is our Lord and mighty; his wisdom is infinite. Adonai raises the humble and casts the wicked down to earth. Answer Adonai with grateful acknowledgment; play music for God with the harp. He covers the sky with clouds, provides rain for the earth, causes grass to grow on the mountains, and gives bread to beasts and to birds who cry out. He does not take joy in the horse's strength, nor take pleasure in man's legs. He takes pleasure in those who fear Him, in those who yearn for his kindness. Exalt Adonai, Jerusalem; praise your God, Zion, for He has strengthened the bars of your gates, blessed your children in your midst. He grants your borders peace, and sates you with choice wheat. He sends his command earthward and his word runs quickly. He grants snow like wool and scatters frost like ashes. He casts out his ice like crumbs; who can stand before his cold? He sends out his word and melts them. By his wind He causes the water to flow. He declares his word to Jacob, his laws and statutes to Israel. He has not done so for every nation, who do not know his statutes. Halleluyah!

PSALM 148

Praise God! Praise Adonai from the heavens; praise Him on high. Praise Him, all his angels; praise Him, all his hosts. Praise Him, sun and moon. Praise Him, all stars of light. Praise Him, heaven of heavens, and the water above the heavens. Let them praise Adonai's name, because by his commandment they were created. He fixed them for ever and ever; He gave a law that shall never pass. Praise Adonai from the earth, sea monsters and all depths. Fire and hail, snow and fog, stormy wind, all fulfill his word. The mountains and all the hills, the fruit tree and all cedars, wild beasts and all animals, bugs and birds and fowl, kings of the earth and all nations, princes and all judges of the earth, young men and women, the old with the young: Let them praise Adonai's name, for his name alone is exalted. His majesty is on earth and in the heavens. He is the strength of his nation, the praise of his faithful, of the children of Israel, the people near to Him. Halleluyah!

Rachel Carson

"WINTER HAVEN"

*Rachel Carson, who writes with the clear and observant eye of the natural-
ist, is best known for her* Silent Spring *(1962), but her earlier works were
about the ocean, including* The Sea Around Us *(1951) and* The Edge of
the Sea *(1954). In* Under the Sea-Wind, *Carson explores with a scientific eye and a lyrical writing style the abundance of life under the sea, following its transitions, its migra-
tions, its fullness, its response to the
world above the oceans, and its
response to the lower seabeds. In
the chapter from this book entitled
"Winter Haven," Carson explores
particularly the coastal regions off
New England and their response
to the onset of winter's cold.*

*It is a mixed response. Many
trout, for example, are caught in
the freezing ice and are killed, but
there is also a kind of playfulness*

> *C*arson explores
> particularly the coastal
> regions off New England
> and their response to the
> onset of winter's cold. . . .
> the whole melee of
> movement and response as
> a kind of beautiful, almost
> glorious spectacle.

*among the birds, and a migration to blue twilight depths for others. Carson
presents the whole melee of movement and response as a kind of beautiful,
almost glorious spectacle brought on by winter. It is, after all, a winter haven.*

WINTER HAVEN

The night of the next full-moon tide, snow came down the bay on a northwest wind. Mile by mile the blanketing whiteness advanced, covering the hills and valleys and marsh flats of the rivers winding toward the sea. Whirling snow clouds swept across the bay, and all through the night the wind screamed over the water, where the flakes were dropping to instant destruction in the blackness of the bay.

The temperature dropped forty degrees in twenty-four hours, and when the tide went out through the mouth of the bay in the morning it left swiftly congealing pools over all the mud flats where it had spread out thinly, and the last of the ebb did not return to the sea.

The cries of the shore birds—twitter of sandpiper and bell note of plover—were silenced, and only the wind's voice was heard, whining over the levels of salt marsh and tide flat. On the last ebb tide the birds had run at the bay's edge, probing the sand; today they were gone before the blizzard.

In the morning, with the snow still whirling out of the sky, a flock of long-tailed ducks, called old squaws, came out of the northwest before the wind. The long-tails were familiars of ice and snow and wintry wind, and they made merry at the blizzard. They cried noisily to one another as they sighted, through the snowflakes, the tall white shaft of the lighthouse that marked the mouth of the bay and saw beyond it a vast gray sheet that was the sea. The old squaws loved the sea. They would live on it throughout the winter, feeding on the shellfish bars of its shallower waters and resting each night on the open ocean, beyond the surf lines. Now they pitched down out of the blizzard—darker flakes among the snow—into the shallows just outside the great salt marsh at the mouth of the bay. Throughout the morning they fed eagerly on the shellfish beds twenty feet below the surface, diving for the small black mussels.

A few of the bay's shore fish still remained in its deeper holes, off the mouths of its lower rivers. They were sea trout, croakers, spots, sea bass, and flukes. These were the fishes that had summered in the bay and spawned, some of them, over its flats or in its river estuaries or its deep holes; the fish that had escaped gilling in the drift nets that came gliding along the bottom on the ebbing tides— the fish that had missed entrapment in the netting mazes that were called pound nets.

Now the bay's waters were in the grip of winter; ice was sealing all its shallows; and its rivers brought down water from the winter hills. So the fishes turned to the sea, remembering with their whole bodies the gently sloping plain that rolled away from the mouth of the bay; remembering the place of warmth, and quiet water, and blue twilight that lay at the edge of the plain.

On the first night of the blizzard a school of sea trout had been trapped by the cold far up in the shallow bay that lay to seaward of the marsh. The thin water chilled so quickly that the warmth-loving trout were paralyzed by cold and lay on the bottom, half dead. When the tide ebbed to the sea, they were unable to follow, but remained in the thinning water. The next morning ice had formed over all the head of the shallow cove or bay and the trout perished by the hundred.

Another school of trout that had lain in deeper water off the salt marsh escaped death by the cold. Two spring tides before, these trout had come down from their feeding grounds higher in the bay and had lain just inside the channel to the sea. There the strong ebb tides brought them the feeling of icy water come down the rivers and drawn off the shallows and mud flats.

The trout moved into a deeper channel that was one of a chain of three valleys shaped like the imprint of a monstrous gull's foot deep in the soft sand of the bay mouth. The floor of the channel led them down, fathom by fathom, into quieter and warmer water, over dense beds of weed that swayed to the tide movements. Here the press of the tides was less than over the slopes of the shoals, with the strongest movement of the flood tides confined to the upper layers of water. The ebbs were the scouring tides that poured down along the floor of the valleys, stirring up the sand and carrying empty cockleshells bumping and rolling down the gentle slopes into the deep valleys.

As the sea trout entered the channel, blue crabs from the upper bay passed beneath them, sidling down the slopes from the shallows, seeking the deep, warm holes to spend the winter. The crabs crept into the thick carpet of seaweeds that grew on the channel floor and sheltered other crabs, shrimps, and small fishes.

The trout entered the channel just before nightfall, at the beginning of the ebb. During the early hours of the night other fish moved into the tide flow through the channel and pressed toward the sea. They swam close to the bottom, advancing through the thickets of weed which swayed to the passage of the myriad fish bodies. The fish were croakers that were coming down from all the surrounding shoals, driven by the cold. They lay in tiers, three or four fish deep, beneath the trout, enjoying the channel water which was many degrees warmer than the water over the shoals.

In the morning, the light in the channel was like a dense green mist, murky with sand and silt. Ten fathoms overhead the last of the flood tide was pushing to westward the red cone of the nun buoy that marked the beginning of the channel as boats came in from the sea. The buoy strained at its anchor chain and tipped and rolled to the surge of water. The trout had come to the junction of the three channels—the heel or spur of the gull's foot that pointed to the sea.

On the next ebb tide the croakers went out through the channel to the sea, seeking waters that were warmer than the bay. The sea trout lingered.

Near the last of the ebb a flurry of young shad passed through the channel, hurrying seaward. They were finger-long fish with scales like white gold. They were among the last of their kind to leave the bay, in the tributaries of which they had hatched from eggs deposited that spring. Thousands of other young of that year had already passed from the shallow, semifresh waters of the bay into the vastness of the sea, which was unknown to them and strange. The young shad moved quickly in the briny water of the bay mouth, excited by the strange taste of salt and by the rhythms of the sea.

Snow had ceased to fall, but the wind still blew out of the northwest, piling up the snow into deep drifts and picking up the unpacked surface flakes to whirl them in fantastic wind shapes. The cold was hard and bitter. All the narrower rivers froze from bank to bank, and the oyster boats were locked in their harbors. The bay lay in a hard rim of ice and snow. With every ebb tide, bringing down new water from the rivers, the cold increased in the channel where the sea trout lay.

On the fourth night after the blizzard, the moonglow was strong on the surface of the water. The wind broke the glow into myriad facets of reflected light, and all the ceiling of the bay was aglow with dancing flakes and shaking streamers of light. That night the trout saw hundreds of fish moving into the deep channel above them and passing seaward as dark shadows beneath the silver screen. The fish were other sea trout that had been lying in a ninety-foot hole ten miles up the bay, part of the channel of an ancient river that once had been drowned by the sea to form the bay. The fish that had been lying in the channel like a gull's foot joined the migrants from the deep hole, and together they passed to the sea.

Outside the channel, the trout came to a place of rolling sand hills. The underwater hills were even less stable than the dunes on a windy coast, for they had no roots of sea oats or dune grass to stay them against the thrust of waves that climbed the slope from the deep Atlantic. Some of the hills lay only a few fathoms under water. At every storm they shifted, tons of sand piling up or washing away during a time as short as a single rising of the tide.

After a day of wandering in the sea dunes, the trout rose to a high and tide-swept plateau that marked the seaward end of the sand-hill region. The plateau was half a mile wide and two miles long and overlooked a steeper slope that rolled down steadily into green depths. The shoal itself lay only thirty feet under the surface. Once a strong tide driven in by a southwest wind had shifted the sand and wrecked a fishing schooner bound for port with a ton of fish in its hold. The wreck of the *Mary B.* still lay on the sands, which had sunk away beneath it. Weeds grew from her spars and her masthead, and their long green tapes streamed into the water, pointing landward on the flood tides and seaward on the ebb.

The *Mary B.* lay partly buried in the sand, listing at a forty-five-degree angle to landward. A thick bed of weeds grew under her sheltered or starboard side. The hatch that had covered her fish hold had been carried away in the breaking up of the vessel when she was wrecked, and now the hold was like a dark cave in the sloping floor of the deck—a sea cave for creatures who loved to hide in darkness. The hold was half-full of the crab-cleaned skeletons of the fish that had not washed out of the hold when the vessel sank. The windows of the deckhouse had been smashed by the waves that drove the *Mary B.* aground. Now the windows were used as passageways by all the small fishes that lived about the wreck, nibbling off its encrusting growths. Silvery lookdown fish, spadefish, and triggerfish moved in endless little processions in and out of the windows.

The *Mary B.* was like an oasis of life in miles of sea desert, a place where myriads of the sea's lesser fry—the small, backboneless animals—found a place of attachment; and the small fish foragers found living food encrusting all the planks and spars; and larger predators and prowlers of the sea found a hiding place.

The sea trout drew near to the dark hulk of the wreck as the last green light was fading to gray. They took some of the small fishes and crabs which they found about the vessel, satisfying the hunger born of the long, swift flight from the cold of the bay. Then they settled for the night near the weedy timbers of the *Mary B.*

The trout school lay in the water over the wreck in the lethargy that passed for sleep. They moved their fins gently to keep their position with relation to the wreck and to each other as the water pressed steadily over the shoal, moving up the slope from the sea.

At dusk the winding processions of small fishes that moved in and out of the deckhouse windows and through holes in the rotting planks dispersed and their members found resting places about the wreck. With the twilight which came early through the winter sea, the larger hunters who lived in and about the *Mary B.* stirred swiftly to life.

A long, snakelike arm was thrust out of the dark cavern of the fishhold, gripping the deck with double rows of suction cups. One after another, arms to the number of eight appeared, gripping the deck as a dark form clambered out of the hold. The creature was a large octopus who lived in the fishhold of the *Mary B.* It glided across the deck and slid into the recess above the lower wall of the deckhouse, where it concealed itself to begin the night's hunting. As it lay on the old, weed-grown planks its arms were never still, but reached out busily in all directions, exploring every familiar crack and crevice for unwary prey.

The octopus had not long to wait before a small cunner, intent on the mossy hydroids which it was nibbling off the planks of the vessel, came grazing along the wall of the deckhouse. The cunner, unsuspicious of danger, drew nearer. The octopus waited, its eyes fixed on the moving form, its groping arms stilled. The small fish came to the corner of the deckhouse, jutting out at a forty-five-degree angle to the sea bottom. A long tentacle whipped around the corner and encircled the cunner with its sensitive tip. The cunner struggled with all its strength to escape the clasp of the suckers that adhered to scales, fins, and gill covers, but it was drawn down swiftly to the waiting mouth and torn apart by the cruel beak, shaped like a parrot's.

Many times that night the waiting octopus seized unwary fish or crabs that strayed within reach of its tentacles, or launched itself out into the water to capture a fish passing at a greater distance. Then it moved by a pumping of its flaccid, saclike body, propelling itself by jets of liquid squirted from its siphons. Rarely did the encircling arms and gripping suction cups miss their mark, and gradually the gnawing hunger in the maw of the creature was assuaged.

When the weeds under the prow of the *Mary B.* were swaying confusedly to the turn of the tide, a large lobster emerged from its hiding place in the weed bed and moved off in a general shoreward direction. On land the lobster's unwieldy body would have weighed thirty pounds, but on the sea bottom it was supported by the water so that the creature moved nimbly on the tips of its four pairs of slender walking legs. The lobster carried the large crushing claws, or chelae, extended before its body, ready to seize its prey or attack an enemy.

Moving up along the vessel, the lobster paused to pick off a large starfish that was creeping over the mat of barnacles that covered the stern of the wreck with a white crust. The writhing starfish was conveyed by the pincer claws of the foremost walking legs to the mouth, where other appendages, composed of many joints and moving busily, held the spiny-skinned creature against the grinding jaws.

After eating part of the starfish, the lobster abandoned it to the scavenger crabs and moved on across the sand. Once it paused to dig for clams, turning over the sand busily. All the while its long, sensitive antennae were whipping the water for food scents. Finding no clams, the lobster moved into the shadows for its night's foraging.

Just before dusk, one of the younger sea trout had discovered the third of the large, predatory creatures that lived in the wreck. The third hunter was Lophius, the angler fish, a squat, misshapen creature formed like a bellows, with a wide gash of a mouth set with rows of sharp teeth. A curious wand grew above the mouth, like a supple fishing rod at the end of which dangled a lure, or leaflike flap of flesh. Over most of the angler's body ragged tatters of skin streamed out into the water, giving the fish the appearance of a rock grown with seaweeds. Two thickened, fleshy fins—more like the flippers of a water mammal than the fins of a fish—grew from the sides of its body, and when the angler fish moved on the bottom it drew itself forward by its fins.

Lophius was lying under the prow of the *Mary B.* when the young trout came upon him. The angler fish lay motionless, his two small, evil eyes directed upward from the top of his flat head. He was partly concealed by seaweed and his outline was largely obliterated by the rags and tatters of loose skin. To all but the most wary of the fish that moved about the wreck Lophius was invisible.

Cynoscion, the sea trout, did not notice the angler fish, but saw instead a small and brightly colored object that dangled in the water about a foot and a half above the sand. The object moved; it rose and fell. So small shrimps or worms or other food animals had moved in the trout's experience, and Cynoscion swam down to investigate. When he was twice his own body's length away, a small spadefish whirled in from the open water and nibbled at the lure. Instantly there was a flash of twin rows of sharp, white teeth where a moment before harmless seaweed had swayed to the tides, and the spadefish disappeared into the mouth of the angler.

Cynoscion darted away in momentary panic at the sudden motion and lay under a rotting deck timber, gill covers moving rapidly to his increased inspiration of water. So perfect was the camouflage of the angler that the trout had not seen his outlines; the only warnings of danger were the flash of teeth and the sudden disappearance of the spadefish. Three times more as he watched the dangling, jerking lure, Cynoscion saw fishes swim up to investigate it. Two were cunners; one was a lookdown fish, high and compressed of body and silvery of color. Each of the three touched the lure and each disappeared into the maw of the angler.

Then twilight passed into darkness, and Cynoscion saw no more as he lay under the rotting deck timbers. But at intervals as the night wore on he felt the sudden movement of a large body in the water beneath him. After about the middle of the night there was no more movement in the weed bed under the prow of the *Mary B.*, for the angler fish had gone out to forage for bigger game than the few small fishes that came to investigate its lure.

A flock of eiders had come down to rest for the night on the water over the shoal. They had alighted first two miles to landward, but the sea ran in broken swells over the rough terrain beneath them and after the tide turn it foamed on the dark water around the ducks. The wind was blowing onshore, and it fought the tide. The ducks were disturbed in their sleep and flew to the outer edge of the shoal, where the water was quieter, and settled down once more on the seaward side of the breakers. The ducks rode low in the water, like laden fishing schooners. Although they slept, some with their heads under the feathers of their shoulders, they often had to paddle with their webbed feet to keep their positions in the swift-running tide.

As the sky began to lighten in the east and the water above the edge of the shoal grew gray instead of black, the forms of the floating ducks looked from below like dark oval shadows encased in a silvery sheen of air imprisoned between their feathers and the surface film. The eiders were watched from below by a pair of small, malignant eyes that belonged to a creature swimming slowly and with awkward motion through the water—a creature like a great, misshapen bellows.

Lophius was well aware that birds were somewhere near, for the scent and taste of duck were strong in the water that passed over the taste buds covering his tongue and the sensitive skin within his mouth. Even before the growing light had brought the surface shadows within his cone-shaped field of vision, he had seen phosphorescent flashes as the feet of the ducks stirred the water. Lophius had seen such flashes before, and often they had meant that birds were resting on the surface. His night's prowling had brought him only a few moderate-sized fishes, which was far from enough to fill a stomach that could hold two dozen large flounders or threescore herring or could pouch a single fish as large as the angler itself.

Lophius moved closer to the surface, climbing with his fins. He swam under an eider that was separated a little from its fellows. The duck was asleep, bill tucked in its feathers, one foot dangling below its body. Before it could waken to knowledge of its danger it was seized in a sharp-toothed mouth with a spread of nearly a foot. In sudden terror the duck beat the water with its wings and paddled with its free foot, seeking to take off from the surface. By a great exertion of strength it began to rise from the water, but the full weight of the angler hung from its body and dragged it back.

The honking of the doomed eider and the thrashing of its wings alarmed its companions, and with a wild churning of the water the remainder of the flock took off in flight, quickly disappearing into the thin mist that lay over the sea. The duck was bleeding spurts of bright-red blood from a severed leg artery. As its life ebbed away in the bright stream, its struggles grew feeble, and the strength of the great fish prevailed. Lophius pulled the duck under, sinking away from the cloud of reddened water just as a shark appeared in the dim light, attracted by the scent of blood. The angler took the duck to the floor of the shoal and swallowed it whole, for his stomach was capable of enormous distension.

Half an hour later Cynoscion, the sea trout, hunting about the wreck for small fishes, saw the angler returning to his hole under the prow of the *Mary B.,* pulling himself over the bottom by his handlike pectoral fins. He saw Lophius creep into the shadow of the vessel and saw the weeds that waved under the prow part to receive him. There the angler would lie in torpor for several days, digesting his meal.

During the day the water chilled by almost imperceptible degrees, and in the afternoon the ebb tide brought a great flood of cold water from the bay. That evening the sea trout, driven by the cold, left the wreck and ran seaward during the entire night, passing down the plain that sloped steadily away beneath them. They moved over smooth, sandy bottoms, sometimes rising to pass over a mound or shoal of broken shell. They hurried on, resting seldom because of the creeping cold. Hour by hour the water above them deepened.

The eels must have passed this way, through the country of underwater sand hills and down the sloping meadowlands and prairies of the sea.

Often during the next few days the trout were overtaken by other schools of fishes when they paused for rest or food and often they met browsing fish herds of many different kinds. The fish had come from all the bays and rivers of many miles of coast line, fleeing the winter cold. Some had come from far to the north, from the coasts of Rhode Island and Connecticut and the shores of Long Island. These were scup, thin-bodied fish with high, arched backs and spiny fins, covered with platelike scales. Every winter the scup came from New England to the waters off the Capes of Virginia and then returned in spring to spawn in the northern waters and be caught in traps and swiftly encircling seines. The farther the sea trout traveled across the continental shelf, the more often they saw the scup herds in the green haze before them, the large bronze fish rising and sinking as they grubbed on the bottom for worms, sand dollars, and crabs and drifted up a fathom or more to munch their food.

And sometimes there were cod schools, come from Nantucket Shoals to winter in the warmer southern waters. Some of the cod would spawn in this place that seemed alien to their kind, leaving their young to the ocean currents, which might never return them to the northern home of the cod.

The cold increased. It was like a wall moving through the sea across the coastal plain. It was nothing that could be seen or touched; yet it was so real a barrier that no fish would have run back through it any more than if it had been solid as stone. In milder winters the fish would have scattered widely over the continental shelf—the croakers well inshore; the flukes or flounders on all the sandy patches; scup in all the sloping valleys, rich in bottom food; and sea bass over every piece of rocky ground. But this year the cold drove them on, mile after mile, to the edge of the continental shelf—to the edge of the deep sea. There in the quiet water, warmed by the Gulf Stream, they found a winter haven.

Even as the fish were running out across the continental shelf from all the bays and rivers, boats were moving south and out to sea. The boats were squat and ungraceful of line and they pitched and rolled in the winter sea. They were trawlers, come from many northern ports to find the fish in their winter refuge.

Only a decade before, the sea trout, the fluke, the scup, and the croakers had been safe from the fishermen's nets once they had left the bays and sounds. Then, one year, boats had come, dragging nets like long bags. The boats had moved down from the north and out from the coast, towing their nets along the bottom. At first they had taken nothing. Mile by mile, they moved farther out, and finally their nets came up filled with food fishes. The wintering grounds of the shore fish—the summer fish of the bays and river estuaries—had been discovered.

From that time on, the trawlers came every season and took millions of pounds of fishes each year. Now they were on their way, coming down from the northern fishing ports. There were haddock trawlers from Boston and flounder draggers from New Bedford; there were redfish boats from Gloucester and cod boats from Portland. Winter fishing in southern waters is easier than winter fishing on the Scotian Banks or the Grand Banks; easier even than on Georges, or Browns, or the Channel.

But this winter was cold; the bays were icebound, and the sea was gale-ridden. The fish were far out; seventy miles out, a hundred miles out. The fish were deep down in warm water, a hundred fathoms down.

The trawls went over the side, from decks that were slippery with freezing spray. The meshes of the trawl nets were stiff with ice, and all the ropes and the cables groaned and creaked with the frost. The trawls went down through the hundred fathoms of water; down from ice and sleet and heaving sea and screaming wind to a place of warmth and quiet, where fish herds browsed in the blue twilight, on the edge of the deep sea.

Sultan Bahu

"On a dark, black night, love lights a lamp" and other Sufi poems

Love blossoms in the spring, we say, but winter is also the irrational season of love. When our minds slow down and our hearts are quieted, we turn expectantly to the "dark, black night" where "love lights a lamp." The Sufi mystical poet Sultan Bahu (d. 1691), whose name reflects his intimacy with God, writes from a particular place: the Punjab region of India. But the longing for love, for God, that he expresses is universal. And winter love, perhaps because it is hard won, exults triumphantly. It claps its hands, it outshines the moon, it faces down every tiger, every fear.

Winter love, perhaps because it is hard won, exults triumphantly. It claps its hands, it outshines the moon, it faces down every tiger, every fear.

On a dark, black night, love lights a lamp.
   You can't hear the voice of the One whose
   love carries your
      heart away.
   Forests, marshes, and frightening swamps,
   where one fears tigers
      with every breath.
   Those whose love is perfect, Bahu, cross
   deserts, seas, and jungles.

———

Love saw me weak and it came, taking over my
      home.
   Like a fussy child, it will not sleep nor let me
      sleep.
   It asks for watermelons in winter, where can I find
      them?
   But all rational thoughts were forgotten, Bahu,
      when love
      clapped its hands.

Arise and shine bright, moon! The stars are
engaged in your
    recollection.
Many moons like you have risen, but without my
Beloved all is
    darkness.
Where my Moon rises, there you have no worth.
The Beloved for whom I lost a lifetime, may I
meet Him just
    once, Bahu.

Everyone asks for firmness in faith, but few for firm-
    ness in love.
They ask for faith and are ashamed of love, such
    arrogant hearts!
Faith has no idea of the place where love transports
    you.
I swear by my faith, Bahu, keep my love firm!

Annie Dillard

"WINTER"

In Pilgrim at Tinker Creek, *Annie Dillard does what she does in many of her books: draws surprising, even shocking connections between things so disparate as to seem to revolve in completely different orbits. In her chapter "Winter," she moves back and forth between the wildness of the world and the beauties of the world, between its dangers and its glories, and points out that perhaps none of these are so very different from the others. As she moves around the countryside near Tinker Creek and observes what extraordinary activity goes on about her, and as she recalls the books she has read, she pictures the world as a surprising whole, a shocking unity.*

She senses the unity, the surprising whole, in moments that she calls gaps that show before the mountains slam together.

She senses the unity, the surprising whole, in moments that she calls gaps that show before the mountains slam together. That startling and even aggressively wild metaphor is of a piece with the whole of Pilgrim at Tinker Creek, *and especially with this section, which suggests that beneath the snow is a world of constant activity and beauty.*

WINTER

I

It is the first of February, and everyone is talking about starlings. Starlings came to this country on a passenger liner from Europe. One hundred of them were deliberately released in Central Park, and from those hundred descended all of our countless millions of starlings today. According to Edwin Way Teale, "Their coming was the result of one man's fancy. That man was Eugene Schieffelin, a wealthy New York drug manufacturer. His curious hobby was the introduction into America of all the birds mentioned in William Shakespeare." The birds adapted to their new country splendidly.

When John Cowper Powys lived in the United States, he wrote about chickadees stealing crumbs from his favorite flock of starlings. Around here they're not so popular. Instead of quietly curling for sleep, one by one, here and there in dense shrubbery, as many birds do, starlings roost all together in vast hordes and droves. They have favorite roosting sites to which they return winter after winter; apparently southwest Virginia is their idea of Miami Beach. In Waynesboro, where the starlings roost in the woods near the Coyner Springs area, residents can't go outside for any length of time, or even just to hang laundry, because of the stink—"will knock you over"—the droppings, and the lice.

Starlings are notoriously difficult to "control." The story is told of a man who was bothered by starlings roosting in a large sycamore near his house. He said he tried everything to get rid of them and finally took a shotgun to three of them and killed them. When asked if that discouraged the birds, he reflected a minute, leaned forward, and said confidentially, "Those three it did."

Radford, Virginia, had a little stink of its own a few years ago. Radford had starlings the way a horse has flies, and in similarly unapproachable spots. Wildlife biologists estimated the Radford figure at one hundred fifty thousand starlings. The people complained of the noise, the stench, the inevitable whitewash effect, and the possibility of an epidemic of an exotic, dust-borne virus disease.

Finally, in January, 1972, various officials and biologists got together and decided that something needed to be done. After studying the feasibility of various methods, they decided to kill the starlings with foam. The idea was to shoot a special detergent foam through hoses at the roosting starlings on a night when weathermen predicted a sudden drop in temperature. The foam would penetrate the birds' waterproof feathers and soak their skins. Then when the temperature dropped, the birds would drop too, having quietly died of exposure.

Meanwhile, before anything actually happened, the papers were having a field day. Every crazy up and down every mountain had his shrill say. The local bird societies screamed for blood—the starlings' blood. Starlings, after all, compete with native birds for food and nesting sites. Other people challenged the mayor of Radford, the Virginia Tech Wildlife Bureau, the newspaper's editors and all its readers in Radford and everywhere else, to tell how THEY would like to freeze to death inside a bunch of bubbles.

The Wildlife Bureau went ahead with its plan. The needed equipment was expensive, and no one was quite sure if it would work. Sure enough, on the night they sprayed the roosts the temperature didn't drop far enough. Out of the hundred and fifty thousand starlings they hoped to exterminate, they got only three thousand. Somebody figured out that the whole show had cost citizens two dollars per dead starling.

That is, in effect, the story of the Radford starlings. The people didn't give up at once, however. They mulled and fussed, giving the starlings a brief reprieve, and then came up with a new plan. Soon, one day when the birds returned at sunset to their roost, the wildlife managers were ready for them. They fired shotguns loaded with multiple, high-powered explosives into the air. BANG, went the guns; the birds settled down to sleep. The experts went back to their desks and fretted and fumed some more. At last they brought out the ultimate weapon: recordings of starling distress calls. Failure. YIKE OUCH HELP went the recordings; snore went the birds. That, *in toto,* is the story of the Radford starlings. They still thrive.

Our valley starlings thrive, too. They plod morosely around the grass under the feeder. Other people apparently go to great lengths to avoid feeding them. Starlings are early to bed and late to rise, so people sneak out with grain and suet before dawn, for early rising birds, and whisk it away at the first whiff of a starling; after sunset, when the starlings are safely to roost bothering somebody else, they spread out the suet and grain once again. I don't care what eats the stuff.

It is winter proper; the cold weather, such as it is, has come to stay. I bloom indoors in the winter like a forced forsythia; I come in to come out. At night I read and write, and things I have never understood become clear; I reap the harvest of the rest of the year's planting.

Outside, everything has opened up. Winter clear-cuts and reseeds the easy way. Everywhere paths unclog; in late fall and winter, and only then, can I scale the cliff to the Lucas orchard, circle the forested quarry pond, or follow the left-hand bank of Tinker Creek downstream. The woods are acres of sticks; I could walk to the Gulf of Mexico in a straight line. When the leaves fall the striptease is over; things stand mute and revealed. Everywhere skies extend, vistas deepen, walls become windows, doors open. Now I can see the house where the Whites and the Garretts lived on the hill under oaks. The thickly grown banks of Carvin's Creek where it edges the road have long since thinned to a twiggy haze, and I can see Maren and Sandy in blue jackets out running the dogs. The mountains' bones poke through, all shoulder and knob and shin. All that summer conceals, winter reveals. Here are the birds' nests hid in the hedge, and squirrels' nests splotched all over the walnuts and elms.

Today a gibbous moon marked the eastern sky like a smudge of chalk. The shadows of its features had the same blue tone and light value as the sky itself, so it looked transparent in its depths, or softly frayed, like the heel of a sock. Not too long ago, according to Edwin Way Teale, the people of Europe believed that geese and swans wintered there, on the moon's pale seas. Now it is sunset. The mountains warm in tone as the day chills, and a hot blush deepens over the land. "Observe," said da Vinci, "observe in the streets at twilight, when the day is cloudy, the loveliness and tenderness spread on the faces of men and women." I have seen those faces, when the day is cloudy, and I have seen at sunset on a clear winter day houses, ordinary houses, whose bricks were coals and windows flame.

At dusk every evening an extended flock of starlings appears out of the northern sky and winds towards the setting sun. It is the winter day's major event. Late yesterday, I climbed across the creek, through the steers' pasture, beyond the grassy island where I had seen the giant water bug sip a frog, and up a high hill. Curiously, the best vantage point on the hill was occupied by a pile of burnt books. I opened some of them carefully: they were good cloth- and leather-bound novels, a complete, charred set of encyclopedias decades old, and old, watercolor-illustrated children's books. They flaked in my hands like pieces of pie. Today I learned that the owners of the house behind the books had suffered a fire. But I didn't know that then; I thought they'd suffered a terrible fit of pique. I crouched beside the books and looked over the valley.

On my right a woods thickly overgrown with creeper descended the hill's slope to Tinker Creek. On my left was a planting of large shade trees on the ridge of the hill. Before me the grassy hill pitched abruptly and gave way to a large, level field fringed in trees where it bordered the creek. Beyond the creek I could see with effort the vertical sliced rock where men had long ago quarried the mountain under the forest. Beyond that I saw Hollins Pond and all its woods and pastures; then I saw in a blue haze all the world poured flat and pale between the mountains.

Out of the dimming sky a speck appeared, then another, and another. It was the starlings going to roost. They gathered deep in the distance, flock sifting into flock, and strayed towards me, transparent and whirling, like smoke. They seemed to unravel as they flew, lengthening in curves, like a loosened skein. I didn't move; they flew directly over my head for half an hour. The flight extended like a fluttering banner, an unfurled oriflamme, in either direction as far as

I could see. Each individual bird bobbed and knitted up and down in the flight at apparent random, for no known reason except that that's how starlings fly, yet all remained perfectly spaced. The flocks each tapered at either end from a rounded middle, like an eye. Over my head I heard a sound of beaten air, like a million shook rugs, a muffled whuff. Into the woods they sifted without shifting a twig, right through the crowns of trees, intricate and rushing, like wind.

After half an hour, the last of the stragglers had vanished into the trees. I stood with difficulty, bashed by the unexpectedness of this beauty, and my spread lungs roared. My eyes pricked from the effort of trying to trace a feathered dot's passage through a weft of limbs. Could tiny birds be sifting through me right now, birds winging through the gaps between my cells, touching nothing, but quickening in my tissues, fleet?

Some weather's coming; you can taste on the sides of your tongue a quince tang in the air. This fall everyone looked to the bands on a woolly bear caterpillar, and predicted as usual the direst of dire winters. This routine always calls to mind the Angiers' story about the trappers in the far north. They approached an Indian whose ancestors had dwelled from time immemorial in those fir forests, and asked him about the severity of the coming winter. The Indian cast a canny eye over the landscape and pronounced, "Bad winter." The others asked him how he knew. The Indian replied unhesitatingly, "The white man makes a big woodpile." Here the woodpile is an exercise doggedly, exhaustedly maintained despite what must be great temptation. The other day I saw a store displaying a neatly stacked quarter-cord of fireplace logs manufactured of rolled, pressed paper. On the wrapper of each "log" was printed in huge letters the beguiling slogan, "The ROMANCE Without The HEARTACHE."

I lay a cherry log fire and settle in. I'm getting used to this planet and to this curious human culture which is as cheerfully enthusiastic as it is cheerfully cruel. I never cease to marvel at the newspapers. In my life I've seen one million pictures of a duck that has adopted a kitten, or a cat that has adopted a duckling, or a sow and a puppy, a mare and a muskrat. And for the one millionth time I'm fascinated. I wish I lived near them, in Corpus Christi or Damariscotta; I wish I had the wonderful pair before me, mooning about the yard. It's all beginning to smack of home. The winter pictures that come in over the wire from every spot on the continent are getting to be as familiar as my own hearth. I wait for the annual aerial photograph of an enterprising fellow who has stamped in the snow a giant Valentine for his girl. Here's the annual chickadee-trying-to-drink-from-a-frozen-birdbath picture, captioned, "Sorry, Wait Till Spring," and the shot of an utterly bundled child crying piteously on a sled at the top of a snowy hill, labeled, "Needs a Push." How can an old world be so innocent?

Finally I see tonight a picture of a friendly member of the Forest Service in Wisconsin, who is freeing a duck frozen onto the ice by chopping out its feet with a hand ax. It calls to mind the spare, cruel story Thomas McGonigle told me about herring gulls frozen on ice off Long Island. When his father was young, he used to walk out on Great South Bay, which had frozen over, and frozen the gulls to it. Some of the gulls were already dead. He would take a hunk of driftwood and brain the living gulls; then, with a steel knife he hacked them free below the body and rammed them into a burlap sack. The family ate herring gull all winter, close around a lighted table in a steamy room. And out on the Bay, the ice was studded with paired, red stumps.

Winter knives. With their broad snow knives, Eskimos used to cut blocks of snow to spiral into domed igloos for temporary shelter. They sharpened their flensing knives by licking a thin coat of ice on the blade. Sometimes an Eskimo would catch a wolf with a knife. He slathered the knife with blubber and buried the hilt in snow or ice. A hungry wolf would scent the blubber, find the knife, and lick it compulsively with numbed tongue, until he sliced his tongue to ribbons, and bled to death.

This is the sort of stuff I read all winter. The books I read are like the stone men built by the Eskimos of the great desolate tundras west of Hudson's Bay. They still build them today, according to Farley Mowat. An Eskimo traveling alone in flat barrens will heap round stones to the height of a man, travel till he can no longer see the beacon, and build another. So I travel mute among these books, these eyeless men and women that people the empty plain. I wake up thinking: What am I reading? What will I read next? I'm terrified that I'll run out, that I will read through all I want to, and be forced to learn wildflowers at last, to keep awake. In the meantime I lose myself in a liturgy of names. The names of the men are Knud Rasmussen, Sir John Franklin, Peter Freuchen, Scott, Peary, and Byrd; Jedediah Smith, Peter Skene Ogden, and Milton Sublette; or Daniel Boone singing on his blanket in the Green River country. The names of waters are Baffin Bay, Repulse Bay, Coronation Gulf, and the Ross Sea; the Coppermine River, the Judith, the Snake, and the Musselshell; the Pelly, the Dease, the Tanana, and Telegraph Creek. Beaver plews, zero degrees latitude, and gold. I like the clean urgency of these tales, the sense of being set out in a wilderness with a jackknife and a length of twine. If I can get up a pinochle game, a little three-hand cutthroat for half a penny a point and a bottle of wine, fine; if not I'll spend these southern nights caught in the pack off Franz Josef Land, or casting for arctic char.

II

It snowed. It snowed all yesterday and never emptied the sky, although the clouds looked so low and heavy they might drop all at once with a thud. The light is diffuse and hueless, like the light on paper inside a pewter bowl. The snow looks light and the sky dark, but in fact the sky is lighter than the snow. Obviously the thing illuminated cannot be lighter than its illuminator. The classical demonstration of this point involves simply laying a mirror flat on the snow so that it reflects in its surface the sky, and comparing by sight this value to that of the snow. This is all very well, even conclusive, but the illusion persists. The dark is overhead and the light at my feet; I'm walking upside-down in the sky.

Yesterday I watched a curious nightfall. The cloud ceiling took on a warm tone, deepened, and departed as if drawn on a leash. I could no longer see the fat snow flying against the sky; I could see it only as it fell before dark objects. Any object at a distance—like the dead, ivy-covered walnut I see from the bay window—looked like a black-and-white frontispiece seen through the sheet of white tissue. It was like dying, this watching the world recede into deeper and deeper blues while the snow piled; silence swelled and extended, distance dissolved, and soon only concentration at the largest shadows let me make out the movement of falling snow, and that too failed. The snow on the yard was blue as ink, faintly luminous; the sky violet. The bay window betrayed me, and started giving me back the room's lamps. It was like dying, that growing dimmer and deeper and then going out.

Today I went out for a look around. The snow had stopped, and a couple of inches lay on the ground. I walked through the yard to the creek; everything was slate-blue and gunmetal and white, except for the hemlocks and cedars, which showed a brittle, secret green if I looked for it under the snow.

Lo and behold, here in the creek was a silly-looking coot. It looked like a black and gray duck, but its head was smaller; its clunky white bill sloped straight from the curve of its skull like a cone from its base. I had read somewhere that coots were shy. They were liable to take umbrage at a footfall, skitter terrified along the water, and take to the air. But I wanted a good look. So when the coot tipped tail and dove, I raced towards it across the snow and hid behind a cedar trunk. As it popped up again its neck was as rigid and eyes as blank as a rubber duck's in the bathtub. It paddled downstream, away from me. I waited until it submerged again, then made a break for the trunk of the Osage orange. But up it came all at once, as though the child in the tub had held the rubber duck under water with both hands, and suddenly released it. I froze stock-still, thinking that after all I really was, actually and at bottom, a tree, a dead tree perhaps, even a wobbly one, but a treeish creature nonetheless. The coot wouldn't notice that a tree hadn't grown in that spot the moment before; what did it know? It was new to the area, a mere dude. As tree I allowed myself only the luxury of keeping a wary eye on the coot's eye. Nothing; it didn't suspect a thing—unless, of course, it was just leading me on, beguiling me into scratching my nose, when the jig would be up once and for all, and I'd be left unmasked, untreed, with no itch and an empty creek. So.

At its next dive I made the Osage orange and looked around from its trunk while the coot fed from the pool behind the riffles. From there I ran downstream to the sycamore, getting treed in open ground again—and so forth for forty minutes, until it gradually began to light in my leafy brain that maybe the coot wasn't shy after all. That all this subterfuge was unnecessary, that the bird was singularly stupid, or at least not of an analytical turn of mind, and that in fact I'd been making a perfect idiot of myself all alone in the snow. So from behind the trunk of a black walnut, which was my present blind, I stepped boldly into the open. Nothing. The coot floated just across the creek from me, absolutely serene. Could it possibly be that I'd been flirting all afternoon with a *decoy*? No, decoys don't dive. I walked back to the sycamore, actually moving in plain sight not ten yards from the creature, which gave no sign of alarm or flight. I stopped; I raised my arm and waved. Nothing. In its beak hung a long, wet strand of some shore plant; it sucked it at length down its throat and dove again. I'll kill it. I'll hit the thing with a snowball, I really will; I'll make a mud-hen hash.

But I didn't even make a snowball. I wandered upstream, along smooth banks under trees. I had gotten, after all, a very good look at the coot. Now here were its tracks in the snow, three-toed and very close together. The wide, slow place in the creek by the road bridge was frozen over. From this bank at this spot in summer I can always see tadpoles, fat-bodied, scraping brown algae from a sort of shallow underwater ledge. Now I couldn't see the ledge under the ice. Most of the tadpoles were now frogs, and the frogs were buried alive in the mud at the bottom of the creek. They went to all that trouble to get out of the water and breathe air, only to hop back in before the first killing frost. The frogs of Tinker Creek are slathered in mud, mud at their eyes and mud at their nostrils; their damp skins absorb a muddy oxygen, and so they pass the dreaming winter.

Also from this bank at this spot in summer I can often see turtles by crouching low to catch the triangular poke of their heads out of water. Now snow smothered the ice; if it stays cold, I thought, and the neighborhood kids get busy with brooms, they can skate. Meanwhile, a turtle in the creek under the ice is getting oxygen by an almost incredible arrangement. It sucks water posteriorly into its large cloacal opening, where sensitive tissues filter the oxygen directly into the blood, as a gill does. Then the turtle discharges the water and gives another suck. The neighborhood kids can skate right over this curious rush of small waters.

Under the ice the bluegills and carp are still alive; this far south the ice never stays on the water long enough that fish metabolize all the oxygen and die. Farther north, fish sometimes die in this way and float up to the ice, which thickens around their bodies and holds them fast, open-eyed, until the thaw. Some worms are still burrowing in the silt, dragonfly larvae are active on the bottom, some algae carry on a dim photosynthesis, and that's about it. Everything else is dead, killed by the cold, or mutely alive in any of various still forms: egg, seed, pupa, spore. Water snakes are hibernating as dense balls, water striders hibernate as adults along the bank, and mourning cloak butterflies secret themselves in the bark of trees: all of these emerge groggily in winter thaws, to slink, skitter, and flit about in one afternoon's sunshine, and then at dusk to seek shelter, chill, fold, and forget.

The muskrats are out: they can feed under the ice, where the silver trail of bubbles that rises from their fur catches and freezes in streaming, glittering globes. What else? The birds, of course, are fine. Cold is no problem for warm-blooded animals, so long as they have food for fuel. Birds migrate for food, not for warmth as such. That is why, when so many people all over the country started feeding stations, southern birds like the mockingbird easily extended their ranges north. Some of our local birds go south, like the female robin; other birds, like the coot, consider *this* south. Mountain birds come down to the valley in a vertical migration; some of them, like the chickadees, eat not only seeds but such tiny fare as aphid eggs hid near winter buds and the ends of twigs. This afternoon I watched a chickadee swooping and dangling high in a tulip tree. It seemed astonishingly heated and congealed, as though a giant pair of hands had scooped a skyful of molecules and squeezed it like a snowball to produce this fireball, this feeding, flying, warm solid bit.

Other interesting things are going on wherever there is shelter. Slugs, of all creatures, hibernate, inside a waterproof sac. All the bumblebees and paper wasps are dead except the queens, who sleep a fat, numbed sleep, unless a mouse finds one and eats her alive. Honeybees have their own honey for fuel, so they can overwinter as adults, according to Edwin Way Teale, by buzzing together in a tightly packed, living sphere. Their shimmying activity heats the hive; they switch positions from time to time so that each bee gets its chance in the cozy middle and its turn on the cold outside. Ants hibernate en masse; the woolly bear hibernates alone in a bristling ball. Ladybugs hibernate under shelter in huge orange clusters sometimes the size of basketballs. Out West, people hunt for these overwintering masses in the mountains. They take them down to warehouses in the valleys, which pay handsomely. Then, according to Will Barker, the mail-order houses ship them to people who want them to eat garden aphids. They're mailed in the cool of night in boxes of old pine cones. It's a clever device: How do you pack a hundred living ladybugs? The insects naturally crawl deep into the depths of the pine cones; the sturdy "branches" of the opened cones protect them through all the bumpings of transit.

I crossed the bridge invigorated and came to a favorite spot. It is the spit of land enclosed in the oxbow of Tinker Creek. A few years ago I called these few acres the weed-field; they grew mostly sassafras, ivy, and poke. Now I call it the woods by the creek; young tulip grows there, and locust and oak. The snow on the wide path through the woods was unbroken. I stood in a little clearing beside the dry ditch that the creek cuts, bisecting the land, in high water. Here I ate a late lunch of ham sandwiches and wished I'd brought water and left more fat on the ham.

There was something new in the woods today—a bunch of sodden, hand-lettered signs tied to the trees all along the winding path. They said "SLOW," "SLIPPERY WHEN WET," "STOP," "PIT ROW," "ESSO," and "BUMP!!" These signs indicated an awful lot of excitement over a little snow. When I saw the first one, "SLOW," I thought, sure, I'll go slow; I won't screech around on the unbroken path in the woods by the creek under snow. What was going on here? The other signs made it clear. Under "BUMP!!" lay, sure enough, a bump. I scraped away the smooth snow. Hand-fashioned of red clay, and now frozen, the bump was about six inches high and eighteen inches across. The slope, such as it was, was gentle; tread marks stitched the clay. On the way out I saw that I'd missed the key sign, which had fallen: "WELCOME TO MARTINSVILLE SPEEDWAY." So my "woods by the creek" was a motorbike trail to the local boys, their "Martinsville Speedway." I had always wondered why they bothered to take a tractor-mower to these woods all summer long, keeping the many paths open; it was a great convenience to me.

Now the speedway was a stillnessway. Next to me in a sapling, a bird's nest cradled aloft a newborn burden of snow. From a crab apple tree hung a single frozen apple with blistered and shiny skin; it was heavy and hard as a stone. Everywhere through the trees I saw the creek run blue under the ledge of ice from the banks; it made a thin, metallic sound like foil beating foil.

When I left the woods I stepped into a yellow light. The sun behind a uniform layer of gray had the diffuse shine of a very much rubbed and burnished metal boss. On the mountains the wan light slanted over the snow and gouged out shallow depressions and intricacies in the mountains' sides I never knew were there. I walked home. No school today. The motorbike boys were nowhere in sight; they were probably skidding on sleds down the very steep hill and out onto the road. Here my neighbor's small children were rolling a snowman. The noon sun had dampened the snow; it caught in slabs, leaving green, irregular tracks on the yard. I just now discovered the most extraordinary essay, a treatise on making a snowman. ". . . By all means use what is ready to hand. In a fuel-oil burning area, for instance, it is inconceivable that fathers should sacrifice their days hunting downtown for lumps of coal for their children's snowmen's eyes. Charcoal briquettes from the barbecue are an unwieldy substitute, and fuel oil itself is of course out of the question. Use pieces of rock, brick, or dark sticks; use bits of tire tread or even dark fallen leaves rolled tightly, cigarwise, and deeply inserted into sockets formed by a finger." Why, why in the blue-green world write this sort of thing? Funny written culture, I guess; we pass things on.

There are seven or eight categories of phenomena in the world that are worth talking about, and one of them is the weather. Any time you care to get in your car and drive across the country and over the mountains, come into our valley, cross Tinker Creek, drive up the road to the house, walk across the yard, knock on the door and ask to come in and talk about the weather, you'd be welcome. If you came tonight from up north, you'd have a terrific tailwind; between Tinker and Dead Man you'd chute through the orchardy pass like an iceboat. When I let you in, we might not be able to close the door. The wind shrieks and hisses down the valley, sonant and surd, drying the puddles and dismantling the nests from the trees.

Inside the house, my single goldfish, Ellery Channing, whips around and around the sides of his bowl. Can he feel a glassy vibration, a ripple out of the north that urges him to swim for deeper, warmer waters? Saint-Exupéry says that when flocks of wild geese migrate high over a barnyard, the cocks and even the dim, fatted chickens fling themselves a foot or so into the air and flap for the south. Eskimo sled dogs feed all summer on famished salmon flung to them from creeks. I have often wondered if those dogs feel a wistful downhill drift in the fall, or an upstream yank, an urge to leap ladders, in the spring. To what hail do you hark, Ellery?—what sunny bottom under chill waters, what Chinese emperor's petaled pond? Even the spiders are restless under this wind, roving about alert-eyed over their fluff in every corner.

I allow the spiders the run of the house. I figure that any predator that hopes to make a living on whatever smaller creatures might blunder into a four-inch square bit of space in the corner of the bathroom where the tub meets the floor, needs every bit of my support. They catch flies and even field crickets in those webs. Large spiders in barns have been known to trap, wrap, and suck hummingbirds, but there's no danger of that here. I tolerate the webs, only occasionally sweeping away the very dirtiest of them after the spider itself has scrambled to safety. I'm always leaving a bath towel draped over the tub so that the big, haired spiders, who are constantly getting trapped by the tub's smooth sides, can use its rough surface as an exit ramp. Inside the house the spiders have only given me one mild surprise. I washed some dishes and set them to dry over a plastic drainer. Then I wanted a cup of coffee, so I picked from the drainer my mug, which was still warm from the hot rinse water, and across the rim of the mug, strand after strand, was a spider web.

Outside in summer I watch the orb-weavers, the spiders at their wheels. Last summer I watched one spin her web, which was especially interesting because the light just happened to be such that I couldn't see the web at all. I had read that spiders lay their major straight lines with fluid that isn't sticky, and then lay a nonsticky spiral. Then they walk along that safe road and lay a sticky spiral going the other way. It seems to be very much a matter of concentration. The spider I watched was a matter of mystery: she seemed to be scrambling up, down, and across the air. There was a small white mass of silk visible at the center of the orb, and she returned to this hub after each frenzied foray between air and air. It was a sort of Tinker Creek to her, from which she bore lightly in every direction an invisible news. She had a nice ability to make hairpin turns at the most acute angles in the air, all at topmost speed. I understand that you can lure an orb-weaver spider, if you want one, by vibrating or twirling a blade of grass against the web, as a flying insect would struggle if caught. This little ruse has never worked for me; I need a tuning fork; I leave the webs on the bushes bristling with grass.

Things are well in their place. Last week I found a brown, cocoonlike object, light and dry, and pocketed it in an outside, unlined pocket where it wouldn't warm and come alive. Then I saw on the ground another one, slightly torn open, so I split it further with my fingers, and saw a pale froth. I held it closer; the froth took on intricacy. I held it next to my eye and saw a tiny spider, yellowish but so infinitesimal it was translucent, waving each of its eight legs in what was clearly threat behavior. It was one of hundreds of spiders, already alive, all squirming in a tangled orgy of legs. Not on me they won't; I emptied that pocket fast. Things out of place are ill. Tonight I hear outside a sound of going in the tops of the mulberry trees; I stay in to do battle with—what? Once I looked into a little wooden birdhouse hung from a tree; it had a pointed roof like an Alpine cottage, a peg perch, and a neat round door. Inside, watching me, was a coiled snake. I used to kill insects with carbon tetrachloride—cleaning fluid vapor—and pin them in cigar boxes, labeled, in neat rows. That was many years ago: I quit when one day I opened a cigar box lid and saw a carrion beetle, staked down high between its wing covers, trying to crawl, swimming on its pin. It was dancing with its own shadow, untouching, and had been for days. If I go downstairs now will I see a possum just rounding a corner, trailing its scaled pink tail? I know that one night, in just this sort of rattling wind, I will go to the kitchen for milk and find on the back of the stove a sudden stew I never fixed, bubbling, with a deer leg sticking out.

In a dry wind like this, snow and ice can pass directly into the air as a gas without having first melted to water. This process is called sublimation; tonight the snow in the yard and the ice in the creek sublime. A breeze buffets my palm held a foot from the wall. A wind like this does my breathing for me; it engenders something quick and kicking in my lungs. Pliny believed the mares of the Portuguese used to raise their tails to the wind, "and turn them full against it, and so conceive that genital air instead of natural seed: in such sort, as they become great withal, and quicken in their time, and bring forth foals as swift as the wind, but they live not above three years." Does the white mare Itch in the dell in the Adams' woods up the road turn tail to this wind with white-lashed, lidded eyes? A single cell quivers at a windy embrace; it swells and splits, it bubbles into a raspberry; a dark clot starts to throb. Soon something perfect is born. Something wholly new rides the wind, something fleet and fleeting I'm likely to miss.

To sleep, spiders and fish; the wind won't stop, but the house will hold. To shelter, starlings and coot; bow to the wind.

Will D. Campbell

FROM *SOUL AMONG LIONS: MUSINGS OF A BOOTLEG PREACHER*

In Soul Among Lions, *Will Campbell—farmer, activist, satirist, storyteller, writer, and preacher—combines a series of short meditations that pointedly search our contemporary culture's ease and complacency: something that Campbell has been doing for half a century. His approach is to combine scriptural passages with a kind of commonsense, straight-to-the-heart stance that brushes aside our easy assumptions about our lives and our values. His goal? To search for what he calls "fragments of compassion."*

The following three short selections from his book are set in winter, and the season takes on surprising qualities. It might seem that winter is hardly the time for "fragments of compassion," given its usual metaphoric meanings. And yet winter—not used ironically—becomes in Campbell's hands precisely the right metaphoric time to reach for such fragments.

> It might seem that winter is hardly the time for "fragments of compassion," given its usual metaphoric meanings. And yet winter—not used ironically—becomes in Campbell's hands precisely the right metaphoric time to reach for such fragments.

FROM *SOUL AMONG LIONS: MUSINGS OF A BOOTLEG PREACHER*

Still we hear talk of despair over racial divisions and teenage crime. There is much to warrant concern, but are there not also promising signs we sometimes overlook? An incident in our rural community recently gave me hope. Two years ago our nearest neighbors, a couple from what is called the blue-collar class, experienced a grim tragedy. Their teenage grandson was murdered by his mother, who also killed herself. This past Christmas Eve, when the grandmother entered the cemetery for her weekly pilgrimage, she saw a young black male standing near the grandson's tomb. She did not recognize him. His dress and bearing would have frightened some, suggesting to them felonious intent. He held something in his hand and moved toward the woman as she approached. What he held was not an Uzi, not a Saturday night special, not a knife. It was a long-stemmed rose, shimmering in the winter's chilly mist. With a smiling greeting, he offered her the rose, and together they leaned down and placed it on the grave.

"I come here often," he said. "Matt was my best friend at school."

An elderly white woman of the yeomanry and a young black man of the urban poor, in solemn accord in a country graveyard. Mourning, loving, remembering. Together. Perplexed, but not despairing.

We shall overcome? Only in ways like that.

A fellow moved in our area some while back who's not exactly polished around the fringes. Very bright, owns a big construction company, and some think he works at being a rube. Mixes casual dress with high fashion, chews tobacco, gets often in the grape and uses flawed grammar on purpose. His name is Pebo. At least, that's the only call he'll answer. He plays a pretty mean guitar, and we have a little country band he calls the MF's. (Our tractors are Massey-Fergusons.) Some evenings we gather in his equipment shop, and Pebo boils peanuts, fries catfish, and makes what he calls swamp gravy, and we pick till midnight.

Pebo has one cultural blemish. He uses the "n" word. I wish he didn't, but he does. An urbane, proper lady came by recently and said our families didn't use that word and Pebo ought to stop it if we are going to be friends and playmates. I reminded her of the violent winter storm that swept through our hollow a few years ago. Roads were blocked and power lines down. While our families spent the night huddled around their fires, sipping sour mash and roasting hot dogs, Pebo was on his bulldozer till daybreak. Clearing the roads, delivering coal, medicine, and food to the poor among our black and white neighbors. She said that didn't excuse his use of the "n" word. I agreed, but reminded her of some words of Jesus: "Not those who say, 'Lord, Lord,' but those who do the will of God." I reckon there's more than one way to use the "n" word, be it verbally or by callous disregard for the neighbor near at hand. There is political correctness, all right. But there is also moral correctness. Deep down, Pebo knows about both. Too many of us, I fear, don't.

It was December 1943, and we were on a crowded troopship bound for the South Pacific. Most of us were in our teens—seasick, homesick, and a little afraid.

I had asked my best pal, Herman Hyman, what he was going to send his girlfriend for Christmas. "Nothing," he answered. Seemed strange. He mumbled something about Hanukkah, and changed the subject. I had no idea what he meant. I was a naive little Baptist boy from rural Mississippi. Herman was from the Bronx.

What had promised to be a bleak Christmas turned even more dreary when the KP list was read over the ship's intercom. I was to be on kitchen duty on Christmas Day. The sergeant told us we would be crossing the international date line, so there would be two December 25ths.

"I'll do it for you," Herman said.

"Why?"

"Because I want to," he laughed, patting me on the head like a mascot. Herman was older than I.

At the end of the second Christmas in a row, Herman found me alone on the stern of the ship, looking back at where we'd been. He looked very tired. He handed me a can of ripe olives he had lifted from the officers' mess. "Merry Christmas," he said, with a feigned and fatigued "Ho-ho-ho."

"Why'd you do that?" I asked. Over and over.

He sighed in a sort of, You really don't know, do you? fashion. Then he answered, "Because I'm a Jew, little buddy. And Jews don't celebrate Christmas." He told me all about Hanukkah: about another war that was fought two hundred years before my Jesus was even born; about how the Maccabees whipped the Syrians, and the big celebration and rededication of the Temple in Jerusalem. He said we would have a big celebration one day. He told me about how his father would light a candle every night for eight nights, about the good food his mother prepared, and he named all the kinfolk who gathered.

There weren't any Jews in my little rural community—no Catholics, Methodists, or Presbyterians either. Just Baptists. But there was a Jew there when I got back. Herman Hyman died for his country in the last days of the Battle of Saipan. When the war was over and I went home to Mississippi, Herman went with me.

Happy Hanukkah, Herman. You would be seventy-six now. I'll light the eighth candle and we'll be together again. And tell Father Abraham it's my time for KP.

William J. Vande Kopple

"THROUGH THE ICE"

William Vande Kopple, essayist and rhetorician, has written widely of fishing and its spiritual connections—which, to the person who doesn't fish, may at first seem rather remote, but in Vande Kopple's hands seem as close as a bluegill dancing just below the surface. In "Through the Ice," Vande Kopple tells the tale of his son and father-in-law, who fish together until, one winter day, it seems that they will fish no more. But there is one more fish to be caught, which in fact will become the first of many more to be caught.

Winter in this piece comes late, and it seems to be a part of disease and death. And yet, in the midst of disease and death and "this pee smell," there is a new beginning of sorts, drawn up from the icy waters of a winter pond, given with understanding and accepted with grace. Here, winter is a time of sorrow but also a time of unexpected and marvelous joy.

> There is a new beginning of sorts, drawn up from the icy waters of a winter pond, given with understanding and accepted with grace.

Through the Ice

I haven't read all the material that the Iowa Division of Tourism makes available to prospective and actual visitors. Still, I'm quite sure that the state has never spent much money advertising Sandy Hollow City Park, which seems almost to be trying to hide in a shallow depression about three miles east of Sioux Center, drawing the fields of corn and soybeans up tightly around itself.

After all, the park is only a matter of three old gravel pits whose shorelines have been smoothed down and spruced up, a picnic area with a campfire pit half full of assorted beer-bottle shards, and a forty-unit campground with pines that still need support wires to stand against the winds that use South Dakota to build their relentless momentum.

Sandy Hollow, however, was always a site of burbling laughter for our son Jason, now thirteen years old. It was there that he spent what he called the "only vacation-like" times of our family's annual summer trips to visit my wife's parents and siblings in northwest Iowa. For Sandy Hollow was where he and the person he called his "Grampa-in-Iowa" went to fish after sneaking away from gatherings that seemed to be developing into full-blown family reunions. Often I sneaked away with them—to fish a little, to read, to watch.

I don't believe Grampa and Jason ever debated what the best way to fool fish was. Largely because of differences in physical capabilities, they simply went about their fishing in markedly different ways.

Grampa had spent decades moving between and behind dairy cows, some of which would kick first and look around later or not at all. Both of his knees were permanently swollen, and his left knee hardly flexed at all anymore. So he would back his pickup as close to the shore of the largest gravel pit as he dared. Then he would use a folded-up aluminum chair for support as he made his halting way onto a sandbar that curved from the shoreline into the water. He would balance his weight on the chair with his left hand, wrench his entire right side around and ahead a foot or so, shift most of his weight to his right leg, and then drag his left foot sideways through the sand until he was ready to reposition the chair and throw his right side ahead once more. When he reached the tip of the bar, he would unfold the chair and fall back into it, gradually listing to one side or the other as the chair settled unevenly into the moist sand.

Jason always brought him his gear, which was simple but effective: a spinning rod and reel, a float that Grampa called a "dobber," a cottage-cheese container full of moist newspaper shreds and worms recently dug from his garden, a small box of hooks, and a stringer for the perch and sunfish that he loved to take home and fry for lunch. Once Grampa was in position, he never moved; he stayed in his chair on the end of that sandbar, leaning to one side or the other but always grinning with patient expectation.

Jason never used anything but artificial lures—usually he alternated among a chartreuse plastic frog, a blue-and-cream floating minnow, and a mottled jitterbug. And he never stayed in one spot for more than a minute or two. He would trot to a small spit of gravel, cast, cast, cast in a semicircle out in front of him, dart down the shoreline to a small cluster of rocks, cast, cast, cast again, and thus make his active way around the pond, often almost stumbling as he reached down to pull burrs off his socks as he hurried from one casting spot to the next.

But each time he either caught a fish or saw that Grampa was fighting one, he would hustle back to Grampa's sandbar. Together they would admire the fish from several angles, debate whether it was a keeper or not, brag about who had so far caught the most impressive fish, and make all sorts of emphatic gestures. After each of these small celebrations, Jason would trot off to another spot along the shore.

And thus our son and his Grampa fished, the boy making several more or less extended forays along the shoreline, his Grampa waiting expectantly for him to return.

Indian Hills Nursing and Rehabilitation Home spreads out its several wings high in the hills on the north side of Sioux City.

When my family and I got out of our van there last December to visit Grampa a few weeks after his cancer surgery, we could see across thousands of acres of farmland to the east. When we got inside room E-12, we could also see that Grampa had probably barely survived the operation.

It can't really be easy for anyone—not even a pastor after hundreds of visits to sick and despairing parishioners—to spend time walking the hallways and visiting people in nursing homes. For Jason, it was traumatic.

While still in the main corridor, he wondered, "What's up with all this pee smell in here?" Once we got into the room, Jason rushed over to give Grampa a big hug, but Grampa warned him quickly but feebly not to bump the feeding tube that "goes plumb through a hole in my chest and into my stomach." When Jason stepped back somewhat gingerly, he noticed that Grampa's feet were sticking out from beneath the sheet and that he had blue booties on, booties that left his big toes with dozens of small puncture wounds exposed. And then Grampa started to cough. It was a deep, racking cough, a cough that brought up a substance unlike any phlegm or vomit any of us had ever seen—smooth and creamy, not chunky and yellow or green at all. As my wife, Wanda, rushed to get a Kleenex and soothingly wipe streaks of this cream off her dad's chin and throat and upper chest, Jason crouched down and began taking ragged breaths.

When Grampa settled down enough to try to talk, he began to worry aloud about his physical therapy scheduled for the next day: "That lady is real bossy, almost mean—and strong too. She says she won't rest until she has me taking some steps back and forth in the hallway with a walker. She doesn't know I never did walk too good. And now I don't think I'll ever walk again."

As Grampa finished saying "walk again," Jason got up and ran out of the room.

Wanda, I, and our other two sons, Jon and Joel, spent a little more time with Grampa, working to believe that he wanted to know what had been keeping us busy lately. But it was clear that he was laboring to look interested, so we told him we'd let him rest and would drive down again from Sioux Center the next day.

When we got back to the van, we found Jason sitting on the rear bumper with his head on his knees. Before we could even begin to think of what to say to him, he looked up, wiped his nose on a shirtsleeve, and announced that he was "never coming back to this place."

We were able to stay in Iowa for only five days of our Christmas vacation, and we had planned to visit Grampa every day if the roads were good. But the next day Jason would not be moved: He refused to see Grampa lying in that crib-like bed in the nursing home again.

In times of stress or crisis in our family, our rhetoric gets chaotic. Wanda and I tried strategy after strategy, each for about thirty seconds. We carefully presented an elaborate case, and we threatened punishment. We cajoled, and we bribed. We pleaded, and we displayed ugly little spikes of anger. But we finally realized that if we were going to get Jason to that nursing home again, we would have to carry him thrashing to the driveway and hurl him onto a seat in the back of the van. We decided it wasn't worth it.

We fretted, though, about leaving him by himself at his uncle and aunt's in Sioux Center, where we were staying. So Wanda and I each spent at least fifteen minutes laying out for him all the things he should not even begin to think of doing while we were away, and then we left for Sioux City with Jon and Joel. While we were away, he found something to do that we had not explicitly forbidden, but that was only because it had never occurred to us that he would ever hatch such a plan.

When we got home, we found out from his Uncle Stan what he had done. He apparently spent most of the morning after we left poking around in Stan's shed. There he dug up a small fishing pole, a few jigging spoons in a stowaway box, a large flathead screwdriver, and a framing hammer.

When Stan came home around noon after finishing his morning chores on the farm, Jason met him at the door and caught him in a barrage of questions: "Can I use all this stuff I found in the shed? Do you still have that old Polaroid camera? Does it work? And is there any way you could drive me out to Sandy Hollow and wait just a bit while I do something important for Grampa?"

Stan, always hospitable, but in this case more than mildly curious, I think, about what his young nephew from Michigan could be up to, said "yes" to all of Jason's questions, provided, he added, that Jason wasn't planning anything risky.

"No way—you know me, right?" came the reply.

So after the two of them packed some heavy clothes, Stan took Grampa's place next to Jason in a pickup headed out to Sandy Hollow.

Once there, Stan asked no questions; he stayed in the pickup, starting it up every few minutes when he needed to run the heater. Jason collected his gear, walked directly to where he knew the arc of Grampa's sandbar was buried under a few inches of crusty snow, and then scuffed around on the ice until, Stan later reported, he looked to be about ten feet off the outside edge of the bar. Then Jason knelt on the ice and started chiseling away at it with the hammer and screwdriver. At least six inches of ice, Stan guessed, and Jason really needed a spud or auger, but he kept at it, occasionally missing the screwdriver and bruising his hand, frequently sending up ice chips hard into his face. After about ten minutes, he broke through to the water. He hadn't found anything to skim off the floating ice chips, so he had to take off his left mitten, cup his hand, and use it to scoop and slosh the chips out of the hole. Finally, he shifted back and forth from knee to knee to ease the pressure against his kneecaps before rigging up a spoon on the small pole, lowering the spoon into the hole, and then jigging the spoon in the water of the gravel pit.

Stan told me later that it was at this point that he decided to set a limit—something like thirty minutes or so—on how long he would be willing to sit out at Sandy Hollow in the dead of winter waiting for his nephew to pursue some adolescent dream. But after only five or six minutes, he could see that Jason was fighting a fish, probably a big one. He grabbed the Polaroid, ran down to the edge of the ice, and then shuffled cautiously out to where Jason was carefully sliding onto the ice about a twenty-eight inch northern pike, one just starting to put on some heavy shoulders.

"Yes! Yes! That's the way we do it!" Jason exulted. "If I hold it up, can you get a picture?"

Jason displayed the fish, Stan took the picture, and then Jason carefully put the fish headfirst down the hole, holding it by the tail to move it gently through the water and get water flowing through its gills. After finally refreshing and releasing the fish, he stood up, brushed the ice and snow off his knees, grinned, and said, "That was awesome. Thanks. We can go back now if you want."

When Jon, Joel, Wanda, and I were still getting out of the car following our trip to Sioux City, Jason met us in the driveway with the pike picture in his hand.

"When you drive down to visit Grampa tomorrow," he said quietly, "show him this."

"What is it?" Wanda wondered. Then with more concern in her voice, she asked, "How on earth did you get this? When did you manage to pull this off? And you want to send just a picture? All by itself? Don't you want to add a little note to explain it to Grampa?"

"No," Jason said as he turned away. "Grampa won't need a note. Just show him." For a moment, Wanda stared at his back, but then she filed the picture away in her purse.

When the four of us walked into room E-12 the next day, it was easy to tell that it was a bad day for Grampa. The physical therapist had been around earlier, he said, to torment him, and he was exhausted. We tried to get him to eat bits of the candied orange slices that we had searched out especially for him, but he complained that lately everything tasted "flau." When we asked him if any doctor had been around earlier in the day to talk about when he might be able to go home, he simply turned on his side away from us, brought the edge of the striped sheet up below his chin, and drew his knees toward his chest.

"Maybe we should just leave for today," Wanda whispered somewhat huskily, emotion starting to choke her from the inside.

"Or maybe we should just show Grampa Jason's Sandy Hollow picture," Jon suggested.

"Yes," Wanda agreed, "how in the world did I forget that?" She found the picture in her purse and then walked around the bed and held it sideways to line it up with Grampa's face.

After he focused on the picture, Grampa was transformed. He reached for the control panel for his bed and raised the top portion until he was sitting up. He took both his upper and lower denture plates out of the glass of water next to the bed and put them hastily into his mouth. He studied the picture for almost a minute. And then he broke into an enormous smile, his eyes glistening, his top plate lying a little crookedly in his mouth and threatening to drop. Finally, he extended his right fist about a foot in front of his right eye and raised the index finger proudly.

"Show Jason this," he said.

"What? What do you mean?" Wanda asked, eagerness and anxiety mixing in her voice. "What should we tell Jason? What do you want him to know?"

"Just show him what I did," Grampa ordered; "he won't need any explanation."

The drive from Sioux City to Sioux Center takes about forty-five minutes. For most of that time, Jon, Joel, Wanda, and I debated what Grampa could have meant by the huge grin and display of his index finger.

"He probably meant something like 'We're number one,'" Joel guessed. But that sounded too much like bragging to the rest of us, at least as far as Grampa was concerned.

Jon had seen a movie in which the gesture had figured: "Maybe he means 'there's one true thing.'" But Wanda was pretty sure that Grampa had never watched a movie in his life. He had grown up hearing that television shows and movies were worldly amusements everyone should avoid, and early on he had made those rules his own.

What we all also thought, I'm pretty sure, was that he could have been pointing toward heaven, and while there was comfort in knowing about the assurance that would lead to a gesture with such meaning, we didn't want to think about this possibility much because it meant we would lose Grampa for ourselves. So we all skirted this interpretation in our talk.

When we got back to Sioux Center, we could tell by his smug expression that Jason thought he was in a position of power. It wasn't acceptable behavior for his older brothers to ask him a question that wouldn't embarrass him, so they never mentioned Grampa's gesture. But it was too important a matter to Wanda for her to let it go.

"What do you and Grampa mean when you do this?" she asked as she approximated Grampa's big smile and his finger position.

"Oh, that. Not much. Nothing really." And he tried to look nonchalant, not realizing that his mother was past any mood for games.

"Please, Jason, please. I really have to know. Please tell me. Right now."

"Oh, all right. That's a signal Grampa and I would give at Sandy Hollow after one or the other of us had caught our first fish of the day. We smiled at each other square in the face and raised that finger."

"But what does it mean?"

"When we did that, we always meant, 'The first of many more to come!'"

This gesture did not come up again in any of our family conversations for about ten weeks—until March, a month cruel enough for us—as we were driving down the long hill past Sandy Hollow on the way to Sioux Center for Grampa's funeral.

It was a dark and stormy day, the clouds scraping their oppressive bottoms on the bare branches in the groves, the fields lying with the brown stubble of last season's harvested crop scattered among the clods. As we passed the drive leading down into Sandy Hollow, Wanda turned to me, brushed my elbow, and whispered: "Do you think he was being ironic?"

"Who?"

"Dad. I mean, do you think he was being ironic when he signaled 'the first of many more to come' to Jason?"

"What's *ironic* mean?" Jason's voice startled us; we thought all three boys were sleeping in the back of the van.

"Didn't you ever have that word on a vocabulary list in school?"

"We don't do vocabulary anymore."

"Well, then, when you're ironic," I explained quietly, "you say the opposite of what you really mean. Like if Grampa said 'the first' when he really meant 'no more.'"

Jason thought for only a second or two: "If that's what ironic is, then that's not what we were, especially when we talked about fishing. Grampa and I never had the time to be ironic."

PART FIVE

Winter As a Time of Delight and Play

INTRODUCTION

In her book *Housekeeping,* Marilynne Robinson writes of what she calls "the life of perished things." Considering this life, she recalls two trees from her childhood.

> I had seen two of the apple trees in my grandmother's orchard die where they stood. One spring there were no leaves, but they stood there as if expectantly, their limbs almost to the ground, miming their perished fruitfulness. Every winter the orchard is flooded with snow, and every spring the waters are parted, death is undone, and every Lazarus rises, except these two. They have lost their bark and blanched white, and a wind will snap their bones, but if ever a leaf does appear, it should be no great wonder. It would be a small change, as it would be, say, for the moon to begin turning on its axis. It seemed to me that what perished need not also be lost.

The principle is a telling one: what perishes is not necessarily lost. The memory can preserve in a very real way those things that have disappeared from the physical landscape for whatever reason—the world, the flesh, or the devil.

Winter may be the season for perishing, but it is also the season of preservation. Patricia Hampl remembers sitting on the cold floor in the vestibule of her grandmother's house, leafing through old photographs of Prague. Her grandmother, coming to call her into the warmth of the kitchen, stoops down to share not just the sepia pictures but also memories of her childhood home. Yet these memories can be expressed only in tears; it falls to her grand-daughter to translate those tears, that past, into memoir and story.

One of the winter stories we tell is of play—the play that we particularly associate with childhood. Here the cold, the snow, the ice are not images of a forlorn and frozen world but instead are elements of winter that are to be embraced and celebrated for their uniqueness, for their surprise, for their unusual quality, and for their place in the annual rhythms of our lives. Here bleakness, which might be conquered through preparation and compassion, is conquered through playfulness and an embracing of that which is built into our world and our temporal lives.

It is what Dylan Thomas recalls so lyrically in his *A Child's Christmas in Wales:* snowballs thrown at cats and fires, dry voices that frighten delightfully, dinners and trees and snow and ice—all wrapped together in a large snowball from which he can draw, all filled with the excitement and exuberance of winter and Christmas. It is what Giorgio Vasari suggests when he tells the story of Michelangelo coming into the courtyard of the Medici one wintry day to build a snowman. It is what is captured in Ezra Jack Keats's *The Snowy Day,* in which young Peter climbs snowbank mountains, throws snowballs, makes snow angels, and smuggles a snowball into his warm house—only to discover that it is not there in the morning. It is what comes in C. S. Lewis's *The Lion, the Witch, and the Wardrobe,* when winter without Christmas is finally defeated, St. Nicholas arrives, and the animals dance and play to celebrate the advent of the day.

This playfulness emerges in old Lakota belief, where the North Wind is represented by the fierce giant Woziya, who kills with his frozen touch, who breathes frozen air, and who throws ice and snow in his bitter war with his brother, the South Wind. Dressed in thick furs, he lives beyond the pines and guards the places of snow and ice. He is a most fearsome giant. Yet, even with all his fierceness, he can also be unexpectedly jolly and winsome. He guards, after all, the entrance to the dance of the shadows of the north: the northern lights.

But it is not only children to whom winter means play. And though winter by February and March may seem old and gray, still the snows of winter bring a wonder to the adult as keen as that experienced by any child. Such a wonder may show itself in passionate play or the quiet delight of seeing a snow-filled landscape, in tracking the snow geese or snuggling up with one's love. That sense of delight and play, always in adulthood shadowed by shimmering loss, coalesces in the dream poem of the sixteenth-century Korean writer Chong Ch'ŏl.

> *Snow has fallen on the pine-woods,*
> *and every bough has blossomed.*
> *I should like to pluck a branch*
> *and send it to where my lord is.*
> *After he has looked at it,*
> *what matter if the snow-flowers melt?*

What matter, indeed, when winter preserves—if only in our memories—its wondrous and terrible beauty?

James Houston

FROM SONGS OF THE DREAM PEOPLE: CHANTS AND IMAGES FROM THE INDIANS AND ESKIMOS OF NORTH AMERICA

In drawing principally from the northwestern tribes of North America, James Houston portrays a people whose poetry and song were intricately, intimately part of the natural world. Images, rhythm, comparisons, tone, narrative responses—all are a part of the relationship between the speaker and the world directly experienced. It might seem, then, that winter, with the hardship that it brings, would be imaged as an adversary. In fact, the opposite is true. In the songs and chants of winter that Houston collected, the season is a time of joy—indeed, of playfulness. There is beauty in the dance of the northern lights; there is beauty in the urgings of the sea ice.

In the songs and chants of winter that Houston collected, the season is a time of joy—indeed, of playfulness. There is beauty in the dance of the northern lights; there is beauty in the urgings of the sea ice.

We will watch the Northern Lights
playing their game of ball
in the cold, glistening country.
Then we will sit in beauty on the mountain
and watch the small stars
in their sleepless flight.
        [Abanaki]

Ayii, Ayii,
I walked on the ice of the sea.
Wondering, I heard
The song of the sea
And the great sighing
Of new formed ice.
Go then go!
Strength of soul
Brings health
To the place of feasting.
        [Eastern Eskimo]

Mark A. Noll

"SNOW"

In his short lyric "Snow," the poet and historian Mark Noll pictures what is, to some, a very frustrating situation: it is snowing, and there is traffic, and the car will not go, and it would be easy to be upset—and more than upset—with the exigencies of the season. But to others—specifically children and "those at peace"—something very different is going on, something close to an exuberant celebration. At the conclusion of the poem, the reader is given an invitation to join the exuberance and so see winter as a time of delight and play.

It is snowing, and there is traffic, and the car will not go, and it would be easy to be upset—and more than upset—with the exigencies of the season. But to others—specifically children and "those at peace"—something very different is going on.

Snow

The snow floats down, fluffing the city to death.
Children and those at peace like sails
catch the surge, mastered giggle-like, and roll
into the snow across the wide, wide spaces
white; the wraith—lovely, inscrutable—calls.
Cars begin to sputter and curse; one by one
withered white they die
as buttoned, capped, and booted, you and I
go dancing, tromping, dancing by.

Annie Dillard

FROM *AN AMERICAN CHILDHOOD*

Annie Dillard begins this selection from An American Childhood *with a call to passion, a call to fling oneself fully and passionately and committedly at life. This makes her a good tackler in backyard football games, but it also serves her well when she and her playmates are chased by an uncompromising man for throwing snowballs at his Buick. Though the chase ends with disappointment— when he finally does catch them, he can only descend into mundane and expected cliché—still, the chase itself is what she remembers. Both the children—the pursued— and the red-headed pursuer are completely and fully and uncompromisingly engaged in what they are doing. There is a single-minded passion about them that brings utter and effusive happiness.*

> *A* call to passion, a call to fling oneself fully and passionately and committedly at life. . . . Here is a winter that provides a very different kind of setting: it is the backdrop to passionate play.

Here is a winter that provides a very different kind of setting: it is the backdrop to passionate play.

FROM *AN AMERICAN CHILDHOOD*

Some boys taught me to play football. This was fine sport. You thought up a new strategy for every play and whispered it to the others. You went out for a pass, fooling everyone. Best, you got to throw yourself mightily at someone's running legs. Either you brought him down or you hit the ground flat out on your chin, with your arms empty before you. It was all or nothing. If you hesitated in fear, you would miss and get hurt: you would take a hard fall while the kid got away, or you would get kicked in the face while the kid got away. But if you flung yourself wholeheartedly at the back of his knees—if you gathered and joined body and soul and pointed them diving fearlessly—then you likely wouldn't get hurt, and you'd stop the ball. Your fate, and your team's score, depended on your concentration and courage. Nothing girls did could compare with it.

Boys welcomed me at baseball, too, for I had, through enthusiastic practice, what was weirdly known as a boy's arm. In winter, in the snow, there was neither baseball nor football, so the boys and I threw snowballs at passing cars. I got in trouble throwing snowballs, and have seldom been happier since.

On one weekday morning after Christmas, six inches of new snow had just fallen. We were standing up to our boot tops in snow on a front yard on trafficked Reynolds Street, waiting for cars. The cars traveled Reynolds Street slowly and evenly; they were targets all but wrapped in red ribbons, cream puffs. We couldn't miss.

I was seven; the boys were eight, nine, and ten. The oldest two Fahey boys were there—Mikey and Peter—polite blond boys who lived near me on Lloyd Street, and who already had four brothers and sisters. My parents approved Mikey and Peter Fahey. Chickie McBride was there, a tough kid, and Billy Paul and Mackie Kean too, from across Reynolds, where the boys grew up dark and furious, grew up skinny, knowing, and skilled. We had all drifted from our houses that morning looking for action, and had found it here on Reynolds Street.

It was cloudy but cold. The cars' tires laid behind them on the snowy street a complex trail of beige chunks like crenellated castle walls. I had stepped on some earlier; they squeaked. We could have wished for more traffic. When a car came, we all popped it one. In the intervals between cars we reverted to the natural solitude of children.

I started making an iceball—a perfect iceball, from perfectly white snow, perfectly spherical, and squeezed perfectly translucent so no snow remained all the way through. (The Fahey boys and I considered it unfair actually to throw an iceball at somebody, but it had been known to happen.)

I had just embarked on the iceball project when we heard tire chains come clanking from afar. A black Buick was moving toward us down the street. We all spread out, banged together some regular snowballs, took aim, and, when the Buick drew nigh, fired.

A soft snowball hit the driver's windshield right before the driver's face. It made a smashed star with a hump in the middle.

Often, of course, we hit our target, but this time, the only time in all of life, the car pulled over and stopped. Its wide black door opened; a man got out of it, running. He didn't even close the car door.

He ran after us, and we ran away from him, up the snowy Reynolds sidewalk. At the corner, I looked back; incredibly, he was still after us. He was in city clothes: a suit and tie, street shoes. Any normal adult would have quit, having sprung us into flight and made his point. This man was gaining on us. He was a thin man, all action. All of a sudden, we were running for our lives.

Wordless, we split up. We were on our turf; we could lose ourselves in the neighborhood backyards, everyone for himself. I paused and considered. Everyone had vanished except Mikey Fahey, who was just rounding the corner of a yellow brick house. Poor Mikey, I trailed him. The driver of the Buick sensibly picked the two of us to follow. The man apparently had all day.

He chased Mikey and me around the yellow house and up a backyard path we knew by heart: under a low tree, up a bank, through a hedge, down some snowy steps, and across the grocery store's delivery driveway. We smashed through a gap in another hedge, entered a scruffy backyard and ran around its back porch and tight between houses to Edgerton Avenue; we ran across Edgerton to an alley and up our own sliding woodpile to the Halls' front yard; he kept coming. We ran up Lloyd Street and wound through mazy backyards toward the steep hilltop at Willard and Lang.

He chased us silently, block after block. He chased us silently over picket fences, through thorny hedges, between houses, around garbage cans, and across streets. Every time I glanced back, choking for breath, I expected he would have quit. He must have been as breathless as we were. His jacket strained over his body. It was an immense discovery, pounding into my hot head with every sliding, joyous step, that this ordinary adult evidently knew what I thought only children who trained at football knew: that you have to fling yourself at what you're doing, you have to point yourself, forget yourself, aim, dive.

Mikey and I had nowhere to go, in our own neighborhood or out of it, but away from this man who was chasing us. He impelled us forward; we compelled him to follow our route. The air was cold; every breath tore my throat. We kept running, block after block; we kept improvising, backyard after backyard, running a frantic course and choosing it simultaneously, failing always to find small places or hard places to slow him down, and discovering always, exhilarated, dismayed, that only bare speed could save us—for he would never give up, this man—and we were losing speed. He chased us through the backyard labyrinths of ten blocks before he caught us by our jackets. He caught us and we all stopped.

We three stood staggering, half blinded, coughing, in an obscure hilltop backyard: a man in his twenties, a boy, a girl. He had released our jackets, our pursuer, our captor, our hero: he knew we weren't going anywhere. We all played by the rules. Mikey and I unzipped our jackets. I pulled off my sopping mittens. Our tracks multiplied in the backyard's new snow. We had been breaking new snow all morning. We didn't look at each other. I was cherishing my excitement. The man's lower pants legs were wet; his cuffs were full of snow, and there was a prow of snow beneath them on his shoes and socks. Some trees bordered the little flat backyard, some messy winter trees. There was no one around: a clearing in a grove, and we the only players.

It was a long time before he could speak. I had some difficulty at first recalling why we were there. My lips felt swollen; I couldn't see out of the sides of my eyes; I kept coughing.

"You stupid kids," he began perfunctorily.

We listened perfunctorily indeed, if we listened at all, for the chewing out was redundant, a mere formality, and beside the point. The point was that he had chased us passionately without giving up, and so he had caught us. Now he came down to earth. I wanted the glory to last forever.

But how could the glory have lasted forever? We could have run through every backyard in North America until we got to Panama. But when he trapped us at the lip of the Panama Canal, what precisely could he have done to prolong the drama of the chase and cap its glory? I brooded about this for the next few years. He could only have fried Mikey Fahey and me in boiling oil, say, or dismembered us piece-meal, or staked us to anthills. None of which I really wanted, and none of which any adult was likely to do, even in the spirit of fun. He could only chew us out there in the Panamanian jungle, after months or years of exalting pursuit. He could only begin, "You stupid kids," and continue in his ordinary Pittsburgh accent with his normal righteous anger and the usual common sense.

If in that snowy backyard the driver of the black Buick had cut off our heads, Mikey's and mine, I would have died happy, for nothing has required so much of me since as being chased all over Pittsburgh in the middle of winter—running terrified, exhausted—by this sainted, skinny, furious red-headed man who wished to have a word with us. I don't know how he found his way back to his car.

Pete Fromm

FROM *INDIAN CREEK CHRONICLES: A WINTER ALONE IN THE WILDERNESS*

The experience that led to Indian Creek Chronicles *began as a college lark: Pete Fromm decided he would accept a position guarding salmon eggs from freezing water and from predators in the Selway-Bitterroot Wilderness on the borders of Idaho and Montana. He would live alone through the winter in a remote and frozen world, with only a canvas tent, for seven months. He quickly realized that this lark could be dangerous. But it would also provide a time unlike any he had ever known, and one unlike the experience of most North Americans.* Indian Creek Chronicles *is a gripping, engaging narrative of his winter in the wilderness.*

Winter comes suddenly to the wilderness, and much of Fromm's early time is taken up by cutting

While he struggles through melancholy and even at times fear, late in the seven months he comes upon a remarkable sense of the liveliness of his world. He follows an otter, listens to a woodpecker, is beguiled by an eclipse and a dog and trout, and comes to the conclusion that this is all part of a world that may be dangerous but is also spectacular.

and storing wood. *From there on he traps, hunts, shovels snow around the tent, cooks, reads, and deals with the loneliness and the terrible cold. But while he struggles through melancholy and even at times fear, late in the seven months he comes upon a remarkable sense of the liveliness of his world, of its beauty, and even of its playfulness. In this selection he follows an otter, listens to a woodpecker, is beguiled by an eclipse and a dog and trout, and comes to the conclusion that this is all part of a world that may be dangerous but is also spectacular.*

FROM *INDIAN CREEK CHRONICLES*

The Forest Service crew never did show up. I wasn't terribly surprised. After going through the work of digging out, something that had to be done to escape, I doubted that a bunch of office workers would do that same kind of work just to mess around in the mountains for a day or two.

I stayed close to my tent though, just in case, and a few miles upstream I discovered an otter den—two holes in the snow across the river, long slide marks connecting the holes to the water. Crushing through the soggy snow, I made a den for myself beneath the sweeping black branches of a spruce, and I waited to spy on the otters. Boone huddled with me in this cave, her coat matted with rain. But the branches kept off most of the drizzle and I staked out the otters for two full days, glad for something to do.

On the third day the first otter popped out of an opening in the ice a hundred yards or so downstream. Once on the snow it ran several steps and launched itself onto its belly, slithering across the snow, pushing with its back feet when it began to lose momentum. Then it would pop up into a run and leap again. As soon as it reached another opening in the ice it disappeared into the water. It was up at the next hole, sliding across the snow until it found another spot to enter the river. I grinned, wondering how it could find its way in that fast, black water.

Eventually I saw the whole family, four of them, and I went back up to the den day after day to watch them play. One came up with a fish—what looked like a sucker—and sat beside the hole in the ice and ate it whole, chewing on it from the head down, like a cold, bony hot dog. The busy crunching came loudly across the snow and ice. Nights were long, cold interruptions keeping me from the play of the otters, but the socked-in weather did hold in radio waves and I spent an hour every night listening to the radio, as much as my battery supply would allow. In one of those hours I learned that in little less than a week Idaho would be right in the path of a full solar eclipse.

I spent a couple of days watching the sun and the clock, picking a spot to watch from, and found that at the scheduled time the sun was neatly framed in the notch between the ridges of Indian Creek. I chose a rocky pinnacle that would get me above the trees and hoped the weather would cooperate.

I was out right after breakfast on the twenty-sixth—eclipse day—but when I climbed up Indian Creek I found that the snow was still crusted hard and I couldn't climb the pinnacle. I stood staring up at the snow-covered point, running my hand over its glossy burnish of ice. Without the pinnacle's height I could only hope to catch glimpses of the sun through the trees, what suddenly seemed like the only view I'd had of anything for months.

I took out my knife and poked at the layer of ice, chipping off bright, brittle shards. Soon I cut a complete foothold and tested it, pushing my foot in and lifting my weight. It held and I cut another, and then another. I cut and climbed until I was at the top.

At the peak there was just enough room for me to sit cross-legged. Boone, stuck below, whimpered for a second or two, then curled up in the snow on the side of the ridge, glaring at me.

The sky was a solid, seemingly hopeless overcast, but I tried to believe that it seemed thinner in the east. Then suddenly the notch really did begin to brighten and I saw the edge of the bright ball of the sun in the haze. It rose quickly, and for a few minutes it seemed as if one side was darker than the other. I waited and nothing changed. I looked at the wind-up clock I had carried with me. Could that have been it? That dull dimming? I glanced around my gray world and felt pretty foolish for cutting my way up here for that, glad nobody was here to see this.

I waited a little longer, staring at the bright gray east. The wind-up clock was less than accurate and I usually set it by guess anyway. Maybe something was still supposed to happen.

By now the sun had burned through to form a clearly defined disk at the top of the notch in the mountains, the haze thick enough I could look at it without being dazzled. Then, too suddenly to be believed, there was a piece missing from its southern edge. I double checked and there was no doubt. This was not a new thickness of clouds, a light dimming on one side or the other. An actual slice was being taken from the side of the sun.

I looked away. The radio had warned and warned about being blinded by watching the eclipse. The world got darker slowly—slowly enough that it was hard to notice. I glanced back and half the sun was gone.

The mountains were darker now. I looked down at my camp and the Selway. It looked like evening, the time of day I would usually be about here, getting back to camp before dark.

Now there was just a sliver of sun edging the left side of the dark ball that had replaced it. That was the moon, I knew, but knowing that didn't mean anything. I stood straight up on my tiny pinnacle and watched as the last of the sun winked out.

Where the sun had been there was only a hazy, fluctuating ring of brightness. That's all. Around me the woods were truly dark. The snow on the open slopes in front of me glowed pure blue, more definite than at any twilight, as if there were some force under there that wouldn't be held back forever. The chickadees were silent for once. It seemed to get a little cooler but I don't think that was possible. Boone whined and then it was completely quiet.

The vague ring of light wavered above the notch in the mountains, the sky blue-purple from horizon to horizon. The green-treed slopes across the creek faded to murky black.

I circled on my pedestal, my fists clenched and my skin tingling. It was truly dark, the snow still glowing blue, nearly pulsing. In the southwest the second dawn of the day began. A first tentative paling grew ruddy red, the color of the darkest wild rose. This spread across the sky but the intensity died, as if there were only so much color to give.

I looked back to the sun as the moon edged aside and day broke again. The snow returned to its normal white, the blue retreating beneath the surface where it was just barely visible. The sun returned to its full orb and there was no longer any trace of the moon. A bird chirped and, tentatively, others followed.

But still I circled, tingling on my little perch, trying to see what was no longer there, what I had not had enough time to see in those too full few minutes—trying to take in all that I had looked over for months, as if the second dawn had shed light on more than just mountains.

I shouted. I raised my fists above my head and shouted. As I continued my demented circling on that spire, I knew that everywhere I could see, and far beyond that, on everything the sun had just transformed, the only footprint on the land that wasn't some animal's was mine. I shouted again, big enough to burst. Whooping, I slid off the pinnacle and Boone charged in. We wrestled around on the crusty snow and then we just flat out ran, as if there was nothing in the world that could ever stop us.

Later that day it rained and I tried to stay busy in my tent, but I couldn't keep away from the pinnacle. By late afternoon I slithered back up, my toeholds grown slushy, and I stood on top, watching the notch and the rest of the world around me. I tried to squint, hoping the blurring would make it easier to picture again the morning's transformation. But that light was gone forever. It was not something that could be captured, even in the mind. Already I was questioning the blueness of the snow, the redness of the sky. But, even though I couldn't see it, I smiled, knowing it had been there, that I had seen what no one else had.

Then, as the day's real dusk closed down on the Selway, I slid back down and strolled to my meat pole. There was only a steak or two left and I meant to cut them down and finish them off in one last feeding frenzy to celebrate the eclipse. But when I reached the pole I found that something had beaten me to the feast. The last bit of spine hung from its rope, the only meat left clinging in thin, frazzled strands. I found the tracks of the marten, saw how it'd climbed one tree and inched along the meat pole, sliding down the rope and gorging itself before dropping straight from the meat to the ground. The drop forced his footprints into the hard snow beneath the bones. I remembered that in the fall, during my trapping initiation, I'd mistaken squirrel tracks for marten. "Be the world's biggest squirrel," I said, shaking my head and cutting down the last trace of the moose and pitching it into the trees. The marten could finish it now without acrobatics.

The next day I hiked down to Paradise and picked up my cured meat. It was much lighter with the water drained away and I was glad of that. Walking back, I whittled slivers off a chunk but I'd gone pretty heavy on the spices and the meat was a little hard to handle. I guessed I'd be making a lot of chili, using the hot meat and the pounds and pounds of beans I still hadn't figured out any real use for. I had three months left here and I wondered just how sick of chili I'd get.

It kept drizzling off and on for the first week of March, the temperature creeping up the thermometer a little higher every day. Finally I stepped out of my tent one morning to find that the sky had cleared. The temperature that day reached forty-four, the highest point since November.

The snow was really beginning to melt and I spent the morning digging it out from around my tent. All winter long I'd used the snow as insulation, but now it was seeping through the canvas and my tent was thick with the smell of wet cloth.

The old snow was hard and stiff and I had to cut blocks to pick up and throw aside. Before I was done I'd stripped off even my union suit top, hardly able to believe how the sun felt full on my back. I smiled, watching my naked arms bulge as I lifted the blocks of snow and felt the coarse, hard crystals melt against my chest. It seemed I could feel everything.

The next day was as clear as the last and when I poked out into the clear blue I took off immediately, even skipping breakfast, my snowshoes strapped across my back for later in the day, when the night's crust would melt off. I hiked all day, stripping off shirts one by one, eventually even unbuttoning the top of my union suit, the air against my skin a wonderful sensation.

From the very top of the mountains I studied the peaks around me, picking out drainages I knew, and though to the east Trapper Peak stood out alone, gleaming white on the edge of the Bitterroot Valley, it no longer drew my eye the way it had before. I turned back to the world I knew, picking out the drainage of the Little Clearwater, hiking south and west until I could see the Selway's path, far below, swinging through a long bend. I knew that curve was the Nez Perce ford, and I grinned, almost surprised by how well I'd learned this country, how I could know it from any angle.

I slid down the mountain, the snow this high taking on a strange, hard slickness. The top inch or two turned soggy in the sun, full of big, wet, slippery crystals. But, beneath that, the frozen crust was still rock hard. Occasionally I'd slip and go all the way down, sliding through the soaking slush without making a dent in the crust, without being able to punch through for any kind of hand-hold. I'd have to slide until I reached a rock or a tree I could grab on to. Though I never picked up great speed, the slips spooked me, my imagination pitching me off cliffs where, dreamlike, I could tumble forever before crushing back to the black spruce and granite-like stretches of snow.

As I got lower, coming down from the mountains that afternoon, the crust gave away and I had to put on my snowshoes. Shuffling along, I ate the last of the little blocks of Wisconsin cheese my aunt had sent in for Christmas, things like Edam and Brick and Gouda that I didn't remember having eaten before, when I lived in Wisconsin. Cheese wasn't something I'd brought in and the new flavors were something I'd tried to dole out to myself, to savor. In the wild, warm sunlight I threw my hoarding to the winds.

I was switchbacking down the last steep southwest slope above the old Nez Perce ford when, at the base of a towering, red-barked, ponderosa pine, I stumbled across open dirt. I just stared at it for a moment. It was the first ground I'd seen in four months.

I chugged across the hill and sat down in the two foot circular patch. The dirt was actually thawed, muddy, covered with pine needles. I dug my fingers into it and laughed. It smelled like mud and wetness, with the hot scent of the dead needles. Some of those things I hadn't quite realized had smells.

Boone rushed over when she saw me on the ground and soon we were rolling in the mud and the snow. I threw snowballs at her that she caught without slowing her mad charges into my chest.

As I picked myself up a sudden whistling, whirring rush filled my ears, and I ducked instinctively, as if someone had launched some kind of missile. I glanced up in time to see a pileated wood-pecker streak by, wings tucked firmly to its sides, screaming through the air. It flared above the trees below me and disappeared in the branches. I'd never seen one fly that way before, and once I recovered from the noise of its rush I wondered if the return of the sun was turning everything a little wild.

I remembered the eclipse, and though I knew it was not an event connected with weather, I couldn't help associating it with the changes taking place. The blue glow of the snow in the momentary darkness seemed to foretell the changes I saw now, as if the energy beneath the ice was finally emerging. I couldn't keep away from it, and I spent the following day up top, too.

This time I went north, chasing herds of mule deer from draw to draw, bumping into an occasional elk or two. I decided to stretch my walk to Sheep Creek, thinking I might be able to see some bighorns, the animal whose picture had drawn me out to Montana in the first place.

The crust acted different today, slushing over the same as ever but occasionally giving away beneath me even way up high. Breaking through unexpectedly was unpleasant, like miscounting the number of stairs, jarring my hip and knee that way, and I strapped on my snowshoes and kept on, worried more about the effect of the coarse, wet snow on the rawhide webbing than I was about the lack of traction the snowshoes gave on the sidehills. On the really steep sidehills I'd take the snowshoes off, kicking in steps with my boots, leaning uphill.

I pushed on for Sheep Creek but the ridges began dropping away in cliffs I couldn't get around and I kept looping farther to the east, until I was worrying about how far away from home I was getting. I worked my way into a corner and I started to hurry a little, not bothering to take off my shoes for the next steep pitch.

My feet went out from under me so fast I hit the ground before I knew I was falling. I built up a head of steam in an instant. I tried to dig my knees and elbows into the snow but the crust was hard here and I only scratched away the surface slush. There was a cliff below me someplace and I thought I was going too fast to ever stop when suddenly my knees grated over rock and I grabbed with everything I had, ripping open my fingertips. I came to a stop, breathing so hard I wasn't sure if I'd ever get another breath.

I waited a minute, making sure I was really there, then reached to my belt for my knife and cut myself a knee hole. With my knee wedged in I cut a handhold. I kept going, as I had up the pinnacle to watch the eclipse, but this time I was trembling, and I concentrated on not looking away from the rough surface of the snow immediately in front of me.

I didn't stop cutting holes for myself until I reached a tree I was able to straddle. With a leg safely around each side of the trunk I peered down my path. The track of my slide—the bright crust wiped clear of slush—went right over the edge of the cliff. I closed my eyes and rested my face against the bark of the tree. My feet must have been dangling in space. My heart began to race, as after a close call in a car, when the driver's had a moment to think of what has just nearly happened.

I stayed there several minutes, wrapped tightly around that tree, before I reached out to unhook my snowshoes. With the snowshoes looped across my back I circled around the way I'd come until I found the first chance to drop down the side of the mountain, leaving the land of the cliffs behind.

Clouds were closing off the sky before I reached my tent that evening and I never did see a sheep that day. And I never did get over how close I'd come to wiping myself out.

The rains resumed during the night and for several days I was content to lie around my tent again, cooking and reading, listening to the steady patter on the canvas. I read all of *Altas Shrugged,* a gift from my sister, and followed it up with *Tales of the French Foreign Legion,* a book my dad had included to lighten up the Graham Greene and Franz Kafka he'd sent in the same box. As the rain mumbled on and on I marched through the baking desert with the legionnaires.

I was just attacking a Muslim-held outpost in the sand when I heard a pair of snow machines whine upstream and abruptly turn silent. I snapped the book shut and grabbed my coat and headed out. In a few moments I saw the warden and a Forest Service ranger walking into my meadow. They'd been running around the new slides, out onto the river ice, threading through the trees on the opposite bank wherever the slides had run clear across the river. But when they reached the last one, just a little way above my meadow, they said the ice looked too rotten, and they'd decided to hoof it in from there.

They carried an armload of mail and apples and oranges, even some eggs and bacon. After the standard channel inspection they stayed long enough to have some sardines and crackers for lunch, the three of us cramped in the small, smoky tent. They were gone within an hour, and, as usual, I was tearing into my mail before I heard the last of their snow machines.

All the mail was great, but the highlight of the whole stack was a rare letter from my little brother, Joe. A senior in high school, he'd been swimming for four years and his letter told of his trip to the state finals. State! I couldn't believe it. The state meet had been nothing but a dream for any of us when I'd been swimming. He'd clipped an article from the school paper, including a photo of him with his head shaved. State and a shaved head! My punky little brother! I just couldn't believe it.

I whooped, startling Boone, but when she saw how excited I was she dove in and we wrestled around like pups. I'd send her flying, shouting, "Can you believe it, Boone? Joe shaved his head! Joe made it all the way to state!" When she'd land Boone would already be turning back to me and we rumbled for nearly an hour. Then I went and read my mail all over again. I read Joe's letter and his article three times, whispering, "Way to go, Joe!"

But that night, for the first time since my first or second mail run, my high was followed by a swooping low. Joe comes out of nowhere to set school records, to go to state. For all I knew Rader was already married to a girl I hadn't even known he was dating. Again it seemed as if everything was slipping away without my having a chance to join in on any of it. That fast I could go from thinking I was living the world's greatest life to feeling I was trapped in here forever.

To take my mind away I dove into a new book that night, *Papillon*. The story of a man condemned to Devil's Island, with long accounts of years of solitary confinement, it did little to help.

When the weather cleared again I unpacked my fishing rod and carried it downstream a few miles, to a wide riffle that had opened up, the first big stretch of open water since early December. Below the riffle the old ice bulged up in blocky chunks against the still frozen river, but I studied the moving water, seeing an alternative to my chili diet. As a kid I'd fished hundreds of lakes, yet I really didn't know what to look for in fast water.

Even so, I'd brought a secret weapon—one of the night's mice. I'd been carrying on a limited battle with the rodents all winter, and with the sudden warming they were everywhere. I trapped them in droves.

As I stood beside the rushing flow of clear water I sank a hook through the entire mouse. I cast it out, letting it bob through the rapids to no avail. My only fishing experience was in Wisconsin, for vicious predators like northern pike, fish that wouldn't think twice about swallowing a mouse, or a squirrel, or probably small dogs. I wondered if the delicate and fabled trout would be different. I wondered how idiotic I was being, expecting them to come charging after an entire mouse. I wondered if their mouths even opened that wide. I didn't know a thing about them.

So I reeled in and I pulled the mouse apart, using only the brightly colored insides as bait. On my next cast I hooked a fish immediately. The fish ran wildly and for a moment I wasn't standing alone in three feet of snow beside a fifty-yard-long opening in river ice. I was back in the north woods, surrounded by my father and brothers, stunned by the first real fish I'd ever caught, a walleye, after years and years of hooking little panfish. I held down an urge to shout, "I got one!" as I had then.

The fish jumped over and over again, clearing the painful sparkles of the sun on the broken water, and I became unduly worried that it might get away. I cranked and cranked on my reel, bulling it through the water, running down as close to the bottom edge of the opening as I dared, trying to take the stress of the water's current off the line. When I finally had the fish beside the bank I realized I couldn't reach in to lift it out. The snow created too steep a bank, the water too deep to step into. Holding my breath, I reached back on the rod and manhandled the fish out of the water, hoping the line and its lip would hold. The fish, a sixteen-inch cutthroat, flopped weakly on the clean bank of snow, large white crystals of the icy snow sticking to its curved side.

I cracked its head and held it up proudly, one of the few trout I'd ever caught, certainly the biggest. That fast I was able to forget the foolishness of casting an entire mouse and congratulate myself for having the smarts to discover mouse guts, a readily available bait. Another feast—a whole new season of feasting—was on its way.

I hooked a finger through the gills of the trout and started back for my tent. Soon I couldn't just walk in the warm, sunny air. I was so excited I began to jog, then finally sprint. The crust was still strong in the shade of the trees, and I cut into the deep timber, running as hard as I could possibly run, swerving through the branches, my moccasined feet as light as air.

I dashed across the rotten ice of Indian Creek, half expecting to crash through, but laughing at the risk, daring the world to try to get me. When I shot clear of the trees and into the rear of my meadow, where the sun had been working on the snow for hours, my feet crashed through the crust and I sprawled out, throwing my fishing rod out in front of me, out of harm's way. The trout slid off my finger too, skittering away across the snow. I was already laughing when Boone crashed into me, running right over my back, chasing the slippery fish. With the run and the laughter, I barely had the wind to call her back before she made off with my fish.

I tried cooking baked potatoes that afternoon, to complement my fish, and after banking the fire I crawled up Indian Ridge to the base of one of its huge ponderosas. I took off my shirts and stretched out in the open dirt there, dried already by the day of sun, and I soaked up the rays. I found a herd of ladybugs milling about in the pine needles and wondered where they had come from. They were bright and colorful in the brown dirt circled by white snow and I watched them until I was afraid I'd burned my potatoes down to hard, black raisins.

Beginning to establish a pattern, the rain resumed as soon as I grew used to the sunshine. I hiked through it, carried by the momentum of the bright days, but soon was spending more time in my tent, reading more and more of *Papillon*'s solitary confinement. I wondered if I'd be able to handle anything like that.

The dawn before the first day of spring I lay in bed, knowing by the dim lighting of my tent that I was faced with another silent gray morning. Instead of throwing back the covers I lay there, studying the mildew stains in the dingy canvas roof of my tent. The stains made patterns, heads and faces, that by now I could trace blindfolded. The grayish light reminded me of the socked-in times of midwinter, long after the crystalline cold snaps had silenced the country. The midday light of the drizzly February avalanche weather had been just like this. I tried to stop thinking of the months of cold and of the thaws, and I wondered if any ice had built up on the channel overnight. There hadn't been any ice-up lately, but chopping it was my only duty. So I lay in bed, looking at the mildew stains, wondering if the winter might not really be ending after all.

And then a cannon shot reverberated down my tight canyon. I sat upright and looked around, as if I could see a sound through the walls of my tent. There were often sonic booms back here, but this was not that.

It was as silent as ever after the shot and I was wondering if I really had heard anything. Then there was a rumble, soft crackings and groanings. I pushed up on my elbows and murmured the word "Ice." The river was opening up.

I dressed as I ran but when I reached the Selway it was over. The river was open. In the last few weeks small spots had been opening, but the ice that broke away jammed up at the first unopened spot. Along with the snow slides that had dammed the river, huge ice dams had formed, blocking the river and flooding some of my old trails. The shot I'd heard had been the last upstream dam bursting after being hit by the rush caused by all the other broken dams farther upriver. Now large blocks of rotting ice battered against the rocks and slipped by and broke apart, or held up until other blocks slammed into them.

The air crackled with the sound. Not the grinding and bashing of the ice, but the sound of the river. The normal gurglings and hissings and rushes of moving water. My world was no longer silent. I remembered in the fall the noise had followed me everywhere, surrounding me. At night, as the lantern fluttered and died, the sounds would change to voices, or music—echoes of my father's symphonies, that wove through the darkness as I shivered waiting for the blankets to warm.

I stayed by the river all day, moving up and down stream,

checking out old favorite spots, smiling stupidly, just listening. Walls of translucent blue ice with white snowcaps still hemmed in the water, but the river roared. Those voices had been buried all winter, under the ice and snow. Somehow, as I'd fished the one open stretch, I hadn't noticed their babble. I'd missed them without knowing it.

That night I lay in bed again, and as soon as the lantern sputtered and went out the voices took over, and I hummed along to the mysterious music I was so glad to have back.

E. B. White

"THE WINTER OF THE GREAT SNOWS"

The essayist and novelist E. B. White is known for the elegance and seeming ease of his style as well as for apparently random movement in his essays, where all comes together in the end in a striking moment of clarity. In "The Winter of the Great Snows," White begins with the seemingly curious and meaningless question of whether a seagull will eat a smelt, but then he moves quickly from that question to an exploration of the wintry landscape of Allen Cove, Maine. "Natural candor," he has said, is the one element that is essential to the essayist. Certainly in this piece that natural candor, that seemingly simple movement of perspective around his farm, is at work.

By the end of the essay, however, what stands in the forefront is the inquisitive and observant eye of the writer. The dogs on patrol, the orange snowshoes of the geese, the firing up of the woodstove—all these become matters of moment in the hands of

> White admits that he loves the cold, and clearly the rituals that he chronicles and the tone in which he chronicles them, the small details he lovingly and carefully describes, are all touched with the element of play and delight—a writer's romp through the season of winter.

the writer. And, most particularly, matters of play. White admits that he loves the cold, and clearly the rituals that he chronicles and the tone in which he chronicles them, the small details he lovingly and carefully describes, are all touched with the element of play and delight—a writer's romp through the season of winter.

The Winter of the Great Snows

Allen Cove, March 27, 1971

Somebody told me the other day that a seagull won't eat a smelt. Even if the gull takes the smelt by mistake, he will disgorge it. I find this hard to believe, but I haven't had a chance to experiment with a smelt and a live gull. I've always supposed a gull would eat anything. If Herbert Tapley were alive, I would put the question to him and be sure of a straight answer. But Herbert is dead, and I find people quite evasive when I ask them if a gull will eat a smelt. I raised a gull chick once, and it never refused anything I handed it. And once, years ago, when I worked in a ship, I used to empty garbage into a chute that discharged overboard. Gulls attended this rite in great numbers, screaming their appreciation. I can't recall ever seeing a gull reject anything that came out of that chute. There were never any smelts in the garbage, though, and this leaves the question wide open. A smelt has rather a sweet taste—there seems to be nothing of the salt sea in its flesh. Perhaps that's why a gull won't eat a smelt, if indeed it is true.

This has not been an ideal winter for pure experimentation here in the East—to see if a gull will eat a smelt. It has been more a time of simple survival, to see if a man can stay alive in the cold. The snows arrived early, before the ground froze. Storm followed storm, each depositing its load and rousing the plowman in the night. And then the cold set in, steady and hard. The ponds froze, then the salt-water coves and harbors, then the bay itself. As far as I know, the ground, despite the deep cold, remains unfrozen: snow is a buffer against the frost, an almost perfect insulating material. A fellow recently reported driving a stake into a snowbank, and when the point of the stake reached ground level it kept right on going. I haven't tested this—it's like the gull and the smelt, a matter of hearsay. But I would have to have a pretty long stake, so remote is the ground.

When snow accumulates week after week, month after month, it works curious miracles. Familiar objects simply disappear, like my pig house and the welltop near the barn door, and one tends to forget that they are there. Our cedar hedge (about five feet high) disappeared months ago, along with the pink snow fences that are set to hold the drifts. My two small guard dogs, Jones and Susy, enjoy the change in elevation and the excitement of patrol duty along the crusted top of the hedge, where they had never been before. They have lookout posts made of snow that the plow has thrown high in the air, giving them a chance to take the long view of things. For a while, the barnyard fence was buried under a magnificent drift. This delighted the geese, who promptly walked to freedom on their orange-colored snowshoes. They then took off into the air, snowshoes and all, freedom having gone to their heads, and visited the trout pond, where they spent an enjoyable morning on the ice. On several occasions this winter, we had to shovel a path for the geese, to make it possible for them to get from their pen in the barn to their favorite loitering spot in the barn cellar. Imagine a man's shoveling a path for a goose! So the goose can loiter!

The door of the woodshed hasn't been open since early in December, the snows having sealed it shut. The house, which always gets banked with spruce brush against the winter, never got banked. The flower beds never got covered. We were simply caught short: the snow arrived ahead of schedule and in large amounts. (I think we've had something like one hundred inches, all told.) We did manage to give the rosebushes decent burial; they are not only out of sight but almost out of mind. It takes an effort of the imagination to conjure up a rose. Only an inch or two of the tall stakes that mark the grave is visible. For most of the winter, the highway has resembled an enormous bobsled run: the passage of the plow builds towering walls of snow higher than the roof of your car, so that you travel through a great white trough, sealed against disaster. (Last summer, my car went off the road and I hit a pole and broke it. The accident was six months too soon—I should have waited till January, when a soft cushion of snow surrounded all poles. I passed my pole the other day and noticed that it had recovered fully from the blow, but I haven't.)

Maine towns take winter seriously. They are ready with money and trucks and men and sand and salt. Derring-do is in good supply, and the roads stay open, no matter what. The things that do not stay open are the driveways of the people. Every new swipe of the plow hurls a gift of snow into the mouth of a driveway, so that, in effect, the plowmen, often working while we sleep snug in our beds, create a magnificent smooth, broad highway to which nobody can gain access with his automobile until he has passed a private miracle of snow removal. It is tantalizing to see a fine stretch of well-plowed public road just the other side of a six-foot barricade of private snow. My scheme for town plowing would be to have each big plow attended by a small plow, as a big fish is sometimes attended by a small fish. There would be a pause at each driveway while the little plow removes the snow that the big plow has deposited. But I am just a dreamer. I have two plows of my own—a big V on the pickup and a lift-blade on the little Cub tractor. Even with this equipment, we were licked a lot of the time this winter and had to call for help. It got so there was no place to put the snow even if you were able to push it around. On the day before Christmas, the storm was so great, the wind so high, people were marooned in my house and had to spend the night. And a couple of days later I had to hire a loader to lift the snow from the mouth of the driveway, scurry across the road with it, and drop it into the swamp.

Except for winter's causing me to become housebound, I like the cold. I like snow. I like the descent to the dark, cold kitchen at six in the morning, to put a fire in the wood stove and listen to weather from Boston. My movements at that hour are ritualistic— they vary hardly at all from morning to morning. I steal down in my wrapper carrying a pair of corduroy pants under one arm and balancing a small tray (by de Miskey) that holds the empty glasses from the night before. The night nurse has preceded me into the living room and has hooked up the thermostat—too high. I nudge it down. As I enter the kitchen, my left hand shoots out and snaps on the largest burner on the electric stove. Then I set the glasses in the sink, snap on the pantry light, start the cold water in the tap, and fill the kettle with fresh spring water, which I then set atop the now red burner. Then comes the real warmup: with a poker I clear the grate in the big black Home Crawford 8-20, roll up two sheets of yesterday's Bangor *Daily News,* and lay them in the firebox along with a few sticks of cedar kindling and two sticks of stovewood on top of that. (I always put on my glasses before stuffing the *News* in, to see who is dead and to find out what's been going on in the world, because I seldom have time in these twilight years to read newspapers—too many other things to tend to. I always check on "Dear Abby" at this dawn hour, finding it a comfort to read about people whose problems are even greater than mine, like the man yesterday who sought Abby's advice because his wife would sleep with him only on Thursday nights, which was all right until his bowling club changed its night to Thursday, and by the time the man got home his wife was far gone in shut-eye.) I drop the match, open the flue to "Kindle," open the bottom draft, and wait a few seconds to catch the first reassuring sound of snap-and-crackle. (That's the phrase around here for a wood fire—always "snap-and-crackle.") As the first light of day filters into the kitchen, I set out the juicer, set out the coffeepot and coffee, set out the pitchers for milk and cream, and, if it's a Tuesday or a Thursday or a Saturday, solemnly mark the milk order blank and tuck it in the milk box in the entryway while the subzero draft creeps in around my ankles. A good beginning for the day. Then I pull my trousers on over my pajama bottoms, pull on my barn boots, drape myself in a wool shirt and a down jacket, and pay a call in the barn, where the geese give me a tumultuous reception, one of them imitating Bert Lahr's vibrato gargle.

The guard changes here at seven: the night nurse goes off (if her car will start) and the housekeeper comes on (if her brother-in-law's truck has started). I observe all this from an upstairs window. It is less splendid than the change at Buckingham Palace but somehow more impressive, the palace guard never having been dependent on the vagaries of the internal-combustion engine in a subzero wintertime.

The chief topics of conversation this winter have been the weather, the schools, and the shadow of oil. Quarreling over the schools has split the town wide open, as it has neighboring towns here on the mainland and over on Deer Isle. Feeling ran so high some people stopped speaking to each other—which is one form of discourse. Forty years ago, when I landed here, we had five one-room or two-room schoolhouses scattered at strategic points. The scholars walked to school. We also had our high school, which was a cultural monument in the town along with the two stores, the Baptist church, the Beth-Eden chapel, and the Rockbound chapel. Times have changed. All through New England, the little red schoolhouse is on the skids, and the small high school that graduates only four or five seniors in June, in a gymnasium decked with lilac and apple blossoms, is doomed. The State Board of Education withholds its blessing from high schools that enroll fewer than three hundred students. Under mounting pressure from the state, the towns organized a school administrative district, usually referred to as SAD. Sad is the word for it. A plan was drawn for an area schoolhouse at a central point near the Deer Isle Bridge, but it was voted down. Too much money and too many frills. Another plan was drawn and failed. Meanwhile, schoolchildren were shuttled around, here and there, in an attempt to close the gap. We no longer have a high school in town; the building is used for the junior-high grades. Most of the children in the ninth, tenth, eleventh, and twelfth grades are carried by bus across to the high school in the town of Deer Isle. A few travel in the opposite direction to a nearby academy. Sending their children over to an island irritated a lot of parents; some disapproved of the building, some had a deep feeling that when you leave the mainland and head for an island in the sea you are headed in the wrong direction—back toward primitivism. Other parents were violently opposed to dispatching their offspring to the academy town, on the score that the place was a citadel of evil, just one step short of Gomorrah. (There was also an ancient athletic rivalry, which left scars that have never healed.) The closing of our high school caused an acute pain in the hearts of most of the townsfolk, to whom the building was a symbol of their own cultural life and a place where one's loyalty was real, lasting, and sustaining. All in all, the schools are a mess.

Feeling about oil is now running high, but it lacks the acute pain of nostalgia that characterizes the school controversy. Oil is the pain of the future. A company called Maine Clean Fuels wants to build a refinery on Sears Island, at the head of Penobscot Bay, bringing barges and 200,000-ton tankers slithering through the fog-draped, ledge-encrusted, tide-ripped waters of one of the most beautiful bodies of water in Maine or anywhere. The proposal sticks in all our crops. Battle lines have been drawn, public meetings have been held. On one side, or in one corner, are Maine's Department of Economic Development, the executives of the oil company (full of joyous promises and glad tidings of a better life and a cheaper fuel), and some people in Searsport who hope that oil will bring jobs and elevate the economy of the town. On the other side, or in the other corner, are Ossie Beal and his Maine Lobstermen's Association, the Audubon Society, the Sierra Club, various conservation groups, the *Maine Times,* several action groups hastily formed for the purpose of beating oil, and thousands of property owners (usually described as "rich" property owners) who just have a feeling in their bones that oil is bad news any way you look at it. A 200,000-ton tanker makes an aircraft carrier look like a dory, and if there were to be a bad spill, it could mean the end of marine life and bird life in the bay.

Searsport was host to a public meeting last week to give the oilmen a chance to present their case. It must have been a barrel of fun. The constabulary was out in full force, CBS News turned up with its cameras, and a carefully selected group of concerned citizens was admitted. The meeting was set up in such a way as to prevent the anti-oil people from releasing their wrath when they rose to speak. It was a powder-keg meeting that failed to explode. Week after next, a hearing is scheduled at which the state's Environmental Improvement Commission will listen to testimony. This body, I believe, now has kingmaking authority and can turn thumbs down on an industrial newcomer if he looks and smells like a pollutant.

Pollution stirred our town a couple of years ago when our harbor became filthy as a result of sewage discharged from a school of theology that had magically turned up in our midst. The school had inherited a big old pipe when it bought the property; at low water the pipe lay on the stinking flats, exposed, broken in three places, and discharging. The town was powerless to act, having no ordinance on the books covering any nuisance of the sort. So the Environmental people were called and came over from Augusta. Testimony was offered by clamdiggers, boat owners, the health officer of the town, and concerned citizens. It took a long while, but the nuisance was finally abated and theology acquired a long-overdue septic tank. (The waste had been backing up into the school's swimming pool, it turned out, making the pool probably the largest and most spectacular tank in the whole county—a real tomato surprise.) Anyway, the water of the harbor is clear again, a classic case of cleanliness next to godliness. Clamming is still restricted.

Town Meeting came early this year—March 1st. I wasn't able to attend but have studied the report. One birth was reported in 1970, and twelve deaths. It would appear from this that although the population explosion is still an issue worldwide, we have it licked locally. The town appropriated $7,000 for snow removal and sanding, in addition to $3,000 from unappropriated surplus—a total of $10,000 to get the snow removed. There was no argument. If there's one thing people are agreed on, it's this: the snow must get removed. A century ago in New England, the approach to snow was quite different. When snow began to fly, people switched to runners. Roads were not plowed out, they were rolled down. A giant roller pulled by horses packed the surface to a fine, smooth glaze. Then the sleighs came out, with their bells. And sleds, to haul wood out from the woodlots. Wheels were laid away for the season. The old pleasure in runners hasn't died, though. The snowmobile is the big new thing—life on runners. It pollutes in two ways with its exhaust fumes and with its noise.

The town voted to enact an ordinance regulating the taking of shellfish. It is now illegal for a nonresident to dig clams, except that he may dig not more than a peck in any one day for the use of himself and his family. A year ago, the town voted to enact an ordinance regulating the use of the town dump. At that meeting, I suggested an ordinance prohibiting the discharge of human waste into ponds and salt water, but it got laid to rest. The selectmen investigated the matter and reported that such an ordinance would be "very complex, extremely difficult to enforce, and possibly declared to be unconstitutional." It seems sad that the town can regulate the taking of shellfish but can't regulate the discharge of the waste that makes the shellfish inedible. But that's the way it is. Years ago, I was sized up as a man who was amiable, honest, and impractical, and I've always agreed with that estimate. Now, I'm not just impractical, I'm unconstitutional.

And I still don't know whether a gull will eat a smelt.

Yun Sŏndo

"When the clouds have passed away" and other poems from *The Fisherman's Calendar*

This beautiful song cycle by the seventeenth-century Korean poet Yun Sŏndo celebrates the changing seasons. "Chigukch'ong, chigukch'ong, ŏshwa!" chants the fisherman, imitating the sound of his oars. Spring, summer, autumn, and winter, he pushes out in his boat, attuned to the delights of heaven and earth, land and sea. Each season brims with its own pleasures, but winter brings a special beauty—bright sun on a frozen landscape, the shimmer of the moon on snow.

There is solitude, to be sure: the hush of the madding crowd. But winter also pulls us back to the hearth, side by side with our beloved.

We anticipate, even yearn for, these crystalline images. They etch their way into our memories, defining the sparse, cool clarity that is winter itself. But winter also bursts with life—the big-mouthed, fine-scaled fish, the red soil refusing its icy coverlet, the fisherman himself singing in his straw cape and reed hat. There is solitude, to be sure: the hush of the madding crowd. But winter also pulls us back to the hearth, to companionship, to the quiet joy of looking out the window, side by side with our beloved.

When the clouds have passed away,
  the sunshine is bright and warm.
     Push out the boat, push out the boat!
Heaven and earth are frozen hard,
  and the lake looks ageless.
     Chigukch'ong, chigukch'ong, ŏshwa!
The boundless, boundless expanse of waves
  is stretched like shimmering silk.

A lone pine by the water—
  how can it stand there so boldly?
     Fasten the boat, fasten the boat!
Do not regret those gathering clouds:
  they will hide the world from us.
     Chigukch'ong, chigukch'ong, ŏshwa!
Do not shun the roaring waves:
  they keep out the noise of crowds.

At last the day has ended,
  it is time to eat and sleep.
     Tie the boat fast, tie the boat fast!
Where red soil in patches shows through
     the wind-strewn snow
  we go singing up the path.
     Chigukch'ong, chigukch'ong, ŏshwa!
Till the moon lights the snow on West Peak
  let's lean on the sill by the pine.

Jane Kenyon

"THIS MORNING"

In her poem "This Morning," Jane Kenyon brings together several different visions of winter and thus brings this biography of the season full circle. At first, this poem seems to be a Currier and Ives print, an idyllic vision of the world of wintertime. There is the barn with the snow, the cows and the milker, the nuthatch feeding happily from the seed scattered by the farmwife—even the drowsy cats dozing near the stove. But beneath that delight—and it is delight—is something else: the barn is bearing weight, and the house trembles.

Winter, like the life of the spirit, is never one thing alone.

> At first, this poem seems to be a Currier and Ives print, an idyllic vision of the world of wintertime. But beneath that delight is something else: the barn is bearing weight, and the house trembles.

This Morning

The barn bears the weight
of the first heavy snow
without complaint.

White breath of cows
rises in the tie-up, a man
wearing a frayed winter jacket
reaches for his milking stool
in the dark.

The cows have gone into the ground,
and the man,
his wife beside him now.

A nuthatch drops
to the ground, feeding
on sunflower seed and bits of bread
I scattered on the snow.

The cats doze near the stove.
They lift their heads
as the plow goes down the road,
making the house
tremble as it passes.

ACKNOWLEDGMENTS

A collection such as this depends so much not only on the collaboration of the editors, but also on the goodwill and high courtesy of those who support them. For this, we wish to thank those who contributed to the gathering of the selections and the piecing together of the manuscript: Kathy Struck, of the Calvin College Library, and Denice O'Heron, of the Department of English, Calvin College. To Jon Sweeney of SkyLight Paths Publishing go praise and thanks for his gracious nurturing of this project. And to our spouses—Anne Elizabeth Schmidt and Douglas Felch—though it seems so very little, we give thanks that, out of your love, you have been willing to put up with yet another book project.

Willis Barnstone and Tony Barnstone, *Literatures of Asia, Africa, and Latin America* (Prentice-Hall, 1999): "Facing Snow" [262] and "River Snow" [289]. Used by permission of Tony Barnstone.

Philip Birnbaum, trans., from the *Amidah,* in *Daily Prayer Book: Ha-Siddur ha-Shalem* (Hebrew Publishing Company, 1977): 562. Used by permission of Hebrew Publishing Company.

Will D. Campbell, reproduced from *Soul Among Lions: Musings of a Bootleg Preacher* (Westminster John Knox Press, 1999): 1–2;

51–52; 60–61. Copyright © 1999 by Will D. Campbell. Used by permission of Westminster John Knox Press.

Rachel Carson, "Winter Haven," from *Under the Sea-Wind: A Naturalist's Picture of Ocean Life* (Oxford University Press, 1941): 232–253. Reprinted by permission of Frances Collin, Trustee u-w-o Rachel Carson. Copyright © 1941 by Rachel L. Carson. Copyright © Renewed 1969 by Roger Christie.

Annie Dillard, from *The Writing Life* (HarperCollins, 1990): 41–44. Used by permission of Annie Dillard. "Winter," from *Pilgrim at Tinker Creek* (HarperCollins, 1974; 1999): 37–54. Used by permission of Annie Dillard. From *An American Childhood* (HarperCollins, 1987): 45–49. Used by permission of Annie Dillard.

Jamal J. Elias, ed. and trans., from *Death Before Dying: The Sufi Poems of Sultan Bahu*. Copyright © 1998 The Regence of the University of California. 72, 92, 58, 30. Used by permission of the University of California Press.

Robert Finch, "A Winter Burial," from *Death of a Hornet and Other Cape Cod Essays,* by Robert Finch. Copyright © 2000 by Robert Finch. Reprinted by permission of PublicAffairs, a member of Perseus Books, LLC.

Pete Fromm, from *Indian Creek Chronicles: A Winter Alone in the Wilderness* (St. Martin's Press, 1993): 141–157. Reprinted by permission of Lyons Press, Guilford, Conn.

Donald Hall, "Winter," from *Seasons at Eagle Pond* (Ticknor and Fields, 1987): 3–19. Reprinted by permission of Donald Hall and Barbara J. MacAdam, Curator of American Art, Hood Museum of Art, Dartmouth College.

Patricia Hampl, from *A Romantic Education* by Patricia Hampl. Copyright © 1981 by Patricia Hampl. Used by permission of W.W. Norton & Company, Inc.

Ron Hansen, "Wickedness," from *Nebraska* (Atlantic Monthly Press, 1989): 3–22. Copyright © 1989 by Ron Hansen. Used by permission of Grove / Atlantic, Inc.

Lawrence A. Hoffman, trans. and ed., *P'sukei D'zimrah (Morning Psalms)* of *My People's Prayer Book: Traditional Prayers, Modern Commentaries* Vol. 3 (Jewish Lights Publishing, 1999): 129–137. Used by permission of Jewish Lights Publishing, Woodstock, Vermont.

Thomas Hopko, *The Winter Pascha: Readings for the Christmas-Epiphany Season* (St. Vladimir's Seminary Press, 1984): 94, 99, 49–50. Used by permission of St. Vladimir's Seminary Press, 575 Scarsdale Road, Crestwood, NY 10707.

James Houston, from *Songs of the Dream People: Chants and Images from the Indians and Eskimos of North America.* Edited and illustrated by James Houston. (Atheneum, 1972): 281. Copyright © 1972 by James Houston. Used by permission of James Houston.

Jim dale Huot-Vickery, "Closing the Circle," from *Winter Sign* (University of Minnesota Press, 1998): 265–285. Copyright © 1998 by Jim dale Huot-Vickery. Reprinted by permission of the University of Minnesota Press and Jim dale Huot-Vickery.

Daniel H. H. Ingalls, trans., "The Moon Bears Likeness," "With Rags upon her Back," and "The Peasant and His Wife," from Daniel H. H. Ingalls, ed., *Sanskrit Poetry from Vidyakāra's "Treasury"* (Harvard University Press, 1965): 112, 116–117. Reprinted by permission of Harvard University Press.

John Jerome, from "November: Old Guys," from *Stone Work* (University Press of New England, 1989). Copyright © 1989 by John Jerome. Reprinted by permission of Chris Jerome.

Jane Kenyon, "Season of Change and Loss" and "Good-by and Keep Cold," copyright © 1999 by the Estate of Jane Kenyon. Reprinted from *A Hundred White Daffodils* with the permission of Graywolf Press, Saint Paul, Minnesota.

Jane Kenyon, "While We Were Arguing," "Apple Dropping into Deep Early Snow," "Depression in Winter," and "This Morning," copyright © 1996 by the Estate of Jane Kenyon. Reprinted from *Otherwise: New and Selected Poems* with the permission of Graywolf Press, Saint Paul, Minnesota.

Jamaica Kincaid, "A Fire by Ice." © 1993 by Jamaica Kincaid. Permission of The Wylie Agency.

Madeleine L'Engle, from *The Irrational Season* (Harper and Row, 1977): 2–3. Copyright © 1977 by Crosswicks, Ltd. Reprinted by permission of HarperCollins Publishers, Inc.

Irving Y. Lo, trans., Po Chü-yi's "Bitter Cold, Living in the Village," in Irving Y. Lo, *Sunflower Splendor: Three Thousand Years of Chinese Poetry* (Indiana University Press, 1975): 203. Reprinted by permission of Irving Yucheng Lo.

Barry Lopez, "Ice and Light," from *Arctic Dreams: Imagination and Desire in a Northern Landscape* (Scribner's, 1986): 240–244. Copyright © 1986 by Barry Holstun Lopez. Reprinted by permission of Sterling Lord Literistic, Inc.

Mark Noll, "Snow," from *Seasons of Grace* by Mark Noll (Baker Book House Company, 1997). Copyright © 1997 by Mark Noll. Used by permission of Baker Book House Company.

Kathleen Norris, from *The Cloister Walk* (Riverhead Books, 1996): 114–115, 181, 106–107. "February 2: Candlemas / Presentation of the Lord," "Triduum Notes," "The Paradox of the Psalms," "February 10: Scholastica," from *The Cloister Walk,* copyright © 1996 by Kathleen Norris. Used by permission of Riverhead Books, a division of Penguin Putnam, Inc.

Kathleen Norris, "Weather Report: February 10," from *Dakota: A Spiritual Geography.* Copyright © 1993 by Kathleen Norris. Reprinted by permission of Houghton Mifflin Company. All rights reserved.

Marilynne Robinson, excerpt from *Housekeeping* by Marilynne Robinson. Copyright © 1981 by Marilynne Robinson. Reprinted by permission of Farrar, Straus and Giroux, LLC.

Richard Rutt, trans., *The Bamboo Grove: An Introduction to Sijo* (University of California Press, 1971; reprint: University of Michigan Press, 1998). Poem by Chong Ch'ŏl, #63. Used by permission of Richard Rutt and the University of Michigan

Press. Poems by Yun Sŏndo, #213, #220, #222. Used by permission of the University of Michigan Press.

Rosemund Tuve, from *Seasons and Months: Studies in a Tradition of Middle English Poetry* (D. S. Brewer, 1933). Reprinted by permission of Boydell and Brewer, Ltd.

John Updike, "The Cold," from *More Matter: Essays and Criticism* by John Updike. Copyright © 1999 by John Updike. Used by permission of Alfred A. Knopf, a division of Random House, Inc.

Makoto Ueda, from *Bashō and His Interpreters: Selected Hokku with Commentary* (Stanford University Press, 1991): 144, 26, 168, 275, 277, 303, 327, 328. Copyright © 1992 by the Board of Trustees of the Leland Stanford Jr. University. With the permission of Stanford University Press, www.sup.org.

William J. Vande Kopple, "Through the Ice." Copyright © William J. Vande Kopple. Used by permission of William J. Vande Kopple.

E. B. White, "The Winter of the Great Snows," from *Essays of E. B. White* by E. B. White (Harper, 1977). Copyright © 1971 by E. B. White. This essay first appeared in *The New Yorker*. Reprinted by permission of HarperCollins Publishers, Inc.

NOTES

Preface

The lines cited from John Greenleaf Whittier's "Snow-Bound" (1866) are ll. 17–178, 210–211, 711–714, and 709–710.

Part One

The folk rhymes are taken from Ethel L. Urlin, *Festivals, Holy Days, and Saints' Days* (London: Simpkin, Marshall, Hamilton, Kent, 1915): 3. The lines from the Sanskrit poem, translated by Daniel H. H. Ingalls, are taken from *Sanskrit Poetry from Vidyākara's "Treasury"* (Cambridge, Mass.: Harvard University Press, 1965): 117. The medieval descriptions of winter appear in Rosemond Tuve, *Seasons and Months: Studies in a Tradition of Middle English Poetry* (Cambridge: D. S. Brewer, 1933): 197, 80, 24, 98. Francisco's complaint comes in Shakespeare's *Hamlet,* I, l, 9–10. The lines from *Sir Gawain and the Green Knight* (724–732, 744–747) are translated by the editors. William Bradford's description of winter appears in his *History of Plymouth Plantation* (Boston: Little, Brown, 1856): 78. The passage by Madeleine L'Engle is from *The Irrational Season* (San Francisco: Harper and Row, 1977): 2–3. "Facing Snow" by Du Fu, translated by Tony Barnstone and Chou Ping, appears in *Literatures of Asia, Africa, and Latin America,* ed. Willis Barnstone and Tony Barnstone (Upper Saddle River, N.J.: Prentice Hall, 1999): 262.

Jamaica Kincaid's "A Fire by Ice" was first printed in *The New Yorker* 69 (February 22, 1993): 64–67.

Matsua Bashō's haiku are collected in *Bashō and His Interpreters,* edited by Makoto Ueda (Stanford: Stanford University Press, 1991): 144, 26, 168, 275, 277, 303, 327, 328.

Barry Lopez, "Ice and Light," from *Arctic Dreams: Imagination and Desire in a Northern Landscape* (New York: Charles Scribner's Sons, 1986): 240–244.

Kathleen Norris, *The Cloister Walk* (New York: Riverhead Books, 1996): 114–115, 181, 106–107.

Jane Kenyon, "While We Were Arguing" and "Apple Dropping into Deep Early Snow," from *Otherwise* (St. Paul: Graywolf Press, 1996): 155, 65.

John Jerome, *Stone Work* (Hanover, N.H.: University Press of New England, 1989): 150–164.

Robert Finch, "A Winter Burial," from *Death of a Hornet and Other Cape Cod Essays* (Washington, D.C.: Counterpoint, 2000): 8–11.

Part Two

The opening lines from the *Second Shepherds' Play* are translated by the editors from the *Secunda Pastorum* in A. C. Cawley, ed., *The Wakefield Pageants in the Towneley Cycle* (Manchester: Manchester University Press, 1958): 43–63. The opening stanza of Christina Rossetti's "In the Bleak Midwinter" is cited from the traditional carol. The description of Deepawali is taken from Rama Devagupta, "Kindling of the Deepa," *Parabola* (Summer 2001): 38–42. The ode sung at Compline is cited from Thomas Hopko, *The Winter Pascha: Readings for the Christmas-Epiphany Season* (Crestwood, N.Y.: St. Vladimir's Seminary Press, 1984): 94; that sung at Matins is also from *The Winter Pascha,* 99. The passages from Lancelot Andrewes are from his *Ninety-Six Sermons* (Oxford: John Henry Parker, 1841): 1: 277–278. The final verse from "Good King Wenceslas" is cited from the traditional carol.

Ron Hansen, "Wickedness," is from his collection of short stories, *Nebraska* (New York: Atlantic Monthly Press, 1989): 3–22.

William Cooper, *Concio Hyemalis. A Winter Sermon. Being a Religious Improvement of the Irresistible Power of God's Cold* (Boston: Draper for Edwards and Foster, 1737).

Jim dale Huot-Vickery, "Closing the Circle," from *Winter Sign* (Minneapolis: University of Minnesota Press, 1998): 265–285. For footnotes from the original article, see pp. 255–256.

"Bitter Cold, Living in the Village," by Po Chü-yi, is translated by Irving Y. Lo; it appears in *Sunflower Splendor: Three Thousand Years of Chinese Poetry* (Bloomington: Indiana University Press, 1975): 203.

Donald Hall, "Winter," from *Seasons at Eagle Pond* (Boston: Ticknor and Fields, 1987): 3–19.

Part Three

Jane Kenyon, "Depression in Winter," from *Otherwise* (St. Paul: Graywolf Press, 1996): 68. The passage from Lancelot Andrewes on the coming of the wise men appears in his *Ninety-Six Sermons* (Oxford: John Henry Parker, 1841): 1: 257–58. The description of Father Alexander Schmemann is cited from Thomas Hopko, *The Winter Pascha: Readings for the Christmas-Epiphany Season* (Crestwood, N.Y.: St. Vladimir's Seminary Press, 1984): 49–50.

Kathleen Norris, "Weather Report: February 10," from *Dakota: A Spiritual Geography* (Boston: Houghton Mifflin, 1993): 25.

John Updike's "The Cold," originally printed in the Brazilian newspaper *Folha de S. Paulo,* is reprinted from his *More Matter: Essays and Criticism* (New York: Alfred A. Knopf, 1999): 133–135.

The Sanskrit poems were originally collected by the great anthologizer Vidyākara, in his *Treasury of Well-Turned Verse* (eleventh century). These translations by Daniel H. H. Ingalls are taken from *Sanskrit Poetry from Vidyākara's "Treasury"* (Cambridge, Mass.: Harvard University Press, 1965): 116–17; 112.

Annie Dillard, from *The Writing Life* (New York: HarperCollins, 1990): 41–44.

Patricia Hampl, from *A Romantic Education* (New York: W. W. Norton, 1981): 51–56.

Jane Kenyon's "Season of Change and Loss" was originally written for the *Concord Monitor.* Her "Good-by and Keep Cold" was originally written for the end page of *Yankee.* Both essays are reprinted from *A Hundred White Daffodils* (St. Paul: Graywolf Press, 1999): 85–87; 43–45.

Henry David Thoreau, "The Pond in Winter," from *Walden;* this passage from Walter Harding's *Walden: An Annotated Edition* (Boston: Houghton Mifflin, 1995): 275–290.

Part Four

Dorothy Wordsworth's observation appears for October 1802 in her journal. It is printed in E. De Selincourt, ed., *Journals of Dorothy Wordsworth* (London: Macmillan, 1952): 1: 181. "River Snow," composed by Liu Zongyuan (773–819), condenses its images into only twenty Chinese characters; it has inspired many landscape paintings. This translation, by

Tony Barnstone and Chou Ping, appears in *Literatures of Asia, Africa, and Latin America,* ed. Willis Barnstone and Tony Barnstone (Upper Saddle River, N.J.: Prentice Hall, 1999): 289. Patricia Hampl's reminiscence appears in *A Romantic Education* (New York: W. W. Norton, 1981): 63. The reference to the Book of Job is from 38.22, the King James Version. The reference to the Psalmist is from Psalm 51.7, also the King James Version. The reference to the "snowy whiteness" comes from the feast of Epiphany on January 6 and appears in the Great Blessing of Water; it is cited from Bishop Fan Stylian Noli, compiler, *The Eastern Orthodox Prayer Book* (Boston: Albanian Orthodox Church in America, 1949): 192. The image of the crow dusting down the snow from the hemlock tree is from Robert Frost's "Dust of Snow." The Lancelot Andrewes passage is from his *Ninety-Six Sermons* (Oxford: John Henry Parker, 1841): 1: 268. The passage from the *Amidah* is cited from Philip Birnbaum, ed. and trans., *Daily Prayer Book: Ha-Siddur ha-Shalem* (Spencertown, N.Y.: Hebrew Publishing Company, 1977): 562.

Psalms 147 and 148 are translated in Lawrence A. Hoffman, *P'sukei D'zimrah (Morning Psalms)* of *My People's Prayer Book* 3 (Woodstock, Vt.: Jewish Lights Publishing, 1999): 129–137.

Rachel L. Carson, "Winter Haven," from *Under the Sea-Wind: A Naturalist's Picture of Ocean Life* (New York: Oxford University Press, 1941): 232–253.

The Sufi poems of Sultan Bahu are taken from *Death before Dying: The Sufi Poems of Sultan Bahu,* translated by Jamal J. Elias (Berkeley: University of California Press, 1998), 72, 92, 58, 30.

Annie Dillard, "Winter," from *Pilgrim at Tinker Creek* (New York: HarperCollins, 1974; 1999): 37–54.

Will D. Campbell, from *Soul Among Lions: Musings of a Bootleg Preacher* (Louisville, Ky.: Westminster John Knox Press, 1999): 1–2, 51–52, 60–61.

William J. Vande Kopple's "Through the Ice" is here printed for the first time.

Part Five

The passage by Marilynne Robinson is from her *Housekeeping* (New York: Farrar, Straus, Giroux, 1980): 124. Patricia Hampl describes this scene in *A Romantic Education* (New York: W. W. Norton, 1981): 3–4. Dylan Thomas, *A Child's Christmas in Wales* (London: Dent, 1954). The incident with Michelangelo is recorded by Giorgio Vasari in *The Lives of the*

Painters, Sculptors, and Architects of Italy (London: Dent, 1963): 4:112–113. Ezra Jack Keats, *The Snowy Day* (New York: Viking Press, 1962). C. S. Lewis, *The Lion, the Witch, and the Wardrobe* (New York: Collier, 1950). The Lakota material is taken from James R. Walker, *Lakota Belief and Ritual,* edited by Raymond J. DeMallie and Elaine A. Jahner (Lincoln: University of Nebraska Press, 1991): 120, 124–125. The poem by Chong Ch'ŏl is translated by Richard Rutt and printed in *The Bamboo Grove: An Introduction to Sijo* (Berkeley: University of California Press, 1971; reprint, Ann Arbor: University of Michigan Press, 1998), #63.

James Houston, *Songs of the Dream People: Chants and Images from the Indians and Eskimos of North America* (New York: Atheneum, 1972): 2, 81.

Mark A. Noll, "Snow," from *Seasons of Grace* (Grand Rapids, Mich.: Baker Books, 1997): 51.

Annie Dillard, from *An American Childhood* (New York: Harper-Collins, 1987): 45–49.

Pete Fromm, from *Indian Creek Chronicles: A Winter Alone in the Wilderness* (Guilford, Conn.: Lyons Press, 1993; reprint, New York: St. Martin's Press, 1993): 141–157.

E. B. White's "The Winter of the Great Snows" is reprinted from his *Essays of E. B. White* (New York: Harper Colophon Books, 1977): 53–59.

The poems by Yun Sŏndo are translated by Richard Rutt and printed in *The Bamboo Grove: An Introduction to Sijo* (Berkeley: University of California Press, 1971; reprint, Ann Arbor: University of Michigan Press, 1998), #213, #220, #222.

Jane Kenyon, "This Morning," from *Otherwise* (St. Paul: Graywolf Press, 1996): 29.

Endnotes to pages 66–82

1. John J. Ozoga, *Whitetail Winter: Seasons of the Whitetail,* book 2 (Minocqua, Wis.: Willowcreek Press, 1995), p. 136.
2. Richard Nelson, *The Island Within* (San Francisco: North Point Press, 1989), pp. 27–28.
3. See Gary Buffalo Horn Man and Sherry Firedancer, *Animal Energies* (Sadieville, Ky.: Dancing Otter Publishing, 1992).

    This booklet attempts to condense traditional and current Native American insights into the spiritual significance of fifty-eight "beings"/species: from alligator through deer (gifts: gentleness and sensitivity) and wolf (balance of dependence and independence) to wolverine. I enjoyed the ideas and possibilities in small doses. Overall, there were just too many animals at Hocoka—an entire mosaic of species in dynamic, daily interaction—for me to attempt, let alone understand, constant specific interpretation.

4.   The largest white pine by this dead doe was struck by lightning the following summer. The tree shattered so forcefully that, halfway up, the trunk burst apart and the tree's great crown fell to the ground near what remained of the doe.

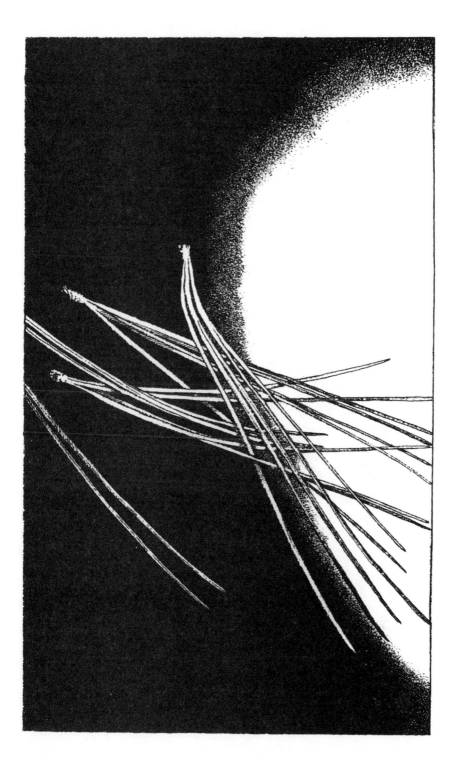

About SKYLIGHT PATHS Publishing

SkyLight Paths Publishing is creating a place where people of different spiritual traditions come together for challenge and inspiration, a place where we can help each other understand the mystery that lies at the heart of our existence.

Through spirituality, our religious beliefs are increasingly becoming a part of our lives—rather than *apart* from our lives. While many of us may be more interested than ever in spiritual growth, we may be less firmly planted in traditional religion. Yet, we do want to deepen our relationship to the sacred, to learn from our own as well as from other faith traditions, and to practice in new ways.

SkyLight Paths sees both believers and seekers as a community that increasingly transcends traditional boundaries of religion and denomination—people wanting to learn from each other, *walking together, finding the way.*

We at SkyLight Paths take great care to produce beautiful books that present meaningful spiritual content in a form that reflects the art of making high quality books. Therefore, we want to acknowledge those who contributed to the production of this book.

PRODUCTION
Tim Holtz, Martha McKinney & Bridgett Taylor

EDITORIAL
Amanda Dupuis, Polly Short Mahoney,
Lauren Seidman & Emily Wichland

COVER DESIGN
Bridgett Taylor

TYPESETTING
Kristin Goble, PerfecType, Nashville, Tennessee

PRINTING & BINDING
Lake Book, Melrose Park, Illinois

Other Interesting Books—
Spirituality/Retreats

Lighting the Lamp of Wisdom: *A Week Inside an Ashram*
by *John Ittner*; Foreword by *Dr. David Frawley*

This insider's guide to Hindu spiritual life takes you into a typical week of retreat inside an ashram to demystify the ashram experience and show you what to expect from your own visit. Includes a discussion of worship services, meditation and yoga classes, chanting and music, work practice, and more.

6 x 9, 224 pp, b/w photographs, Quality PB, ISBN 1-893361-52-7 **$15.95**;
HC, ISBN 1-893361-37-3 **$24.95**

Waking Up: *A Week Inside a Zen Monastery*
by *Jack Maguire*; Foreword by *John Daido Loori, Roshi*

An essential guide to what it's like to spend a week inside a Zen Buddhist monastery.

6 x 9, 224 pp, b/w photographs, HC, ISBN 1-893361-13-6 **$21.95**

Making a Heart for God: *A Week Inside a Catholic Monastery*
by *Dianne Aprile*; Foreword by *Brother Patrick Hart*, OCSO

This essential guide to experiencing life in a Catholic monastery takes you to the Abbey of Gethsemani—the Trappist monastery in Kentucky that was home to author Thomas Merton—to explore the details. "More balanced and informative than the popular *The Cloister Walk* by Kathleen Norris." —*Choice: Current Reviews for Academic Libraries*

6 x 9, 224 pp, b/w photographs, Quality PB, ISBN 1-893361-49-7 **$16.95**;
HC, ISBN 1-893361-14-4 **$21.95**

Come and Sit: *A Week Inside Meditation Centers*
by *Marcia Z. Nelson*; Foreword by *Wayne Teasdale*

The insider's guide to meditation in a variety of different spiritual traditions. Traveling through Buddhist, Hindu, Christian, Jewish, and Sufi traditions, this essential guide takes you to different meditation centers to meet the teachers and students and learn about the practices, demystifying the meditation experience.

6 x 9, 224 pp, b/w photographs, Quality PB, ISBN 1-893361-35-7 **$16.95**

**See our website: www.skylightpaths.com
for book covers, full descriptions, sample chapters, and more.**

Spirituality/Biography

Inspired Lives: *Exploring the Role of Faith and Spirituality in the Lives of Extraordinary People*
by *Joanna Laufer* and *Kenneth S. Lewis*
Contributors include *Ang Lee, Wynton Marsalis, Kathleen Norris,* and many more

How faith transforms the lives and work of the creative and innovative people in our world.

In this moving book, soul-searching conversations unearth the importance of spirituality and personal faith for more than forty artists and innovators who have made a real difference in our world through their work.
6 x 9, 256 pp, Quality PB, ISBN 1-893361-33-0 **$16.95**

The Life of Evelyn Underhill
An Intimate Portrait of the Groundbreaking Author of Mysticism
by *Margaret Cropper;* Foreword by *Dana Greene*

Evelyn Underhill was a passionate writer and teacher who wrote elegantly on mysticism, worship, and devotional life. This is the story of how she made her way toward spiritual maturity, from her early days of agnosticism to the years when her influence was felt throughout the world.
6 x 9, 288 pp, 5+ b/w photos, Quality PB, ISBN 1-893361-70-5 **$18.95**

Zen Effects: *The Life of Alan Watts*
by *Monica Furlong*

The first and only full-length biography of one of the most charismatic spiritual leaders of the twentieth century—now back in print!

Through his widely popular books and lectures, Alan Watts (1915–1973) did more to introduce Eastern philosophy and religion to Western minds than any figure before or since. Here is the only biography of this charismatic figure, who served as Zen teacher, Anglican priest, lecturer, academic, entertainer, a leader of the San Francisco renaissance, and author of more than thirty books, including *The Way of Zen, Psychotherapy East and West* and *The Spirit of Zen.*
6 x 9, 264 pp, Quality PB, ISBN 1-893361-32-2 **$16.95**

Simone Weil: *A Modern Pilgrimage*
by *Robert Coles*

The extraordinary life of the spiritual philosopher who's been called both saint and madwoman.

The French writer and philosopher Simone Weil (1906–1943) devoted her life to a search for God—while avoiding membership in organized religion. Robert Coles' intriguing study of Weil details her short, eventful life, and is an insightful portrait of the beloved and controversial thinker whose life and writings influenced many (from T. S. Eliot to Adrienne Rich to Albert Camus), and continue to inspire seekers everywhere.
6 x 9, 208 pp, Quality PB, ISBN 1-893361-34-9 **$16.95**

See our website: www.skylightpaths.com
for book covers, full descriptions, sample chapters, and more.

Prayer/Meditation

Finding Grace at the Center: *The Beginning of Centering Prayer*
25th Anniversary Edition
by *M. Basil Pennington*, OCSO, *Thomas Keating*, OCSO, and *Thomas E. Clarke*, SJ

The book that helped launch the Centering Prayer "movement." Explains the Prayer of *The Cloud of Unknowing*, posture and relaxation, the three simple rules of centering prayer, and how to cultivate centering prayer throughout all aspects of your life.

5 x 7¼, 112 pp, HC, ISBN 1-893361-69-1 **$14.95**

Three Gates to Meditation Practice
A Personal Journey into Sufism, Buddhism, and Judaism
by *David A. Cooper*

Shows us how practicing within more than one spiritual tradition can lead us to our true home.

Here are over fifteen years from the journey of "post-denominational rabbi" David A. Cooper, author of *God Is a Verb,* and his wife, Shoshana—years in which the Coopers explored a rich variety of practices, from chanting Sufi *dhikr* to Buddhist Vipassanā meditation, to the study of kabbalah and esoteric Judaism. Their experience demonstrates that the spiritual path is really completely within our reach, whoever we are, whatever we do—as long as we are willing to practice it.

5½ x 8½, 240 pp, Quality PB, ISBN 1-893361-22-5 **$16.95**

Praying with Our Hands: *Twenty-One Practices of Embodied Prayer from the World's Spiritual Traditions*
by *Jon M. Sweeney;* Photographs by *Jennifer J. Wilson;*
Foreword by *Mother Tessa Bielecki;* Afterword by *Taitetsu Unno, Ph.D.*

A spiritual guidebook for bringing prayer into our bodies.

This inspiring book of reflections and accompanying photographs shows us twenty-one simple ways of using our hands to speak to God, to enrich our devotion and ritual. All express the various approaches of the world's religious traditions to bringing the body into worship. Spiritual traditions represented include Anglican, Sufi, Zen, Roman Catholic, Yoga, Shaker, Hindu, Jewish, Pentecostal, Eastern Orthodox, and many others.

8 x 8, 96 pp, 22 duotone photographs, Quality PB Original, ISBN 1-893361-16-0 **$16.95**

Women Pray
Voices through the Ages, from Many Faiths, Cultures, and Traditions
Edited and with introductions by *Monica Furlong*

Many ways—new and old—to communicate with the Divine.

This beautiful gift book celebrates the rich variety of ways women around the world have called out to the Divine—with words of joy, praise, gratitude, wonder, petition, longing, and even anger—from the ancient world up to our own time. Prayers from women of nearly every religious or spiritual background give us an eloquent expression of what it means to communicate with God.

5 x 7¼, 256 pp, Deluxe HC with ribbon marker, ISBN 1-893361-25-X **$19.95**

See our website: www.skylightpaths.com
for book covers, full descriptions, sample chapters, and more.

Spirituality

Spiritual Perspectives on Globalization:
Making Sense of Economic and Cultural Upheaval
by *Ira Rifkin*

A balanced introduction to the issues of globalization. Explains in clear and nonjudgmental language the beliefs that motivate religious leaders, activists, theologians, academics, and others involved on all sides of the issue. Many different perspectives are represented: Bahá'ís, Buddhists, Protestants, Catholics and other Christian groups, Earth-based tribal and neo-pagans, Hindus, Jews, Muslims, and more.

5½ x 8½, 160 pp, Quality PB, ISBN 1-893361-57-8 **$16.95**

Labyrinths from the Outside In
Walking to Spiritual Insight—a Beginner's Guide
by *Donna Schaper* and *Carole Ann Camp*

The user-friendly, interfaith guide to making and using labyrinths— for meditation, prayer, and celebration.

Labyrinth walking is a spiritual exercise *anyone* can do. This accessible guide unlocks the mysteries of the labyrinth for all of us, providing ideas for using the labyrinth walk for prayer, meditation, and celebrations to mark the most important moments in life. Includes instructions for making a labyrinth of your own and finding one in your area.

6 x 9, 208 pp, b/w illus. and photographs, Quality PB, ISBN 1-893361-18-7 **$16.95**

Earth, Water, Fire, and Air: Essential Ways of Connecting to Spirit
by *Cait Johnson*

Spiritual nourishment at its most basic— the elemental approach to spirituality

You can't help but be drawn into the elemental approach to spirituality so gracefully detailed in this book. It identifies the four basic elements as humanity's first ways of knowing Spirit and reminds us of their value as keys to self-healing and re-connection. Offers a fascinating look at element-based symbols, traditions, and ceremonies, with creative activity suggestions for both individuals and groups.

6 x 9, 224 pp, HC, ISBN 1-893361-65-9 **$19.95**

White Fire: A Portrait of Women Spiritual Leaders in America
by *Rabbi Malka Drucker*; Photographs by *Gay Block*

In thirty-one profiles, this remarkable book gives voice, face, and image to the often ignored, invisible, or overlooked narrative of women's spiritual leadership in America today. Insightful interviews and compelling photographic portraits include Bishop Leontine Kelly, Iyanla Vanzant, Marianne Williamson, Elaine Pagels, Jean Houston, Sylvia Boorstein, and many more.

7 x 10, 240 pp, b/w photographs, HC, ISBN 1-893361-64-0 **$24.95**

See our website: www.skylightpaths.com
for book covers, full descriptions, sample chapters, and more.

SkyLight Illuminations
Andrew Harvey, series editor

Offers today's spiritual seeker an enjoyable entry into the classic texts of the world's spiritual traditions. Each is presented in an accessible translation, with facing pages of guided commentary from experts, giving you the keys you need to understand the history, context, and meaning of the text. This series enables readers of all backgrounds to experience and understand classic spiritual texts directly, and to make them a part of their lives.

The Way of a Pilgrim: *Annotated & Explained*
Translation and annotation by *Gleb Pokrovsky*
This delightful account is the story of one man who sets out to learn the prayer of the heart—also known as the "Jesus prayer"—and how the practice transforms his existence. This SkyLight Illuminations edition guides you through the text with facing-page annotations explaining names, terms, and references.
5½ x 8½, 160 pp, Quality PB, ISBN 1-893361-31-4 **$14.95**

Bhagavad Gita: *Annotated & Explained*
Translation by *Shri Purohit Swami*; Annotation by *Kendra Crossen Burroughs*
"The very best Gita for first-time readers." —Ken Wilber
Millions of people turn daily to India's most beloved holy book, whose universal appeal has made it popular with non-Hindus and Hindus alike. This SkyLight Illuminations edition of the Gita introduces readers to the characters; explains references and philosophical terms; shares the interpretations of famous spiritual leaders and scholars; and more.
5½ x 8½, 192 pp, Quality PB, ISBN 1-893361-28-4 **$15.95**

Dhammapada: *Annotated & Explained*
Translation by *Max Müller*; Annotation by *Jack Maguire*
The Dhammapada—words spoken by the Buddha himself over 2,500 years ago—is notoriously difficult to understand for the first-time reader. Now you can experience the Dhammapada with understanding even if you have no previous knowledge of Buddhism. Enlightening facing-page commentary explains all the names, terms and references, giving you deeper insight into the text. An excellent introduction to Buddhist life and practice.
5½ x 8½, 160 pp, Quality PB, ISBN 1-893361-42-X **$14.95**

See our website: www.skylightpaths.com
for book covers, full descriptions, sample chapters, and more.

SkyLight Illuminations
Andrew Harvey, series editor

The Gospel of Thomas: *Annotated & Explained*
Translation and annotation by *Stevan Davies*

The recently discovered mystical sayings of Jesus—now with facing-page commentary that illuminates and explains the text for you.

Discovered in 1945, this collection of aphoristic sayings sheds new light on the origins of Christianity and the intriguing figure of Jesus, portraying the Kingdom of God as a present fact about the world, rather than a future promise or future threat. This edition guides you through the text with annotations that focus on the meaning of the sayings, ideal for readers with no previous background in Christian history or thought.
5½ x 8½, 192 pp, Quality PB, ISBN 1-893361-45-4 **$15.95**

Selections from the Gospel of Sri Ramakrishna
Annotated & Explained
Translation by *Swami Nikhilananda*; Annotations by *Kendra Crossen Burroughs*

Introduces the fascinating world of the Indian mystic and the universal appeal of his message that has inspired millions of devotees for more than a century. Selections from the original text—originally recorded in Bengali by M, a disciple of the Master—and insightful yet unobtrusive commentary highlight the most important and inspirational teachings. Ideal for readers without any prior knowledge of Hinduism.
5½ x 8½, 240 pp, b/w photographs, Quality PB, ISBN 1-893361-46-2 **$16.95**

Zohar: *Annotated & Explained*
Translation and annotation by *Daniel C. Matt*

The cornerstone text of Kabbalah, now with facing-page commentary that illuminates and explains the text for you.

The best-selling author of *The Essential Kabbalah* brings together in one place the most important teachings of the *Zohar*, the canonical text of Jewish mystical tradition. Guides readers step by step through the midrash, mystical fantasy and Hebrew scripture that make up the *Zohar*, explaining the inner meanings in facing-page commentary. Ideal for readers without any prior knowledge of Jewish mysticism.
5½ x 8½, 176 pp, Quality PB, ISBN 1-893361-51-9 **$15.95**

See our website: www.skylightpaths.com
for book covers, full descriptions, sample chapters, and more.

Children's Spirituality

Where Does God Live?

For ages 3–6

by *August Gold* and *Matthew J. Perlman*

Using simple, everyday examples that children can relate to, this colorful book helps young readers develop a personal understanding of God.
10 x 8½, 32 pp, Quality PB, Full-color photo illus., ISBN 1-893361-39-X **$7.95**

God's Paintbrush

For ages 4 & up

by *Sandy Eisenberg Sasso*; Full-color illus. by *Annette Compton*

Invites children of all faiths and backgrounds to encounter God openly in their own lives. Wonderfully interactive; provides questions adult and child can explore together at the end of each episode. "An excellent way to honor the imaginative breadth and depth of the spiritual life of the young." —Dr. Robert Coles, Harvard University
11 x 8½, 32 pp, HC, Full-color illus., ISBN 1-879045-22-2 **$16.95**
Also available:
A Teacher's Guide 8½ x 11, 32 pp, PB, ISBN 1-879045-57-5 **$8.95**
God's Paintbrush Celebration Kit 9½ x 12, HC, Includes 5 sessions/40 full-color Activity Sheets and Teacher Folder with complete instructions, ISBN 1-58023-050-4 **$21.95**

Where Is God? (A Board Book)

For ages 0–4

by *Lawrence and Karen Kushner*; Full-color illus. by *Dawn W. Majewski*

A gentle way for young children to explore how God is with us every day, in every way.
5 x 5, 24 pp, Board, Full-color illus., ISBN 1-893361-17-9 **$7.95**

What Does God Look Like? (A Board Book)

For ages 0–4

by *Lawrence and Karen Kushner*; Full-color illus. by *Dawn W. Majewski*

A simple way for young children to explore the ways that we "see" God.
5 x 5, 24 pp, Board, Full-color illus., ISBN 1-893361-23-3 **$7.95**

How Does God Make Things Happen? (A Board Book)

For ages 0–4

by *Lawrence and Karen Kushner*; Full-color illus. by *Dawn W. Majewski*

A charming invitation for young children to explore how God makes things happen in our world.
5 x 5, 24 pp, Board, Full-color illus., ISBN 1-893361-24-1 **$7.95**

What Is God's Name? (A Board Book)

For ages 0–4

by *Sandy Eisenberg Sasso*; Full-color illus. by *Phoebe Stone*

Everyone and everything in the world has a name. What is God's name?
5 x 5, 24 pp, Board, Full-color illus., ISBN 1-893361-10-1 **$7.95**

Naamah, Noah's Wife (A Board Book)

For ages 0–4

by *Sandy Eisenberg Sasso*; Full-color illus. by *Bethanne Andersen*

We know the story of Noah, but what about Naamah, Noah's wife? When God tells Noah to bring the animals onto the ark, God also calls on Naamah to save each plant. Ideal for young girls and boys, this simple, beautiful book will help you explore the spirituality of this ancient story with your children.
5 x 5, 24 pp, Board, Full-color illus., ISBN 1-893361-56-X **$7.95**

**See our website: www.skylightpaths.com
for book covers, full descriptions, sample chapters, and more.**

Children's Spirituality

What You Will See Inside... Series

This important new series of books is designed to show children ages 6–10 the Who, What, When, Where, Why, and How of traditional houses of worship, liturgical celebrations, and rituals of different world faiths, empowering them to respect and understand their own religious traditions—and those of their friends and neighbors. Each full-color volume is ideal for orienting children within the faith—and introducing young people from other faiths—to what happens. Clergy and other experts of each tradition will author each volume, ensuring that these are valuable, authoritative resources as well as visual guides for younger-to-middle readers.

What You Will See Inside a Catholic Church

by *Reverend Michael Keane;* Photographs by *Aaron Pepis;*
Foreword by *Robert J. Kealey, Ed.D.*

For ages 6–10

A fun, easy-to-read introduction to the traditions of Catholic worship and faith. Includes full-page photographs and concise but informative descriptions of what is happening, the objects used, the clergy and laypeople who have specific roles, the spiritual intent of the believers, and more. For ages 6–10.
8½ x 10½, 32 pp, HC, Full-color photographs, ISBN 1-893361-54-3 **$17.95**

Lo que se puede ver dentro de una iglesia católica

by *Reverend Michael Keane;* Photographs by *Aaron Pepis;*
Foreword by *Robert J. Kealey, Ed.D.*

For ages 6–10

What You Will See Inside a Catholic Church also available in a Spanish language edition.
8½ x 10½, 32 pp, Full-color photographs, ISBN 1-893361-66-7 **$16.95**

What You Will See Inside a Mosque

by *Aisha Karen Khan;* Photographs by *Aaron Pepis*

For ages 6–10

A colorful, fun-to-read introduction that explains the traditions of Muslim worship, faith, and religious life. Includes full-page photographs and concise but informative descriptions of what is happening, the objects used, the clergy and laypeople who have specific roles, the spiritual intent of the believers, and more. For ages 6–10.
8½ x 10½, 32 pp, HC, Full-color photographs, ISBN 1-893361-60-8 **$17.95**

In God's Name

by *Sandy Eisenberg Sasso;* Full-color illus. by *Phoebe Stone*

For ages 4 & up

Like an ancient myth in its poetic text and vibrant illustrations, this award-winning modern fable about the search for God's name celebrates the diversity and, at the same time, the unity of all the people of the world. "What a lovely, healing book!" —Madeleine L'Engle
9 x 12, 32 pp, HC, Full-color illus., ISBN 1-879045-26-5 **$16.95**

El nombre de Dios

by *Sandy Eisenberg Sasso*
Full-color illus. by *Phoebe Stone*

For ages 4 & up

In God's Name also available in a Spanish language edition.
9 x 12, 32 pp, HC, Full-color illus., ISBN 1-893361-63-2 **$16.95**

See our website: www.skylightpaths.com
for book covers, full descriptions, sample chapters, and more.

Children's Spirituality

Ten Amazing People: *And How They Changed the World*
by *Maura D. Shaw;* Foreword by *Dr. Robert Coles*
Full-color illus. by *Stephen Marchesi*

For ages 6–10

Black Elk • Dorothy Day • Malcolm X • Mahatma Gandhi •
Martin Luther King, Jr. • Mother Teresa • Janusz Korczak • Desmond Tutu •
Thich Nhat Hanh • Albert Schweitzer

This vivid, inspirational, and authoritative book will open new possibilities for children by telling the stories of how ten of the past century's greatest leaders changed the world in important ways.
8½, x 11, 48 pp, HC, Full-color illus., ISBN 1-893361-47-0 **$17.95**

Becoming Me: *A Story of Creation*
by *Martin Boroson*
Full-color illus. by *Christopher Gilvan-Cartwright*

For ages 4 & up

Told in the personal "voice" of the Creator, here is a story about creation and relationship that is about each one of us. In simple words and with radiant illustrations, the Creator tells an intimate story about love, about friendship and playing, about our world—and about ourselves. And with each turn of the page, we're reminded that we just might be closer to our Creator than we think!
8 x 10, 32 pp, Full-color illus., HC, ISBN 1-893361-11-X **$16.95**

Noah's Wife: *The Story of Naamah*
by *Sandy Eisenberg Sasso*
Full-color illus. by *Bethanne Andersen*

For ages 4 & up

This new story, based on an ancient text, opens readers' religious imaginations to new ideas about the well-known story of the Flood. When God tells Noah to bring the animals of the world onto the ark, God also calls on Naamah, Noah's wife, to save each plant on Earth.
"A lovely tale.... Children of all ages should be drawn to this parable for our times."
—Tomie de Paola, artist/author of books for children
9 x 12, 32 pp, HC, Full-color illus., ISBN 1-58023-134-9 **$16.95**

For ages 4 & up

In Our Image: *God's First Creatures*
by *Nancy Sohn Swartz*
Full-color illus. by *Melanie Hall*

A playful new twist on the Creation story—from the perspective of the animals. Celebrates the interconnectedness of nature and the harmony of all living things. "The vibrantly colored illustrations nearly leap off the page in this delightful interpretation." —*School Library Journal*
"A message all children should hear, presented in words and pictures that children will find irresistible." —Rabbi Harold Kushner, author of *When Bad Things Happen to Good People*
9 x 12, 32 pp, HC, Full-color illus., ISBN 1-879045-99-0 **$16.95**

See our website: www.skylightpaths.com
for book covers, full descriptions, sample chapters, and more.

Religious Etiquette/Reference

How to Be a Perfect Stranger, In 2 Volumes
A Guide to Etiquette in Other People's Religious Ceremonies
Ed. by *Stuart M. Matlins* and *Arthur J. Magida* **AWARD WINNERS!**

Explains the rituals and celebrations of North America's major religions/denominations, helping an interested guest to feel comfortable, participate to the fullest extent possible, and avoid violating anyone's religious principles. Answers practical questions from the perspective of *any* other faith.

Vol. 1: North America's Largest Faiths

VOL. 1 COVERS: Assemblies of God • Baptist • Buddhist • Christian Church (Disciples of Christ) • Christian Science • Churches of Christ • Episcopalian/Anglican • Greek Orthodox • Hindu • Islam • Jehovah's Witnesses • Jewish • Lutheran • Methodist • Mormon • Presbyterian • Quaker • Roman Catholic • Seventh-day Adventist • United Church of Canada • United Church of Christ
6 x 9, 432 pp, Quality PB, ISBN 1-893361-01-2 **$19.95**

Vol. 2: More Faiths in North America

VOL. 2 COVERS: African American Methodist Churches • Baha'i • Christian and Missionary Alliance • Christian Congregation • Church of the Brethren • Church of the Nazarene • Evangelical Free Church • International Church of the Foursquare Gospel • International Pentecostal Holiness Church • Mennonite/Amish • Native American/First Nations • Orthodox Churches • Pentecostal Church of God • Reformed Church • Sikh • Unitarian Universalist • Wesleyan
6 x 9, 416 pp, Quality PB, ISBN 1-893361-02-0 **$19.95**

Also available:

The Perfect Stranger's Guide to Funerals and Grieving Practices
A Guide to Etiquette in Other People's Religious Ceremonies
Edited by *Stuart M. Matlins*
6 x 9, 240 pp, Quality PB, ISBN 1-893361-20-9 **$16.95**

The Perfect Stranger's Guide to Wedding Ceremonies
A Guide to Etiquette in Other People's Religious Ceremonies
Edited by *Stuart M. Matlins*
6 x 9, 208 pp, Quality PB, ISBN 1-893361-19-5 **$16.95**

See our website: www.skylightpaths.com
for book covers, full descriptions, sample chapters, and more.

Other Interesting Books—Spirituality

God Within: *Our Spiritual Future—As Told by Today's New Adults*
Edited by *Jon M. Sweeney* and *the Editors at SkyLight Paths*

Our faith, in our words.

The future of spirituality in America lies in the vision of the women and men who are the children of the "baby boomer" generation—born into the post-New-Age world of the 1970s and 1980s. This book gives voice to their spiritual energy, and allows readers of all ages to share in their passionate quests for faith and belief. This thought-provoking collection of writings, poetry, and art showcases the voices that are defining the future of religion, faith, and belief as we know it.

6 x 9, 176 pp, Quality PB, ISBN 1-893361-15-2 **$14.95**

Releasing the Creative Spirit: *Unleash the Creativity in Your Life*
by *Dan Wakefield*

From the author of *How Do We Know When It's God?*— a practical guide to accessing creative power in every area of your life.

Explodes the myths associated with the creative process and shows how everyone can uncover and develop their natural ability to create. Drawing on religion, psychology, and the arts, Dan Wakefield teaches us that the key to creation of any kind is clarity—of body, mind, and spirit— and he provides practical exercises that each of us can do to access that centered quality that allows creativity to shine.

7 x 10, 256 pp, Quality PB, ISBN 1-893361-36-5 **$16.95**

Spiritual Innovators: *Seventy-Five Extraordinary People Who Changed the World in the Past Century*
Edited by *Ira Rifkin and the Editors at SkyLight Paths;* Foreword by *Dr. Robert Coles*

Black Elk, H. H. the Dalai Lama, Abraham Joshua Heschel, Krishnamurti, C. S. Lewis, Thomas Merton, Elijah Muhammad, Aimee Semple McPherson, Martin Luther King, Jr., Simone Weil, and many more.

Profiles of the most important spiritual leaders of the past one hundred years. An invaluable reference of twentieth-century religion and an inspiring resource for spiritual challenge today. Authoritative list of seventy-five includes mystics and martyrs, intellectuals and charismatics from the East and West. For each, includes a brief biography, inspiring quotes and resources for more in-depth study.

6 x 9, 304 pp, b/w photographs, Quality PB, ISBN 1-893361-50-0 **$16.95**;
HC, ISBN 1-893361-43-8 **$24.95**

See our website: www.skylightpaths.com
for book covers, full descriptions, sample chapters, and more.